The New Religions of Japan

HARRY THOMSEN

the New Religions of Japan

Charles E. Tuttle Company: Publishers
RUTLAND, VERMONT   TOKYO, JAPAN

European Representatives
Continent: BOXERBOOKS, INC., Zurich
British Isles: PRENTICE-HALL INTERNATIONAL, INC., London

Published by the Charles E. Tuttle Company
of Rutland, Vermont and Tokyo, Japan
with editorial offices at
15 Edogawa-cho, Bunkyo-ku, Tokyo

Layout & typography
by Ken Tremayne
Printed in Japan

to
KARL LUDVIG REICHELT
in gratitude

Contents

CONTENTS (continued)

Foreword

THE PUBLICATION of this book will meet a conscious need among students of Japanese religion and culture because it presents in a series of factual and scholarly, yet not pedantic, expositions one of the significant developments of postwar Japan: the emergence and development of *shinko shukyo,* or "new religions." Mr. Thomsen, who has given himself to the study of these religions and is one of the younger missionaries who herald a return to the scholarly tradition so greatly neglected among postwar Christian missionaries and students, estimates that the new religions have about eighteen million followers, or one out of every five Japanese. Probably never before in the history of Japan have there been so many kinds of religious innovations and interests.

This book is significant on several counts: it reflects the vitality of Japanese religion through the new religions, which perhaps are as representative of this vitality as any of the older traditional religions. It seriously considers this unique phenomenon of Japanese culture, which because of fanatical and superstitious acts among some of the followers has been treated with a reproach mingled with contempt, and because of obvious materialism and even charlatanry has led many to dismiss them with a quip or a laugh. On the other hand, some of the older religious groups are obviously alarmed over the increasing power of the new religions because they are seemingly able to meet many of the felt needs of the Japanese people. Mr. Thomsen considers the religious and sociological factors that have created these movements—the roots from which they have sprung—and goes a considerable distance toward establishing their common bonds.

The book is important for the Christian student because it not only describes the encounter which Christianity has had with these new religions, but it also makes clear the difficulties missionaries have had in facing the Oriental syncretic concept of religion. How- **9** ever much the Christian must feel compelled to reject such syn- cretism, he can clearly see the reasons for both Christianity's ap- peal and its offence. Sympathetic insight together with a sincere desire to understand the religious orientation of these religions with their extensive borrowings from others is necessary if there is to be confrontation or even conversation. It is the merit of this book that it greatly helps in such a task. It is quite suited for use by theological seminaries, Bible schools, and other institutions.

I hope that a further significance of this book is in its being the forerunner of other serious studies of Japan's religious and cultural heritage. Harry Thomsen's background as editor of "Jap- anese Religions," a quarterly issued by the Christian Center for the Study of Japanese Religions, and as an active missionary of the Christian Mission to the Buddhists ably qualifies him from the viewpoint of study as well as experience for this and future books.

There is no doubt that this work will stimulate and educate the reader to a greater understanding of the religious phenomenon which is shinko shukyo.

St. Paul, Minnesota   Olaf Hansen

Preface

THE NEW religions of Japan are as yet more or less *terra incognita,* and few people are aware of the political and religious impact and potential strength of the 171 religions that come under this title. To most observers they are "an interesting and exotic phenomenon," but I feel that they constitute the third major milestone in the religious history of Japan. A study of these new religions is an absolute necessity for any student of the religious situation in Japan. Furthermore, the financial and political strength of several of these religions is such that students and other observers of the Japan of today would do well to devote time and effort toward an understanding of this startling development.

The task of compiling this book has not been an easy one as there has been no such previous English-language work in this field. I am conscious of the limitations of this volume and aggravated by the fact that the rapidly developing religions are likely to render many of the details recorded here obsolete in short time. However, as the time is at hand where such a work is needed, I have attempted this book conscious of these limitations.

As far as has been possible, I have allowed the new religions to speak for themselves. That is, I have quoted original sources as often as possible, only adjusting the English translations where awkward phrasing occurred. Most of my sources, however, had to be translated from the original Japanese. I have tried to give some objective evaluation as to the reasons for the success or failure of each religion, and have tried to give some idea as to what might be expected in the future. My source material, listed in the notes and in the bibliography, should make it possible for the student to go beyond the scope of this book into a deeper penetration of the relatively unplowed soil of the new religions.

The outline of the book follows a grouping that is natural **11** and functional. The first section includes those new religions that might be called the "old" new religions. The second group consists of those that have a close connection to Nichiren Buddhism. The third is a group that descends from one "old" new religion, Omotokyo, but which is large enough to warrant a separate section. The last section includes religions which are not classifiable under the previous three groups. No attempt has been made to cover all the 171 new religions, only those which have shown themselves to be influential and important, or which have such a potential.

The sources for the present work are the following:

1. All existing English literature. This consists mainly of articles and pamphlets as only one or two of the new religions have been treated in book form. In this connection the author wishes to express his gratitude for the use of the valuable materials published by the International Institute for the Study of Japanese Religions, under its Director of Research William P. Woodard.

2. The most important works of the existing Japanese-language works on the new religions.

3. The information supplied by the various religions themselves. I have thought it of the utmost importance to establish personal contact with these groups and have spent a few days at the headquarters of each religion in order to penetrate into the peculiar atmosphere of every one. This included conversations with the founder or present leader of each religion as well as visits to outlying churches or temples in order to round out my impressions and get a balanced look at the respective religions.

I wish to express my gratitude to Rev. Sakae Kobayashi, assistant professor of Kansai Gakuin, for his valuable assistance in various ways during the preparation of this work.

Kyoto 1963   Harry Thomsen

The New Religions of Japan

NOTE:

Though many readers will be familiar enough with Japan and the Japanese language that they will not stumble over pronunciation and certain other problems that crop up in a book of this nature, it is advisable that some effort be made at the outset for those who do not speak Japanese or who have had little practical experience in Japan.

Pronunciation: Japanese vowels are pronounced as in Spanish or Italian. Consonants are much as in English, except that *g* is always hard. Some vowels, such as the first *o* in Kyōto are extended, being indicated by the long mark over the vowel in question. These marks have been omitted from the text, but appear in the index.

Names: Complete Japanese names are given in the Japanese fashion, that is, the family name precedes the given name. Once they have been introduced, however, the author refers to them in the way least likely to create confusion.

Yen equivalents: Generally, figures such as those connected with constructing of religious centers or annual budgets are given in yen. At the time of publication, one U.S. dollar equals 360 yen.

The New Religions

ONE OF the most significant religious developments in postwar Japan is undoubtedly the emergence of the so-called "new religions," the *shinko shukyo*. Mushrooming into prominence at the end of the Second World War, the new religions at present claim to have about eighteen million believers, or one out of every five Japanese. Although this figure may be subject to doubt, no serious observer can afford to ignore the present influence and future potential power of the new religions. It is even possible that the emergence of these religions is the third major milestone in the history of Japanese religion—the first milestone being the introduction of Buddhism in the sixth century, and the second, the appearance of the popular branches of Buddhism in the 13th century.

Neither New nor Religion

The term "new religions" has been subject to much discussion, and there is no denying the fact that it is a misleading and inaccurate name. Consequently new names have been suggested—for example, "modern religions," "modern religious movements," etc.—however, the current term continues to be "new religions."

As for age, the new religions are *not* startlingly new. Some of them, like Tenrikyo, Omotokyo, and Konkokyo started in the 19th century, and even those that came into existence after the Second World War more often than not have a long history behind them within the framework of Shinto or Buddhism. Still, compared to the age of the so-called established religions (Buddhism, Shinto, and Christianity), the "new religions" may be considered rather new.

As for the content of the new religions, it follows that in the strict sense of the word they also cannot be called new. Mainly **15** their doctrines and teachings are simply popularized versions of Shinto and Buddhism. However, there is one important new element in the new religions, namely Christianity, or rather Christian doctrines and teachings taken out of their original context and more or less skilfully mixed with thoughts from Buddhism and Shinto.

In form the new religions *are* most certainly new. One of the main characteristics of the new religions is that they endeavor to present their teaching in a new and striking way with new rites, new buildings, new methods of evangelism, and new interpretations of anything old.

As for calling them religions, it must be pointed out that a large number of the new religions do not meet any definition of the word that includes a regular doctrinal system, an established liturgy, and a certain measure of stability in organization. However, Shinto, which is generally handled as a religion, does not measure up to many definitions of religion either. Further these groups are recent developments, and those that are not already strictly speaking religions are, mainly, moving toward the status of religion. In any case, Tenrikyo and a few others are established to the point where there can be little objection to applying the term religion now. Due to their extraordinary variety there may be no term completely satisfactory, but since the term "new religions" is already in current use, it will be used in this book. Where there may be some doubt as to its correctness, justification will be offered in the appropriate place.

Numerical Strength

It is difficult to give the exact number of the new religions, not to mention giving the number of their believers. Practically all figures available are those supplied by the religions themselves, and although some of these figures are accurate, most of them cannot be relied upon. The numbers given in the *Year Book of Religions* (Shukyo Nenkan), published by the Ministry of Education, cannot be trusted either since they are only reproductions from reports submitted to the ministry by the religious groups concerned.

The number of new religions registered with the Ministry of

Education at present is 171. A little more than one-third of them are registered under Shinto, about one-third under Buddhism, two or three under Christianity, and the rest (thirty) are simply listed as "miscellaneous." Besides the 171 new religions, which are found in most prefectures of the country, there are many smaller religious groups found in only one prefecture and accordingly are registered only on the prefectural level. The exact number within the latter category is not known.

The believers of the thirty new religions listed as "miscellaneous religions" by the Ministry of Education totaled 3,597,599 as of January 1, 1958. The followers of the remaining 141 new religions listed under Shinto, Buddhism, and Christianity run to a little less than 15,000,000, making a total of 18,000,000. However, as mentioned above, the figures have been reported by the new religions themselves and cannot be heavily relied upon. The only thing that can be said with certainty is that the actual number of believers is not above the figures quoted.

Approximately eight percent of the believers belong to the bottom of the social pyramid—farmers and workers. However, the percentages were much higher in this field some years ago since several new religions have made serious attempts to attract the middle class and the intelligentsia. Prime example of this is Tenrikyo, which partly due to its enormous library and its educational program, has succeeded in attracting a fair number of people from the top of the pyramid. On the whole the vast majority of new religions seem to concentrate on the farmers and workers in the first stage of their development and then gradually shift some of the emphasis to the middle and upper classes as the religions in question get older and more firmly established.

The main strength of the new religions is concentrated in the cities of Tokyo, Kyoto, Osaka, and the rural areas of Kyushu, Hokkaido, Okayama Prefecture, Hiroshima Prefecture, and Yamaguchi Prefecture.

The financial strength of the new religions is considerable, The budget of Tenrikyo for 1958 was 880,000,000 yen; that of Rissho Kosei Kai, 600,000,000 yen; PL Kyodan, 380,000,000 yen; Konkokyo, 300,000,000 yen. The rate of increase for the budgets of the various new religions is considerably faster than for the established religions, and the contributions of each member are generally much higher. Tenrikyo, Sekai Kyusei Kyo, and some others are extremely wealthy. The total financial strength of the new religions makes them a factor to reckon with in the future life of the nation.

Reasons Behind Development

The majority of the new religions have their roots in prewar Shinto and Buddhism: the fifty-five old Buddhist denominations and the thirteen old Shinto sects. But while the new religions have such a historical background, their postwar acceleration, their fantastic mushrooming in the space of a few years must be accounted for. The defeat in the war is the key. This can be divided into three facets: a reaction against estranged religion; an answer to a crisis; and a new freedom made possible by the removal of religious restrictions.

The times of crisis during and after World War II led, on a world-wide scale, to the emergence of all kinds of religions and sects which might minister to the needs of man. The defeat of Japan, the first in its long history, left the nation in a state of moral and economic chaos. War's destruction and defeat's blow to national self-confidence combined to create for many a need for religion. Some turned to Shinto, Buddhism, and Christianity to satisfy these needs. But many more found their answer in the new religions.

On the whole there was a religious vacuum at the end of the war. Shinto, with its connection to the head of state, the Emperor, suffered a great loss of face on defeat. Buddhism was not a vital religion—a situation that had been true for many years before the war. Christianity stood ready to enter the spiritual vacuum, but only a small number of people thought they could find their answer in it, probably partly because Christianity was yet felt to be a foreign religion. In the midst of this situation of disillusionment and turmoil what seems to have happened is that events have shaped up to put Japan on the threshold of a period of religious development that bears a striking resemblance to that of 13th-century Japan.

This seeming historical parallel may become clearer with a

brief review of the events of the second great milestone in the history of Japanese religion—the birth of the popular Buddhist sects in the 13th century.

By 1200, the seven schools of Nara Buddhism, as well as the later sects of Shingon and Tendai Buddhism, were waning. They had never reached the level of the common people and, in the hands of the priviledged courtiers and clergy, had become increasingly corrupt and lacking in vitality by the end of the Heian period. Political foment and a rising national feeling only widened the already large gap between the involved, ceremonious, and esoteric doctrines and practices of Buddhism and the unlearned and uninitiated masses. The farmer and the worker needed bread instead of stones, however beautiful the stones might be. Against this background and within the space of sixty years, arose the popular sects of Jodo, Shin, and Nichiren Buddhism, which taught about salvation in terms that anyone could understand and showed a way towards this salvation that even the most sinful could follow. Within a few decades they had become the religions of the farmer and the worker. And Zen, with its practical approach to Buddhism, became a sect of high appeal to the rising warrior class.

The parallels are not hard to see. The established religions at war's end were generally in a state of impotency as far as the masses were concerned, or outside forces had combined to destroy their confidence in the old way. Buddhism was out of the race. Shinto had been part and parcel of the ultra-nationalism of the war and fell into disrepute at surrender, its tremendous influence on education and social behavior being withdrawn soon after. Christianity suffered from its connection with the West and had been hampered by the wartime government. Whatever efforts at retrenching they could muster could not immediately fill the vacuum. The removal of religious restrictions that occurred under the Occupation in 1945 was the final event that allowed the budding new religions to grow and multiply. The 1939 Religious Bodies Law had held all such development in check.

Once the way was clear the new religions, with their easy-to-understand doctrines of popular appeal, began to spread among the people—mainly among farmers and workers, but also getting a foothold in the upper levels of Japanese society. This emergence may be more momentous than most religious observers seem to think, so that today we may stand at the third great milestone in the history of Japanese religion.

Characteristics

No foolproof classification of the new religions is possible due to their extraordinary variety. The following eight characteristics will vary in degree of strength and importance in the different religions, and in the case of a few religions some of the points may be misleading. However, to some extent they constitute the major characteristics of the 171 new religions.

1. They Center Around a Religious Mecca

In the case of most of the larger new religions an imposing headquarters has been constructed, a central point where all the believers go on special occasions. There is the huge Tenrikyo headquarters near Nara, which in its architecture points back to the past of Japan. There is the impressive center of Soka Gakkai near Mt. Fuji, which reflects the modern day in its large ferro-concrete building. There is the colossal headquarters of Rissho Kosei Kai, scheduled for completion in 1964, which combines the past and the present in its architecture with a modernistic ferro-concrete building that is topped by ancient Indian-style temple domes. The Rissho Kosei Kai headquarters will house more than 50,000 people and will probably be the largest building for religious use in the Far East.

The importance of the impressive headquarters is manifold. The centers, with the various ceremonies taking place there, lend to the religion a special atmosphere; they are a bulwark against frequent secessions—a weakness of several new religions; they give the believers a center towards which to proceed on pilgrimages and festive occasions; and they give to the faithful a sense of pride, dignity, and a feeling of being part of something big.

2. They are Easy to Enter, Understand, and Follow

With a few notable exceptions, these organizations are exceedingly easy to enter—there are no entrance examinations, no special requirements, no baptisms, and no promises. It is true that in a few religions there is an entrance fee, and in the case of a few others of these that the prospective member needs recommendation by a present member. Once entered, the main requirement is to pay the monthly fee, which might be five or ten yen, and to buy various religious articles—such as, the sutras or holy scriptures of the particular religion, a shoulderband, a rosary, or some other object.

One of their most important characteristics is the simple and uncomplicated doctrinal structure, which makes it possible for even the most unlearned farmer or worker to understand. Nothing is regarded as useful unless it can be understood by everybody belonging to the religion. We are reminded of Nelson's words: "The speed of a fleet is that of its slowest ship," although the new religions turn the words around to have a more positive ring: "the slower the doctrinal speed, the more efficient the religion."

In so far as the dogmas of Buddhism have been taken over by these groups they have been simplified and are expressed in a terminology that can be grasped by anybody—for example: "God's world and that of maggots [non-believers] are as different as two trains passing each other going in opposite directions. The celestial ship is about to depart for Heaven from a maggot harbor while the maggot ship of mud is floundering. If you realize that you are on board the ship of mud, the only thing for you to do is to transfer to the ship of God."[1]

Often the doctrine is coupled with a kind of visual demonstration, and in this way difficult Buddhist doctrines which were formerly understood by only a small minority have become popularized. Thus the *muga* (non-self) doctrine of Buddhism is demonstrated, or given expression, by the *muga no odori* (non-self dance) in the group known as the Dancing Religion (Odoru Shukyo). And in Tenrikyo the removal of the dust (sin or evils) from the heart is illustrated by sweeping hand movements, and this forms part of the daily worship.

The service in the new religions usually consists of the following elements: some ceremonies, often colorful and interesting, and wherever possible typical of the religion in question; a speech or sermon; and the *zadankai* (a get-together). The speech, which could be called a popular sermon (formerly regarded as the monopoly of Christianity), is simple and easy to understand. It is applied to everyday problems and often is mixed with humorous anecdotes. The zadankai is probably the most important part of the service. Over a cup of tea the believers experience a sense of fellowship and belonging, they exchange testimonies, and discuss common problems, such as, how to educate their children, how to become happy, how to win new followers.

3. They Are Based on Optimism

In contrast to Buddhism (or at least to original Buddhism) the new religions are basically optimistic. There is no room for life-pessimism and negativism. Life is beautiful, and there is always a sun above the clouds.

Man is regarded as "a being of happiness," and several of the new religions call themselves "religions of happiness." "How to Live a Happy Life" or "Towards Happiness" are titles used for many books and pamphlets. The happiness is emphasized by numerous festivals, often on a stupendous scale. Thus PL Kyodan has the greatest display of fireworks seen anywhere in the nation on the occasion of their annual summer festival, and the annual celebrations of such groups as Tenrikyo, Rissho Kosei Kai, and Kurozumikyo have become nationally known.

The aura of *festivitas,* the stupendous festivals, and the various colorful dances and ceremonies undoubtedly account for much of the popular appeal of the new religions to the Japanese, with whom the pessimism of Buddhism has never harmonized.

4. They Want to Establish the Kingdom of God on Earth, Here and Now

Practically all the new religions claim to be working for, or to be able to attain, the establishment of the Kingdom of God on earth—not in the distant uncertain future, but right here and now. They promise freedom from various evils: "Sickness, poverty, and unhappiness will become things of the past, and a happy life with the fulfillment of every human need lies ahead." Kitamura Sayo, the foundress of the Dancing Religion, expresses this in the following way: "If you come to God's world, you will find all the necessary supplies you need piled up in quantities ready to be allocated. Greedy self-deluded fools are groping around in the dark and are failing to take in these rich heavenly supplies. Come and see the Kingdom of God! There is no worry, agony, sickness, or suffering in God's land. There you can enjoy a heavenly life with the body you now possess. God's Kingdom is nowhere remote. It sprouts in your heart and grows within yourselves."[2]

Innumerable quotations could be added. The following is the seventh article in the creed of Seicho no Ie: "We wish to overcome diseases and all other miseries of mankind by a true conception of man's life, by a true way of living, and by a true method of education; and we want to devote ourselves to propagating the idea that all men are children of God, in order to establish on earth the Heaven of Mutual Love and Assistance." It should also be noted that Tenrikyo at an early stage of its development owed part of its growth to the promise of painless childbirth, and the Soka Gakkai has spread among the rank and file coal miners in Hokkaido and elsewhere by promising freedom from disease, safety from mine accidents, and automatic wage raises without resorting to strikes.

Healing by faith and prevention of sickness by faith are main characteristics of the new religions. In connection with this various forms of magic have been practiced in some groups, often resulting in much-publicized sudden deaths. Although numerous accounts of miraculous healings are published in the respective religious news organs every day—quite a few cases—especially those due to nervous diseases, probably authentic—there is no doubt that a large number of the believers go to an untimely grave because they refrain from consulting a doctor. Still, faith-healing remains one of the main attractions, a fact that may be partly explained by the ancient connection between religion, the healing of diseases, and the reversal of disasters.

As the various organizations gradually develop and change their emphasis from farmers and workers to the middle and upper classes, a change takes place in the doctrine of faith-healing. Thus Soka Gakkai at first discouraged its followers from consulting doctors. "Don't waste your money on the doctors," they said, "go to Soka Gakkai." But now the motto seems to be "first go to the doctor, and if he cannot cure it, then come to Soka Gakkai."

Tenrikyo too has changed its emphasis on faith-healing, which has now come from being one of the main doctrines to its present more peripheral status. Tenrikyo and a few others have even built hospitals, whose doctors more often than not are non-believers.

The promise of a heaven on earth has been particularly emphasized by Sekai Kyusei Kyo (formerly Meshiyakyo), which has built two miniature prototypes of an earthly paradise, one in Atami and one in Hakone, both well-known Japanese resort areas. The one in Atami is situated on a hill commanding a beautiful view of Atami bay and is combined with an art museum designed to convey to the believers the feeling of happiness through beauty. The other in Hakone also has an impressive museum of art objects as well as one of the most beautiful gardens in Japan.

In the "Kingdom of God," world peace is a necessity, and accordingly this is emphasized in the official writings of practically every new religion. In some cases the emphasis on world peace seems genuine, but in other cases it seems to be more an appeal to popular sentiment than a central dogma. Near Hiroshima it is prerequisite for any religion that wants popular support to emphasize world peace and recommend itself as a means towards this goal.

5. They Emphasize that Religion and Life are One

In most of the new religions the believers are taught that religion in itself has no value if it is not intimately connected with daily life to the point where they merge into one. Thus Ittoen, a new religious movement, refuses to be called a religion but uses the term *seikatsu* (life, living).

The connection of life and religion works both ways: religion being thought of in terms of daily life, and daily life being filled with religious contents. Kitamura Sayo of the Dancing Religion expresses it in this way: "Religion is not merely to worship and believe in God, but also to advance along the Road to God by practicing God's teaching. Human life is holy, and therefore one's home and community are the places where the soul must be polished. No religion can exist which is not intimately related to one's daily life."[3] Miki Tokuchika, leader of PL Kyodan, expresses the same idea in the terminology characteristic of his religion:

"Life is art, and every occupation and every action must be carried out artistically. Man is an artist, and God is the artist of artists." Taniguchi Masaharu, founder and leader of Seicho no Ie, maintains that many religions are only book-and-church religions and cannot be applied to practical life."[4]

An interesting attempt to express the union of life and teaching in religious terminology, while at the same time intimating that Christianity does not practice this union, is found in the Dancing Religion. The title used for one of their most important books, the biography of the founder, has the same pronunciation as the word used by the Christians for the Bible, namely *seisho*. But whereas the Chinese characters used by the Christians mean holy writing, the characters used by the Dancing Religion convey the meaning of living book. Similarly the words used for "faith" have the same pronunciation in the two religions, but whereas the *shinko* of Christianity has the meaning of to believe, or to worship, the characters used by Kitamura Sayo convey the meaning of holy action.

This characteristic has been treated in length because of its importance when the success and popular appeal of the new religions are estimated. It must also be pointed out in this connection that most of these religions are lay movements.

Many new religions are well known for their emphasis on social services of various kinds. Best known in this respect are Ittoen, Tenrikyo, and Rissho Kosei Kai. Ittoen members, living in the village of Kosenrin near Kyoto, go out one day a week to clean toilets in the neighboring towns and villages in what they call "prayer in action" or "prayer for world peace." Rissho Kosei Kai sends its members out every week to clean various public places in Tokyo, and Tenrikyo believers twice a year clean the huge park in Nara, close to their headquarters. It should also be mentioned that Reiyukai recently constructed a large hall at the cost of 200,000,000 yen and presented it to the city of Tokyo for social welfare work.

6. They Rely upon a Strong Leader

Most of the new religions are centered around a leader who is so closely identified with his religion that his death usually causes drastic changes and in several cases has led to the dissolution of the religion.

Whereas the relationship between the believers is thought of in horizontal terms, the relationship between the leader and the believers is vertical and is based on the *oyako* principle, the absolute authority of father over son. This authority cannot be questioned, and to some extent it may be said that whereas democracy is evident in the reationship between the believers, the old feudalism lingers on in the relationship between leader and believer. Some observers point out that the reverence paid to the emperor to the end of World War II has been transferred to these leaders.

In about sixty of the new religions the authority of the leader is based on a revelation in which the divinity of the religion appeared and asked the leader to initiate the movement. The authority of the leader based upon such a close connection with the divinity leads the believers to regard the founder as divine. Thus Kitamura Sayo of the Dancing Religion is called Goddess (*Ogami-sama*), and her son is known as the young god.

These *ikigami* (living gods), found in the streets or fields of today's Japan, have their roots in the history of Japanese religion, where the distinction between God and man never has been very clear. To the Japanese there never was a Jahveh of Sinai, there never was the gulf between man and God which is found in the West. In Japanese religion man and God have always been regarded as a whole. In Buddhism, man is conceived of as having inside of him the Buddha-seed or as being Buddha himself. And in Shinto the term *kami* (god) is given to men as well. Consequently in Japanese religion the man-God conception has more or less leveled out the difference between man and God—man being the image of God, and God being the image of man. With this background it is easy to see how the leaders of many new religions have come to be regarded as gods. Even from the beginning of Japanese religion, the gods have been walking in the street or working in the field.

One of the greatest problems for the new religions is the matter of succession. In many cases the leader is followed by his eldest son, but in other cases a board of directors takes over, and the line of succession is broken. In the case of Ananaikyo, Nakano Yonosuke has adopted a young woman who will succeed to the leadership of this religion. An even more interesting case is that of the Dancing Religion's Kitamura Sayo, who announced that her yet unborn grandchild would be her successor. The grand-daughter, now ten years old is known by the title Ohimegami-sama, the Princess-goddess.

Finally it should be mentioned that whereas most of the new religions are centered around one strong leader, there is a notable exception in the case of Soka Gakkai, which started with Maki-guchi and later on Toda as the central figure but at present has a number of strong leading personalities. This fact seems to ac-count for some of the success of Soka Gakkai up to now, but may in the future become the source of a splintering-off process in this religion.

7. They Give Man a Sense of Importance and Dignity

Most of the new religions could be called religions of "I-ism."

The new follower is made to feel that he is an important per-son, that in fact he is the center of his own universe, that he is basically strong and good, not weak and bad.

From the moment he enters, everything is done for his conven-ience. Services are held at times adapted to his leisure, early in the morning or in the evening; the church, shrine, or temple of the religion is always open to him or his children; the minister or teacher is at any time ready to speak with him and help him with his problems; if he is poor, a minimum of expense is asked from him; and he is told again and again that he is the "master of his own destiny." This optimistic estimation of man, together with the attention paid to the single believer, accounts for much of the popularity of the new religions, but also indirectly has been one of the reasons behind the secession movements that so fre-quently occur within them.

It can also turn out to be a boomerang and a major stumbling-block when the believer meets with difficult problems in his daily life and finds that he is *not* always "the master of his own destiny."

In several religions the believer is given the opportunity to con-fess and talk things over frankly. On such occasions he tells of his problems and mistakes, and at the same time he receives answers and advice. The best known in this respect is Rissho Kosei Kai. In the headquarters of this religion in Tokyo there is a daily crowd of thousands of believers—mostly middle-aged women—divided into small groups of from ten to twenty people and led by a teacher or counselor. In each group the people are given a chance of presenting their problems and difficulties, while at the same time listening to the problems of others. The leader then gives an answer or solution to the questions, and testimonies are given by the most ardent believers. To Western observers the counselling and the frank testimonies may seem rather un-Japanese, however, what is happening is that the Japanese through this counselling gradually are freeing themselves from the typical Japanese code of behavior imposed upon them during the Tokugawa period. The tremendous success of group counselling is a significant factor in the development of the new religions, and in the further development of the Japanese character. We are perhaps witnessing the first beginnings of a change from national religion into personal religion, a development that could cause drastic changes in the present Japanese religious system.

8. They Teach the Relativity of All Religions

Most of the new religions teach the doctrine of inclusiveness and relativity in regard to other religions. The main exception to this is Soka Gakkai, a fanatically intolerant group attached to the equally intolerant Nichiren sect of Buddhism. Otherwise, the traditional religions, Buddhism and Shinto, have always been tolerant, their feelings being summed up in a Japanese version of an old Buddhist thought: We are all climbing Mt. Fuji, some from one starting place, some from others, so we cannot see each other now because the mountain is between us, but we will all see the same moon when we finally arrive at the top.

Consequently most of the new religions regard each other as of equal standing, and have formed the Union of the New Religious Organizations of Japan, in which they are co-operating in various ways. Nevertheless, for the greater number of new religions there is a limit to the inclusiveness, for while they regard all religions as being basically equal, they are still convinced that their own "way to the top" is slightly superior; and their inclusive way of thinking does not prevent them from waging extremely vigorous propaganda in Japan as well as outside.

There is no doubt that inclusive thinking and tolerance are not limited to Japanese religion, but are essential parts of all Eastern religions. Throughout Asia the religious tolerance reflects the inability or reluctance of the Eastern mind to think in exclusive terms. However, it would be of the greatest interest to know to what extent the inclusive attitude of Japanese religion has been molded by the influence of the joining of Shinto and Buddhism, which almost a thousand years ago resulted in the syncretic Ryobu (dual) Shinto. Both of these religions came to be seen as manifestations of the truth, and probably this connection has done much to shape the Japanese religious mind, which so often is quite willing to accept the best of any new thought and combine it with the old—that is, religions do not exist as entities in themselves for the Japanese religious mind, but as parts of a whole which may be united or mixed as one sees fit.

What can be called the selective and combinative religious mind of the Japanese is quite evident in the new religions. Old Shinto and Buddhist doctrines have been mixed with Christian thoughts and Biblical events. To some extent it may even be said that the innovations of the new religions are from Christianity.

It is amazing to see various versions and parts of Christianity embedded in the heart of the new religions. The new religions have actually placed much of Christianity within the framework of Japanese religion as a whole in a different way from that done by the various Christian churches in Japan. Christ is mentioned with the greatest respect and reverence in the majority of the new religions, and it can be said that most of the phases of the life of Christ are to be found in one form or another. There are versions of the stilling of the sea, the Sermon on the Mount, and the Lord's Prayer. Christian terminology is used extensively, and words from the Bible are quoted freely—thus, the official monthly publication of Seicho no Ie uses a Biblical quotation as its motto.

Further, as might be suspected, some of the high-ranking leaders of the new religions are former Christians.

Are the New Religions Here to Stay?

Generally, the significance of the new religions has been underestimated. Until the sensational Soka Gakkai victory in the Upper House elections in 1959, most people did not think too seriously about the possibility that the new religions might turn out to be one of the main developments in the religious history of Japan rather than just a temporary phenomenon. A second look enables one to see that in many ways the new religions have become permanent parts of the social, religious, and now, political picture of postwar Japan.

It is true that a large number of bizarre and rather strange groups appeared after the end of World War II, and that a large number of them have disappeared as suddenly as they came. 1951 saw 156 miscellaneous new religions registered with the Ministry of Education (besides those listed under Buddhism, Shinto, and Christianity), but after the enactment of the Religious Jurisdiction Law of the same year, the number went down from 156 to 98 by December, and today the number is 30.

Among those that disappeared was Denshinkyo, which worshipped electricity as the main deity and Thomas Alva Edison as one of four lesser deities. Other short-lived religions were Boseikyo, in which sex apparently played a role in healing practices, and Jiyukyo, which established its own cabinet for the country (among them, the famous sumo wrestler Futabayama). Jiyukyo finally was raided by the police and dissolved.

However, those religions that disappeared were the most extreme and bizarre ones, and it can be assumed that the majority of the present 171 are here to stay, at least in the foreseeable future. Some of them will undoubtedly diminish, some of them disappear, but it is just as certain that some of them will develop and may in the future be counted among the strongest religions of the country.

Even at present the numerical strength of the new religions is anything but negligible. The three largest count between them ten percent of the population of Japan, and the largest one, Soka Gakkai, is at present the fastest growing religion in the world, with a monthly increase of up to 100,000 people.

Japan's established religions, particularly Buddhism, are aware of the threat of the new religions to take over the leading position in the religious arena of the future. The General Secretary of the Soto branch of Zen Buddhism, Mr. Sasaki, remarked in his annual report of March 7, 1957: "Buddhism is now beset by a *danger such as it has never known since its beginning.* This danger comes from the new religions and their astonishingly effective propaganda methods. To survive it will take all our zeal and all our financial resources."

Rather than giving the death blow to the established religions it seems probable that the new religions will force the other Japanese religions, particularly Buddhism, into an era of accelerated accommodation and streamlining. This will cause Buddhism in Japan, which even at present differs considerably from continental Buddhism, to deviate even further from its origin. However, without this streamlining process it is doubtful whether Buddhism will be able to survive the challenge of the new religions.

The "Old" New Religions

HAVING decided on the term "new religions" it immediately becomes necessary to distinguish a group which might be called the "old" new religions. These were established about a hundred years ago and were actually carried on the Japanese government's official list of Shinto sects, or they owe much of their form or content to the indigenous Shinto religion. Tenrikyo, though it is not the oldest of these, is the largest and one of the most influential forces in the religious sphere. In addition, it is typical in many ways of the entire new-religion movement. Because of this I feel that Tenrikyo will serve as the most striking and informative introduction to the material included in this book.

1

天理教 / Tenrikyo

Tenrikyo, which started more than 120 years ago, is probably the best known of the new religions, having more than two million believers, a streamlined and effective propaganda machine, and the most established organizational form and doctrinal structure. *Tenri* means divine or heavenly wisdom; *kyo* is a word meaning teaching or religion. (It is the last character in the names of most of the new religions.) Hence, Tenrikyo means the

Religion of Divine Wisdom. This religion is certainly one of the strongest religious forces in Japan today, but even so it would be going too far to agree with van Stralen when he calls it "Japan's most powerful religious movement."[1]

Tenrikyo developed within the framework of Shinto, and its ceremonies and much of its external form show this relationship. However, in the doctrines of Tenrikyo we will find elements from both Buddhism and Christianity as well.

Founding and History

The founder (*kyoso*) of Tenrikyo was a woman, as indeed is the case in a considerable number of new religions. Her name was Nakayama Miki. She was born in 1798, the first daughter of Maekawa Hanshichi Masanobu, and acquired the name of Nakayama by marriage. This has been the name of all preceding patriarchs (*shimbashira*) of Tenrikyo.

As a girl, Miki was deeply religious and was initiated as a devout lay Buddhist of the Pure Land sect (Jodo-shu). From her childhood on, her mind was thus molded by the teachings of Buddhism, and undoubtedly here we find the beginnings of her religious development, although most Tenrikyo believers will maintain that her ideas and concepts are entirely original.

For the details of Miki's life we must rely upon information supplied by Tenrikyo itself. According to their beliefs Miki had her first revelation in 1837. An itinerant priest had been called to perform some mystical ritual to cure Miki, her husband Zembei, and their son Shuji of sudden attacks of pain, and in the process Miki served as medium. Suddenly she entered a trance and presently said, "I am the True and Original God. I have been predestined to reside here. I have descended from Heaven to save all human beings, and I want to take Miki as the Shrine of God and the mediatrix between God and men."[2] Miki's husband asked the deity to withdraw, but it refused. A family council was held, and after much deliberation they decided that it would be necessary to accept the deity. Only then did Miki awake from her trance.

This was only the first of such experiences, and Miki's behavior gradually changed. She began to practice charity by giving furniture, food, and family heirlooms to the poor. Her husband, relatives, and friends tried to dissuade her, and the villagers were convinced she was possessed of a demon.

In a later revelation she was told to tear down her house in order that she might attain ultimate poverty, and at the same time, give her possessions to the poor. She asked her husband to do this, and he finally consented to destroy part of the house. After her husband's death in 1863 she had the demolition completed. She gave away practically everything she had and was in the absolute depths of poverty.

Miki's concept of charity has been the object of much discussion. There are those who think she gradually lost her mind, but to the Tenrikyo believer this is out of the question. Her actions are seen as a carrying out of God's will so that she could attain ultimate poverty and help the less fortunate people in her area.

This state of affairs lasted for about nine years, after which period Miki began propagating the teaching which by now had matured in her mind. At the same time she began practicing various healings by faith, as well as a method of aiding in painless childbirth. As a result of these activities she gradually began to gain followers. Among these was the master carpenter, later called Master Iburi, who was destined to become Miki's successor and the only one besides her to produce canonical writings. However, persecution by the Buddhists and, after the Meiji Restoration, by the Shintoists, continued and led to severe harassment by the government, partly because the rise of Tenrikyo was synchronous with a wave of peasant revolts. The characteristic dance of Tenrikyo, the *Kagura Tsutome,* which was often accompanied by violent scenes of ecstasy, especially aroused the suspicion of the authorities, and finally the dance was prohibited. During these years Miki wrote the main canonical writings of Tenrikyo—the liturgical prayer *Mikagura Uta* and the seventeen books of *Ofudesaki.*

In 1887 Miki died after a long life, during which she had her full share of sufferings, persecutions, jail sentences, and poverty. However, it was also a life of final success, for she saw her religion established in spite of many obstacles. Master Iburi assumed leadership and held it until his death in 1907. The Nakayama family again took over, the present leader being Miki's great-grandson.

Headquarters

The center of Tenrikyo is in a city bearing the name of the religion, Tenri City. It is near Nara and has a population of about fifty thousand, most of whom belong to the religion. It is a very impressive mecca, and no other new religion, except Rissho Kosei Kai and Soka Gakkai, has anything comparable. Tenrikyo's compound takes up a square kilometer of the town and is known as God's Residence (Oyasato). Through an immense black *torii* the thousands of daily visitors enter into the Tenrikyo compound of temple buildings. The most important is the *honden,* or main sanctuary, in the center of which is the Jiba, a large square recess in the floor which only a few select persons are allowed to approach. The Jiba is regarded as the original home of the human race, the place where the earth was created, and the holy spot to which in the future all mankind will return.

In the middle of this square hole in the floor is the Kanrodai or "Sweet Dew Stand." The Kanrodai is a column of hexagonal shape, consisting of thirteen wooden pieces. Its height is 2.48 meters, and the mystical interpretations given to its size, shape, and measurements are numerous. On top of it is a wooden vessel of more than two gallon capacity. According to Tenrikyo doctrine this vessel as well as the whole Kanrodai will some day be changed into stone, the *kanro,* or "sweet dew," will pour down from heaven, and Tenrikyo will become the religion of all mankind. The roof over the Kanrodai has a square opening through which, in time, the kanro, and meanwhile, snow, hail, and rain, can pour down. When the kanro has arrived, happiness will reign in the world, and all men shall live to the age of 115.

Connected with the main sanctuary by an extremely long and carefully dusted corridor is the Kyosoden, or "Sanctuary of the Foundress." In this building, according to Tenrikyo believers, Miki is still living, waiting for the sweet dew to pour down on the Kanrodai. Meals are served for her three times a day, a hot bath is made ready every evening, and to enable the foundress to benefit from the inventions of the modern age, a television set has been installed in her room. Twenty-four hours a day in front of this room, priests, alternating every half-hour, perform a sort of perpetual adoration.

Behind these two sanctuaries stands the amazing Oyasato Yakata, one of the largest buildings for religious use in the East. It is a ferro-concrete, five-story structure with a total floor space of 52,880 square meters and various offices and other rooms for more than fifteen thousand persons. It was built in 1.5 million man-days of work, all supplied by believers, who did their *hinokishin* (free labor) in this way. Seeing this stupendous edifice, one is rather astounded to hear that it is only one of sixteen identical buildings which upon completion will form an imposing frame around God's Residence, with the Jiba as the geographical and spiritual center. That this tremendous task is being planned and gradually carried out bears witness to the strength and influence of Tenrikyo.

In the compound there is a school system complete from kindergarten through university. The Tenri University, connected with the Tenrikyo Institute of Asiatic Culture, has nearly two thousand students. It is rather well known, not least for its physical education, which is so effective that it has enabled Tenri to run off with many trophies in nation-wide contests in sports such as baseball, judo, and swimming. In swimming, Tenri now holds several national women's records.

Furthermore there is a remarkable museum with some of the best collections of archaeological and ethnological material in Japan as well as one of the largest libraries in the East. The latter has close to 700,000 volumes and an unequaled collection of rare books, especially 16th- and 17th-century literature on the Far East missionary work of the Portuguese and the Spanish.

Worship and Practices

At the main sanctuary in Tenri, services are performed twice daily, once at sunrise and once at sunset. There is a festival on the 26th of each month, and grand festivals are held three times a year: on January 26 to celebrate the Ascension of the Foundress;

on April 18, the birthday of the Foundress; and on the anniversary of the founding of Tenrikyo, October 26.

The service for festive occasions is made up of the following:

1) *The Offertory.* This is a prelude to the services. It is the same as that performed at all Shinto shrines—the offering of vegetables, fish, fruit, rice cakes, and saké (rice wine) at the various altars. A number of priests take part in the ceremony, which lasts about an hour.

2) *The Procession.* The shimbashira leads, followed by the most prominent high priests from various congregations. Then comes a similar number of women—the wives of the shimbashira and the priests. They all bow in front of the Kanrodai and proceed, the men to the left and the women to the right, and take seats.

3) *The Prayer.* This is recited by the shimbashira, who is squatting in front of the Kanrodai. He is assisted by a deacon and a subdeacon. One hands him a paper with a prayer (*saibun*) on it; the other hands him a branch from the sacred sakaki tree. While this is going on, sacred music on such traditional instruments as the *taiko, shoko, sho,* and *fue* begins.

4) *The Kanrodai Dance.* The dance follows the Prayer and is the climax of the festival. It takes place at the bottom of the square recess around the Kanrodai, and since it is below the floor level, nobody can see it. They can only hear the shuffling of the dancers' feet as they dance over small grey stones that have been strewn on the dancing surface.

There are always ten performers, five men and five women, including the shimbashira and his wife. He stands in the northern corner facing south and takes the role of the male deity Kunito-kotachi-no-mikoto, and his wife stands in the south facing to the west and takes the role of the female deity Omotari-no-mikoto. The other eight performers stand four on the eastern side facing their four counterparts on the west. They are all masked while doing the mystical Kanrodai Dance.

It is supposed to be a re-enactment of the creation of the world and can only be performed at the Jiba of the Tenri headquarters, where the followers of Tenrikyo believe mankind was created.

5) *The Mikagura Uta Dance, or Teodori.* This dance, which follows the Kanrodai Dance, can be seen at any Tenri church. It is

performed in front of the altar by three men and three women who are accompanied by the music of the *jampon, fue, koto,* and *samisen* besides the rhythm of various drums. This music, usually lasting about fifty minutes, is fascinatingly punctuated by an unusual beat. Through graceful movements of hands, arms, and manipulation of a fan, the dancers express various sentiments—pain and suffering, joy and ecstasy. There is an atmosphere of dynamism and religious zeal which can be fanned into frenzy by the rhythmic percussion. The climactic end of the dance is brought about by a series of ear-rending drum beats.

6) *The Sermon.* The shimbashira's sermon is not merely a message from a pulpit. The sermon, besides being broadcast all over God's Residence by means of loud-speakers, is also taped for later use. There is often the popping of flash bulbs so that the latest publicity photos can be made, or so that the leaders of Tenrikyo can be eternalized by the camera.

The sermon usually concerns the life of the foundress, her sufferings, her love for mankind, and how to follow her example. She is the *hinagata,* the divine model for all mankind. Here is a typical example:

"The way of God means joyful life (*yokigurashi*). This was the intention of God the Parent when he created mankind. because man finds his real self in a joyful life. However, for selfish purposes man has misused his mind—the only faculty he can freely exercise—and has piled dust (*hokori*) on his soul. This dust is now covering the world and has made it a world of competition, suffering, and war. The only way to a joyful life is to convert our mind and to sweep off the dust. When we are cleansed from all sorts of dust, and when we perform the Kanrodai Dance [this, of course, is the best means] we shall be reborn."

Besides these six elements of the Tenrikyo service a seventh must be mentioned. It is the backbone of the daily service in the temple as well as in the homes of the believers. This is the prayer *Ashiki o harote tasuke tamae, Tenri-o-no-mikoto,* which means "Sweep away all evils and save us, Parent Tenri-o-no-mikoto." This prayer is accompanied by hand movements intended to show how the dust is brushed away from the soul and how the grace of the Parent God is received. Its popularity is immense, and to the common believer it takes the place the Lord's Prayer occupies in Christianity.

Writings and Doctrines

The canonical writings of Tenrikyo are contained in three books: the *Mikagura Uta,* the *Ofudesaki,* and the *Osashizu.* The first two were written by Miki, and the last one by Master Iburi. The originals have been preserved, and the edition commonly used by the believers is a microphotograph from the original. The canonical writings of Tenrikyo therefore not only give the words of Miki and Master Iburi, but also reflect the various shades of mind which Japanese brush calligraphy reveals. Tenrikyo believers are very proud of this, and often in discussions with Christians they claim that this proves the superiority of Tenrikyo over Christianity.

The Mikagura Uta

All but a few lines of the *Mikagura Uta* were written between 1866 and 1880. It is a song consisting of one prelude, which is divided into twelve parts and is probably the most important text used in Tenrikyo worship, being chanted in every Tenri church at morning as well as at evening service. The gestures and melody designed by the foundress to accompany the song are primitive, yet dignified and fascinating, and there is no doubt that the *Mikagura Uta* is one of the most important sources of inspiration for the believers. Fukaya, a prominent Tenri writer, says: "We Tenrikyo believers will never forget our Mikagura Uta. It is the first thing taught upon entering our religion, and we sing it day and night. Whenever we chant this sacred song, miraculous salvation descends upon us. This song is the source and essence of our religious life, and it is as necessary to us as rice."[3] It is claimed that the Mikagura Uta is a new and entirely original creation of Miki; however, it seems highly probable that there is a historical connection with the *ee ja nai ka* dances so popular among farmers in the middle of the 19th century. The popularity of the Mikagura Uta and its connection with a familiar type of dance did much to make the farmers cast their lot with Tenrikyo.[4]

The *Mikagura Uta* is so important as source material for the study of Tenrikyo that I have included an English translation here:

Prologue

Sweep away all evils and save us, oh God our parent![5]
I will speak a word to you. Listen to the Word of God.
Listen, for I never tell you anything wrong.
In the manner of Earth and Heaven I created man and wife,
    the dawn of human life.
Sweeping all evils away I hasten to save you all,
And when the world is purified, the heavenly nectar will
    come.[6]
Since creation I have looked through all the world, but no-
body understands my heart.
This is only natural, as nobody ever taught you;
But this time I, your Parent, appear to you all to explain to
    you all things in full.
You have spoken of the Jiba, God's home in Yamato,[7]
But concerning its origin you know nothing.
Whoever learns in full about the origin of the Jiba
    cannot but long and yearn for it.
If you want to learn, come to me,
And you shall know all about the origin of all beings.
I, God the Parent, reveal myself unto you and explain every-
    thing,
And the whole world shall bloom.
I hasten to save you all,
Therefore, all souls of the world, rejoice and be happy.

Part I

How wonderful is the gift bestowed at New Year:
The fertilizer of great effect.[8]
Smiles come with the gift from me,
How happy you all shall be.
Your mind should always be like that of a three-year-old baby.
Fortunes of full harvest,
Blessings flooding you all.
Surprising abundant crops will be produced.

Sow and reap with care.
Always full harvest in Yamato.
Now come and follow me here.
The harvest is assured.[9]

Part II

With a "tong, tong, tong" we begin the New Year dance,
Oh, so delightful.
Since we started the mysterious building[10]
How merrily we shout.
Everything will be yours.
Your fortune will be created again and again.
For anyone who follows me
Must cut the roots of evil.
Since I save you all from distress,
Every root of disease must be cut off.
If your souls are strong and firm,
Peace will reign throughout the world.

Part III

The place of holy service in the Land of the Sun
Will be the foundation of the world.
So mysterious a temple of holy service
I never before asked anybody to create.
Here, gathering from all over the world,
They build the temple to the wonder of all.
From far you have followed me to this time,
From now the actual salvation will begin.
For years and years I have been scoffed and slandered,
Yet, now I will work a wondrous miracle and save you all.
Never ask me for unnatural and unreasonable things,
But come to me with an innocent soul.
Whatever you do, with all your heart and soul
Lean on your Parent and trust in Me.
There is no greater hardship than to have disease,
I will also devote myself to holy labor.

Although you may have believed in me up to now,
Yet never could you know me until now.
At long last She has appeared,
The true and real Parent of all.

Part IV

Fear not, however people may slander you,
I, your Parent, keep watch over you all.
Every couple of you, live in harmony of soul,
Then everything will become clear to you.
Those of you near to me, look at me,
See how your Parent serves and works wonders.
Day and night our service goes on,
Annoying those around us.
I am always in haste to save you all,
Come, hasten to Me with a cheerful heart.
First I want to save the villagers,
But they cannot understand my heart.
All our lives are ever getting closer,
Meditate it deeply in your innermost souls.
Then all the roots of disease will be cleared away,
Let all your hearts from now on be bright and gay.
Now this is the paradise of the world,
I myself long to be there in haste.
Thankful be you all,
Now our souls have been purified.

Part V

Wherever you live in this world,
There will be places of salvation.
Yet, here is a most mysterious salvation for you:
I grant you painless childbirth, and free you from smallpox.
God the Parent and water are alike,
They both clean away stains from man.
For none can escape avarice and greed,
But in the Presence of God no greed will be found.

As long as you are devoted to me,
Be always bright and cheerful.
Free your hearts from all violent thoughts,
And come to me with a soft and gentle mind.
I will let no distress come near you,
This is the place of salvation, there is no place like this.
Yamato, but not only here,
To every corner of the earth my salvation will reach.
Know ye, that the origin of this world, the Jiba,
This most wonderful place, has now been revealed.
If you are ever devoted, whatever may come,
Let us live in this our brotherhood.

Part VI

As you know, human nature, the heart of every man,
Is prone to doubt and suspect.
Because I perform miraculous salvation,
There is nothing my eyes cannot see.
The hearts of all the people in the world
Are reflected to me as in a mirror.
Until now you have performed my service well,
The foundation of salvation.
Forever the sacred song and dance go on,
Therefore I grant you wonderful salvation.
You have asked me, and even excessively,
And in a thousand ways your prayers have been granted.
Therefore, whoever you are, if devoted to Me,
Never let your hearts harbor thoughts of wrong.
Be ever devoted to Me, your Parent,
And if you fail, you must start anew.
Since you have given Me your devotion so far,
A special gift will be given unto you.
At long last invocation through a fan has been revealed,
How miraculous this is!

Part VII

I tell you the secret of *hinokishin*[11]

And pour over you the holy perfume.
This is done from my inmost soul,
And I pray you will never refuse it.
Throughout the world there is no one,
Who does not desire to own farm land.
If there is a good field,
All you will be eager to own it.
For all through the world the heart is the same,
Even I would yearn for such a field.
I never force you to do anything,
All is left to the free decision of your heart.
My desire is to own the land,
No matter what the cost may be.
The seed sown in the rice field of God,
Shall come out and sprout.
Since God's field is the land for all men of the earth,
I Myself shall sow the seed with care.
Now, at last, we are here, come from all over the world,
And all of you who have sown the seed with me
   shall harvest a rich crop, even without fertilizer.

Part VIII

How can it be that throughout the world,
There were no stone nor timber?
A mysterious building, without stone or timber, I build,
But I do not expect anybody to help me.
Yet, from all over the world people will come,
And the building will grow up by itself.
Forget all greed,
And let firmness stay in your heart.
For a long time I have been waiting,
And pray you: do not let it be built by Me alone.
Yet be not too much in haste,
But meditate deeply in your heart.
So, that when your heart has become purified,
You can begin to build.
Deep in the mountains,

I have marked all the stones and timber for My need.
All are left in your Parent's mind,
The timber to fell and the stone to cut.
Together, through all the world,
Our souls have been purified now.

Part IX

For I will wander around in the wide world,
Until I have saved you all.
I save you from all discomfort,
So trust in God the Parent.
When I look into the hearts of men,
I find it marred with greed.
Fling away all your avarice,
Since I receive nought but the pure.
All the people in the world are the same,
Think of this and then come and follow me.
I do not compel you to come,
But wait till you so desire.
Therefore I say to all of you,
Meditate seriously on this in your heart.
Everywhere, even in the mountains,
The service to Me shall be heard.
But although you will be serving me here,
No one can read the depth of my heart.
When you begin to call for the name of God the Parent,
Then come in haste to Me, your original home.

Part X

The human heart, by its nature,
Is difficult to understand.
Although I have wrought wondrous salvation before,
This is the first time I reveal Myself.
I pray you all to take away
The dirty mud in the water.
Fathomless deep is the abyss of greed,

But purify the spirit and paradise is yours.
These words of mine, for ever and ever,
Shall be the source of your every day's thought.
I have also spoken severe words at times
Because I am in haste to save you all.
Suffering is rooted in your own mind,
Blame not others, the fault is yours.
Although disease causes so much suffering,
No one knows of its root.
Never before until this day, unto you,
Has the root of disease been disclosed.
But now the truth has been brought to light,
The root of disease is your own mind.

Part XI

For here in Japan, the Land of the Sun,
The Jiba, home of the Parent, has been built.
Man and wife, united in holy labour,
This is the first seed of human happiness.
Wherever I look in the world I see more people
With baskets on their shoulders, carrying out holy work.
Forget your greed and hasten to do holy work,
This is the first fertilizer of faith.
Every day you must carry earth,
If work remains, I will come Myself and help.
But do not call others to join,
Unless they themselves want to come.
How wonderful this work of carrying earth,
Since it is done in holy *hinokishin*.
We dig out the soil from the grounds of the Holy Home
And carry it to another place.
So far, until this day, alack,
No one understood my heart.
This year we did not use fertilizer,
Yet we have reaped such a plentiful harvest,
How joyful and thankful we are!

Let us leave everything to the Master Carpenter[12]
In utmost trust to Him.
Since you are building so wondrous a temple,
Give the instructions after consulting with Me.
Come here, all master workmen, from all the world,
And I will pour over you the Holy Perfume.
The best master workmen you can find,
Call them here to the Original Home of Man.
We need four Master Carpenters,
Consult with me without losing time.
I will never speak to compel them to come,
But they will come of their own free will.
This building is most mysterious,
Once the work is started, it never ends.
Go deep into the mountains,
Along with the Master Carpenter, the feller of the trees.
Here comes the Master Workman, the sawer of the planks,
The Master Workman, the builder of the House,
And the Master Workman, the planner of it all.
Thus now, at last, throughout the world,
All the working team is complete.[13]

The Ofudesaki

The *Ofudesaki* was written from 1869 to 1882 and consists of
seventeen volumes with a total of 1,711 verses. Like the *Mikagura
Uta* and the *Osashizu,* the *Ofudesaki* was written in the Japanese
phonetic syllabary *hiragana* without the use of the Chinese ideo-
graphs (kanji).[14] The *Ofudesaki* deals with the same subjects as
the *Mikagura Uta*: the blessings of the Kanrodai, the problems of
sin and Salvation, the Jiba as the center of the earth and the healing of disease.

The Osashizu

The *Osashizu* (Divine Directions) is the most valuminous of
the three canonical writings. There are thirty-three books with

a total of 7,790 pages. It was written by Master Iburi during the period 1887 to 1907.

The *Osashizu* is much more elaborate than the *Mikagura Uta* and the *Ofudesaki* and reflects the development of Tenrikyo. It contains numerous detailed explanations for the believers and tells them how to propagate their faith. The doctrinal system of Tenrikyo takes its beginning here, as does its apologetics. The following example written in 1887 is from one of the earliest *Osashizu*: "You will never be able to understand My will or probe My mind. I will tell you that the normal lifespan of human beings is 115 years, even though Miki passed away at the age of ninety. Why should that happen? It will be impossible for you to understand this. I hastened to save mankind, and for this reason I opened the doors of heaven and came down to cure all the ills of the world. This has been done with My own almighty will, and nobody could prevent me from doing so. God can never lie. Take all these things and keep them in your hearts. I will surely make this world a place of happiness."[15] This and many other examples show how Tenrikyo well before the end of the 19th century conceived of itself as a full-fledged religion with a philosophy and a doctrinal system.

God

The center of worship in Tenrikyo is Tenri-o-no-mikoto (Lord of Divine Wisdom), who is conceived of as the sole deity of all, the creator of all things, and the gracious sustainer of life. He is also referred to as Oya-gami (God the Parent). This god, according to Tenrikyo doctrine, chose Nakayama Miki as his dwelling and revealed his purpose to the world through her. Thus Miki has come to be identified with God the Parent, and she herself during the latter part of her life came to the conviction that she was divine, a conviction that caused her to wear distinctive red clothes and to refuse food which was not cooked in a special pot.

Tenrikyo teaches that God first revealed Himself as Kami, which here means the creator of this world and all human beings, or the original, true God. Later God revealed himself as Tsuki-hi (Moon-sun God), the god who used the heavenly bodies to give life and warmth to this earth. The final stage of the revelation of God was the appearance of Miki, through whom God was revealed as a parent (*oya*) who loves his children on earth.

God the Parent is conceived of in the following way: "My daily concern is solely how best I may help My children."[16] The doctrine states:

"He associates his parental love with that of ours, with which we bring up our children, and taught that He is not only the Supreme Being to be worshipped as God, or Tsuki-hi to be looked up to in heaven, but also our true parent in Whom we can safely trust and confide our joys and sorrows."[17]

"We are born between heaven and earth and live amidst the exquisite harmony of the universe. Just as we are all bathed in the light of both moon and sun, so we are indiscriminately under the blessing of both heaven and earth. Heaven and earth, as well as the moon and the sun, are the manifestations of God the Parent. Thus we live between the embrace of heaven and earth, in the very bosom of our real Parent, basking in His benevolence that knows no bounds."[18]

Although the center of Tenrikyo worship is God the Parent, the Creator of the Universe, and the Father of Mankind, a multitude of other gods are mentioned. At present Tenrikyo emphasizes only one deity, but it started within the framework of polytheistic Shinto and still retains part of the Shinto pantheon—for example the Tohashira no Kami (Ten Gods) which play such a dominant part in the creation story of Tenrikyo.

Creation

The strong influence of Shintoism on Tenrikyo in the early days of its development is particularly evident in the creation story of Tenrikyo.[19] The following passages, excerpts from *The Doctrine of Tenrikyo*, will remind many a reader of the ancient Japanese chronicles, the *Nihon Shoki* and especially the *Kojiki*. These are the Shintoistic stories that give the myths and legends of early Japanese history. The Tenrikyo version is related to it in that most of the names used are the same as those in the Shinto text as well as some of the contents:

"Originally this world was an immense expanse of muddy waters.

Tsukihi, God the Parent, found this chaotic condition unbearably tasteless and thought of creating human beings so that He might share their joy. One day He searched through the muddy waters to see what materials He could find for the creation and found a merman and a white snake, both with human faces. He asked that they undertake the roles which He envisioned for them. He called a dolphin from the northwest and a tortoise from the southeast, took them up with their consent and ate them to taste their mental flavor. He decided to use the former as the 'first organ' of the sterner sex and as the skeleton to support the body, and the latter as the 'first organ' of the gentler sex and as skin to cover the body. They were given the names of Izanagi-no-mikoto and Izanami-no-mikoto. In a similar way Tsuki-hi called an eel from the east, a flat-fish from the southwest, a black snake from the west, and a globe-fish from the northeast, and gave them the respective functions of being the instrument of breathing and speaking, the instrument of pulling out, and the instrument of severing (the latter two functions to be used at the birth of human beings). He now entered into the body of Izanagi-no-mikoto as Tsuki-sama (moon) and into that of Izanami-no-mikoto as Hi-sama (sun) and taught them how to procreate. Seeds, in the number of 900,099,999, were put into the womb of Izanami-no-mikoto, who after three years and three months delivered the first 900,099,999 species of mankind. The off-spring, however, only reached a height of three inches in a period of ninety-nine years, after which they all passed away together with the father. Izanami gave birth to the same number of children twice more, and the height increased to three and a half and finally to four inches, after which human beings were reborn 8,008 times in the form of all kinds of animals, all of whom died except a female monkey. She gave birth to ten human beings, who stood half an inch at their birth and grew taller, half an inch at a time, until they reached the height of eight inches. At that time the bottom of the muddy sea began to develop so that land and sea, heaven and earth, sun and moon could be dimly discerned. Once these humans would grow to a height of one foot eight inches, they started to be born in pairs, but when they reached a height of three feet, they came to be conceived one at a time, and began to speak. When at last they came to stand full five feet, the whole universe, land

and sea, heaven and earth, was completed and they began to dwell there.

According to Tenrikyo doctrine the place where Izanami and Izanagi met and saw the dawn of the human race is the Jiba, the center of what is now Tenri City, the "cradle and the future center of the world." Further, the time of the first meeting of Izanami and Izanagi is said to have been 900,099,999 years before Tenri-o-no-mikoto came down to Miki. In the explanations of the Tenrikyo creation story the supremacy of the Japanese race as the oldest in the world is often stressed, and the story was frequently used during the war when patriotism was strong in Tenrikyo.

Kashimono-karimono

Kashimono-karimono (thing lent, things borrowed) is the Tenrikyo doctrine according to which everything man possesses, including his body, has been lent to him by God the Parent. If man realizes that he depends entirely upon God the Parent, happiness will be his, but if he relies upon his own strength, all kinds of adversities will meet him: "People live as if all the treasures, joys, their own bodies and all that they possess are their own property. To act in this way is to break the harmony and order that should exist between man, society and the universe. In doing so we are betraying the will of God, and He will warn us in various ways, such as by sending us sickness and other adversities."[20]

The origin to the doctrine of *kashimono-karimono* is found in the writings of Miki and Master Iburi:

"I lend you your body. Know you not of the almightiness of God the Parent?"[21] "You borrow your body from Me; the mind alone is yours. And out of this mind of yours arises daily all your mental actions of every variety. But I hope that you will listen to Me with understanding when I say that I estimate each of these actions at its true value and help with My omnipotent hand only those whose sincerity is acceptable in My sight."[22]

Tenrikyo scholars and teachers put strong emphasis on this doctrine, and maintain that in this point they have gone further than all other religions: "The old religions also preach that clothes, food, and shelter are given by God or Buddha, but they have not gone so far in their teaching as to state that the human body is a loan from

God."[23] This is a statement that few non-Tenrikyo scholars would agree with.

An interesting application of the kashimono-karimono doctrine is the attempt to explain the miseries of the human race in the light of this doctrine.

"Bodily ailment is an act of injunction by God the Parent against the unnatural action of man who tries to make selfish use of what he has only borrowed, according to the reason of the ego; it is a taboo God the Parent has placed on free use of what He has given in trust. That we cannot dispose of disease or misfortune after our own will, no matter how much we may try, chafe, fret, fume, or strive is the proof that our body is a thing, not of our own, but borrowed."[24] The doctrine is used to explain all the miseries of mankind, and on the other side, all the miseries of mankind are used to prove the doctrine.

Sin

If we use our mind and body as if it were our own, the result will be accumulation of hokori (dust) on our soul and everywhere else in the world. Hokori is the Tenrikyo term equivalent to the Christian conception of sin, although Tenrikyo believers maintain that man is essentially good and without serious sin. Miki expressed it in the following way: "Looking over all ages and climes, I find not a single human being essentially bad. No, there is not a single person who is born bad. The so-called bad are only those whose minds are stained with specks of dust."[25]

However, although Tenrikyo denies the existence of sin, the way they *speak* about hokori does not seem much different from the way other religions speak about sin. Tenrikyo mentions eight kinds of dust: greed, stinginess, partiality, hatred, animosity, anger, covetousness, and arrogance. No attempt is made to explain the various evils of this world as, for example, in Buddhism. Nevertheless, the hokori of Tenrikyo is essentially different from the Christian conception of sin. Hokori is not regarded as something which parts man from God, something that can never be removed. It is rather regarded as something which does not belong to the nature of man, but as something which can be easily removed, thus dust that briefly covers the soul but from an outside source.

While the Twelve Links of Ignorance and the concept of Karma of Buddhism never really penetrated to the common people, the doctrine of hokori has become part and parcel of the daily life of all Tenrikyo believers—to these workers, farmers, and housewives, hokori has become as real a thing as dust.[26]

Salvation

As there is no real evil, and as man is not constitutionally bound in sin, the path to salvation is broad and not too strenuous to follow. If the dust is swept away, the way will be open to the land of yokigurashi, a term which means a happy life, but often is used synonymously with salvation or paradise. Sometimes it appears that God the Parent will sweep the dust away, sometimes it is said that man must do it himself, and sometimes it is said that the dust will be swept away by itself: "Behold, I shall cleanse the minds of all mankind, acting Myself as a broom."[27] "Particles of dust are essentially things so light and minute that we can blow them away with a single puff of breath—so light and minute that we can clear them away with perfect ease, provided only that we dispose of them soon enough."[28] "When once you understand this appearance, the dust of your minds, whoever you may be, shall be swept away of itself."[29] The latter idea, that the dust shall be swept away of itself, is probably due to influence from Buddhism, where sin is regarded as ignorance or illusion which disappears as soon as the mind is enlightened with true knowledge.

The meaning of salvation has undergone some change during the history of Tenrikyo. In the beginning it meant deliverance from sickness and pain; later on, it received a connotation of deliverance from economical, social, and domestic troubles; and at present the idea of spiritual salvation is getting stronger. Further, the salvation of the world (tasuke-ichijo) is gradually getting a more prominent place. The following is from a speech by the present shimbashira of Tenrikyo, Nakayama Shozen: "Thinking in this way, the Tenrikyo doctrine consists indeed in the development of the parental love of the Creator of Mankind. Thus we are enabled to have constant opportunities to encourage the growth and animation of our minds by means of the parental love. When we become aware of this point, we come to realize that it is our mission to encourage one another with our mind serene and cheerful. I believe that herein lies the true peace of the world and the salvation of mankind."[30]

According to Tenrikyo the salvation of mankind started at the creation of the earth. After that came "indirect salvation" through Buddha, Christ, and other deities. Finally, full and direct salvation came through Miki Nakayama by Tenri-o-no-mikoto.

The main idea of salvation in Tenrikyo is expressed by the term yokigurashi, that is, a happy life without disease and suffering. This is easily seen from the various *otsutome* and *osazuke,* or ways to obtain yokigurashi. Of the otsutome at least six are connected with agriculture—a reflection of the early stage of Tenrikyo when almost all believers were farmers, They include: *koe no tsutome,* or the service which grants miraculous manure; *haede no tsutome,* or the service of germination; *amagoi zutome,* or the ceremony held to ask for rain; *mushibari no tsutome,* or the service held to extirpate such things as worms or insects. Most such ceremonies have now disappeared, and the services and ceremonies held today to obtain yokigurashi are the osazuke (divine grantings). Among them are: *koe no sazuke,* the granting of a fertilizer of extraordinary efficacy; the *iki no sazuke,* the granting of divine breath to heal diseases; and above all, the *Kanrodai no tsutome,* the service around the Kanrodai, which is said to grant believers all kinds of gifts, spiritual as well as material.

By means of the various *tsutome* and *sazuke,* and by the grace of the Foundress, they believe in the coming of a new world where sickness and suffering shall be a thing of the past:

"This grace, the granting of which depends upon the sincerity of your minds, is a safeguard against becoming sick, against dying, and against decaying. This gift is an expression of My earnest desire to fix a length of 115 for man's natural term of existence."[31] The latter words refer to the Tenrikyo doctrine that man was created to have a natural life span of 115 years, which he will be able to obtain again once the dust has been swept away from the world and the tasuke-ichijo—the salvation of all—has taken place.

Afterlife and Transmigration

Tenrikyo is mainly interested in this life on earth, and little has been written on the subject of afterlife. Whenever this subject is treated, it is done in simple and easily understood terms—for example, "when you die your soul passes into the body of a baby born in the same instant."

However, even if Tenrikyo believers are mainly concerned with this present life on earth, still they believe in transmigration. "Do not think that a man lives only one life. He will be reborn over and over again. Hark and listen carefully: your offspring will inherit the consequences of your previous lives."[32] But Tenrikyo attempts to take away from transmigration the rather sombre and sinister stamp it has been given in Buddhism; death is not spoken of as a disappearance, but as a taking off of old clothes and putting on of bright new ones (*denaoshi*). And the six Worlds of transmigration in Buddhism (Hell, World of Hungry Spirits, World of Beasts, World of Fighting and Bloodshed, World of Man, and World of Heavenly Beings) have been simplified into one: the World of Man.

According to Buddhism man is the prisoner of karma until he obtains enlightenment, but according to Tenrikyo all will be released from the world of transmigration when the world has been cleansed from dust, and the heavenly dew has descended upon the Kanrodai. From that moment eternal happiness shall be the lot of all men. There shall be no suffering to disturb their peace, and when they reach the age of 115 they shall give back their borrowed body to God the Parent, at which time they will immediately return in the form of a newborn baby to live another 115 years—in other words, they envision a circle of happiness to continue forever.

Propagation

Each believer of Tenrikyo is expected to be a missionary, but special missionaries and teachers are also trained. The missionaries and teachers are called *yoboku,* or beams—one of the many terms from housebuilding used in Tenrikyo.[33]

The task of a yoboku is to save others by *nioigake,* which literally means to pour perfume but is actually synonymous with propagating the teaching of Tenrikyo and helping others by administering the various osazuke. The yoboku is not doing this by himself, but entirely through the power of God the Parent: "The yoboku is in no way a saviour but only the instrument. The mission of a yoboku may be said to be truly fulfilled, when he earnestly follows in the wake of the Foundress."[34]

In order to become a missionary of Tenrikyo a special training course emphasizing Tenri doctrines must be taken. This training course has played an important role in the development of Tenrikyo and accounts for much of its impetus.

The missionary training course is mentioned as early as 1892 in the following passage from the *Osashizu*:

"Listen to me. One full course of instruction requires ninety days. To complete the instructions three courses are required. Each of the three lessons takes thirty days. These three lessons must be repeated three times. If the people study in this way, their knowledge will be sufficient and their healing power over others will be strong enough."[35] This was changed in 1898 by a new osashizu: "If you teach too long, the students will get tired. In this way you will get nowhere. Therefore it is my wish that you should instruct the people only during thirty days and repeat this nine times. For everyone will certainly remember the things that are told him nine times."[36]

However, this has been changed again so that believers who live more than four-hundred kilometers from Tenri are allowed to take the thirty-day course only once; people more than 280 kilometers away, twice; and the people who are so fortunate as to live in the town of Tenri itself must come and be taught the stipulated nine-times-thirty days.

The curriculum consists of: the Doctrine of Tenrikyo, Court Music, Course on the Life of the Foundress, Religious Observance, History of the Church of Tenri, Testimonial Procedure, Morals, Sermons, and—most important of all—hinokishin, or daily donation of labor. Through hinokishin the huge compound of Tenrikyo is cleaned, buildings and roads are constructed and repaired, and the cleanliness of public places, especially the deer park of Nara, is maintained.

There are only two qualifications for entering the missionary training course. The person in question must be a member of Tenrikyo and must be over seventeen years of age. Every month a crowd of about fifteen hundred people of all ages from all parts of the country takes part in the training course. Upon completion of the class, examinations are held, and the osazuke, which are supposed to give various miraculous powers, are awarded to the believers by the patriarch himself at a short ceremony.

In the propagation of its teachings, Tenrikyo probably avails itself of all modern mass communication methods more than any of the other new religions. A weekly radio program originates from the headquarters. Besides coverage on eight major radio stations, there are many programs carried on local stations. Tenrikyo distributes more than twenty 16mm documentary films showing all phases of Tenri life and doctrine. It has two troupes traveling throughout the country staging dramas and shows, and it publishes more books, pamphlets, weeklies, and other magazines than any other new religion in Japan.

In this connection the library of Tenrikyo must be mentioned. It is one of the largest libraries in Asia with close to 700,000 volumes and is the center of Tenrikyo's endeavors to develop from being a "farmers'" religion into a modern streamlined religion acknowledged by the intellectual world in, as well as outside of Japan. For this purpose Tenrikyo contributed more than ten percent of all the money raised in Japan towards the expenses of the Ninth International Congress of the History of Religions (in 1958), during which all the delegates visited the headquarters of Tenrikyo near Nara. The Tenri University was established as another important link in the attempt to become recognized by the intellectual classes. It was built in 1926 as a school of foreign languages for the training of missionaries and obtained full university status only in 1949.

The mission of Tenrikyo is also to reach areas outside Japan. 225 churches are located in the United States, Brazil, Korea, China, the Philippines, and other countries, but the vast majority of the members of those churches are of Japanese ancestry.

To increase the effectiveness of the mission abroad, Tenri missionaries study 16th-century Christian mission literature (their library has the best collection on this subject in the world); they study modern mission strategy of various religions in Japan as well as abroad; and they imitate foreign culture, architecture, and ways of thinking when establishing churches in other countries. The motto of Tenrikyo mission abroad is to accommodate their religion to foreign ways so it will become as appealing to other peoples as it has become to so many people of Japan.

Tenrikyo and Christianity

There is no denying the fact that there are numerous points of similarity between Tenrikyo and Christianity, in form as well as in content. Consciously or unconsciously Tenrikyo leaders have borrowed extensively from the form and teachings of Christianity. Some people even go so far as to maintain that Miki herself was under the influence of a little secret group of *hanare Kirishitan*—Japanese Christians who in the greatest secrecy and in danger of their lives stuck to the faith transmitted to them by Francis Xavier in the middle of the 16th century, even though it was strictly forbidden by the government from the beginning of the 17th century. So far no proof of the latter theory has been found.

Similarities with Christianity are seen in the phraseology of Tenrikyo, the use of such expressions as "we shall reap what we have sown," "soldiers of God," "how inscrutable are the ways of God," as well as the words "ascension," "sacrament," "mediatrix," all found in Tenrikyo texts. It is seen in the prayers, which often sound like prayers heard in Christian churches, for example, "Thou, oh God, hast created man as well as this world out of a shapeless chaos, and Thou hast conserved us up to this very day. Never, not in all eternity, shall I forget all the graces Thou hast bestown upon me." Further, the creation story of Tenrikyo, with its mention of "a muddy sea of chaos" and its "let us create man," reminds us somewhat of Genesis.

The circumstances surrounding the death of Miki, when the temple doors were wide open although nobody had opened them; the explanation by Tenrikyo scholars that Miki's attempted suicide was due to the fact that God the Parent was so set upon saving mankind that he even wanted to sacrifice his own life; or the messianic expectance of an advent, after which neither temples nor prayers will be necessary, are but a few of the many other similarities that could be listed.

Tenrikyo has a remarkable gift for modification and accommodation that has carried it some way from its original teaching and may take it still further in the future as it follows developments in Buddhism, Shintoism, and Christianity.

Summary and Future

Of course it is impossible to pinpoint all the reasons for Tenrikyo's success. However, a few points which undoubtedly are partly responsible for it can be listed:

1) Simple and practical dogmas which are easy to understand and not too strenuous to follow.

2) Systematic study of these dogmas during the missionary course, the nature of which unites the believers in study, work and play.

3) Effective and zealous propaganda using up-to-date mass communication media.

4) Emphasis on yokigurashi, a happy life without extremely strict moral commandments.

5) The tremendous importance of the mecca at Tenri City as a focal point that gives the believers a sense of importance and convinces them of the grandeur of Tenrikyo.

6) The donation of labor (hinokishin), which gives the believers a sense of fellowship and increases their willingness to serve.

7) The oneness of life and teaching—that is, that religion is not something that can be taken apart from daily life, but belongs to it, or is even identical with it.

8) The healing of diseases by faith—a characteristic that especially in the earlier history of Tenrikyo accounted for much of its fame.

The rapid progress of Tenrikyo seems to have leveled off. During the past few years the number of churches and believers has varied only slightly. According to the yearbook published by the Ministry of Education, Tenrikyo now has approximately 2,350,000 believers and about 15,000 churches.

Future development depends to some extent on the degree to which the splintering-off process divides and diffuses the total strength of the religion. It seems probable that Tenrikyo, which in 120 years has shown less tendency to divide than most other new religions, will in the foreseeable future continue to maintain its leading position as one of the strongest of Japan's new religions.

2

黒住教 / Kurozumikyo

Many new religions emphasize international relationships and take in ideas and thoughts from abroad. Kurozumikyo, however, is only interested in things Japanese, particularly those of the past and calls itself "the most genuine Japanese religious faith." It is an older member of the new religions, having been founded almost 150 years ago, and is listed as one of the thirteen Shinto sects, though it differs from them enough that it can be considered separate. Its leaders consider it quite separate.

History and Background

Kurozumikyo was founded on November 11, 1814, by Kurozumi Munetada, a Shinto priest of the Imamura Shrine, which is near Okayama City in central Japan.

The Kurozumi family had furnished priests to Okayama Prefecture for generations and was well known in the area. Born in December, 1780, Munetada was destined to follow in the family tradition. He assisted his father in the latter's capacity as chief priest of the Imamura Shrine. Munetada, a deeply religious man, experienced three dramatic events in his life, the third one, in 1814, resulting in the creation of his religion.

His first such experience is said to have been a revelation experienced when he was twenty. The Sun Goddess appeared before him and told him to live according to his conscience and in filial piety. The second experience was the death of his parents when he was thirty-three, an event that shook him so seriously that he al- **61** most died himself. The third was a severe attack of a pulmonary disease that was almost fatal. Kurozumikyo tells us of his cure:

"In 1814 his condition grew hopeless, and conscious of this, he offered his last thanksgiving to the Sun Goddess and the spirits of his ancestors for the mercies granted him during his life on earth. Then he peacefully waited for the moment when his end would come. At this very instant our Founder thought to himself that such serious illness might have been caused by too much grief and depression after the death of his parents, and that he might recover if he tried to bring cheerfulness and happiness into his mind. He now began to turn over in his mind every grace granted him by Heaven, until at last he recovered."[1]

Soon after his recovery the final revelation came: "On the winter solstice of the same year, while Holy Munetada was worshipping the sun as usual, in spite of himself he opened his mouth so wide as if to swallow up the sun, and felt in the same moment how his breast became filled with life-giving warmth and light. At this moment a sudden inspiration flashed into his mind, by which he experienced within himself that God and Man, heaven and earth, within and without, were one and undivided. The whole universe became a living being in him. He called this profound experience *tenmei jikiju,* that is 'the direct reception of the will of heaven.' "[2]

Munetada expressed his experience in the following poem:

> *Amaterasu Kami no Mitoku o shiru toki wa*
> *Nete mo samete mo arigataki ka na.*

(When we understand the virtue of Amaterasu-o-mikami
Whether asleep or awake—oh, what a wonderful thing!)

Munetada immediately decided to impart his experience to others. He announced his revelation, and as revelations were more unique in the beginning of the last century than now, crowds of people came to see this man who claimed to be one with the Sun Goddess. Munetada held meetings six times a month, where he preached, taught, and performed various miracles, especially healings. As his believers increased (a considerable number of them were influential samurai of the Okayama clan) Kurozumikyo soon reached the status of a Shinto sect and was officially recognized as such in 1846.

After Munetada's death in 1850, his disciples continued to preach his teaching. The posthumous name of Munetada Daimyojin was granted by the Imperial House in 1856. At the newly-named Munetada Shrine in Kyoto, court nobles, samurai, and even occasionally members of the Imperial Household Agency paid him homage.

In 1876 the sect took the name of Kurozumikyo and reorganized. It continued to be one of the thirteen Shinto sects, but it developed its own characteristics. In addition to the two Munetada shrines, one in Kyoto and one in Okayama, four hundred meeting places (*kyokaisho*) were set up. This system remains intact for the almost 750,000 believers Kurozumikyo now claims.

Worship, Ceremonies, and Services

The believers of Kurozumikyo worship the Sun Goddess in their homes, at the local shrine, and at the main Munetada shrine at the headquarters of the religion in Okayama City. Besides the shrine dedicated to the Founder, there is a large *daikyo-den* (main preaching hall), where all believers are supposed to come and worship at least once during their lifetime.

The worship is the same as in other Shinto sects—prayers, offerings, purification rites, etc.—the only special rite of Kurozumikyo being the "sun-swallowing rite," which is based on the experience of the founder. It is explained as follows:

"Every day the believers shall worship the Sun, and while doing this inhale the fresh air as if to swallow the Sun that is the divine spirit of God. By repeating this they shall arrive at the mystic consciousness of oneness with Amaterasu-o-mikami. By this practice, health of body as well as of mind shall be attained without fail."[3]

Kurozumikyo has three festivals each year. Most famous is the Founder's Festival on April 17 and 18, the *Kyososai,* when the Munetada Shrine Procession takes place.

To provide priests for the shrines and the activities of Kurozumikyo the sect maintains the Omoto Gakuin (Omoto Institute), which is an institution for the training of young people in the doctrines of the religion.

Notable among social activities carried out by Kurozumikyo is their orphanage the Tenshin-ryo. It is located in the town of Akasaka in Okayama Prefecture and is one of the oldest and largest orphanages in that part of the country. At present about one hundred orphans are enrolled there. Besides this, Kurozumikyo has a middle school, five nurseries, and a large number of children's clubs.

Doctrines

The doctrines of Kurozumikyo were all created by Munetada, and hardly anything new has been added to them since his death.

God

The center of worship is the Sun Goddess, Amaterasu-o-mikami, who is regarded as the absolute deity of the universe, the creator of heaven and earth. This is a slight deviation from Shinto, which gave supremacy to the Three Gods of Creation. Thus Kurozumikyo seems to be monotheistic. However, the Eight Million Gods of Shinto are also recognized, although they are said to be only manifestations of Amaterasu-o-mikami and unable to exist apart from her. The relationship between the Sun Goddess and the Eight Million Gods is explained as follows: "One God is embodied in a million gods, and a million gods are found in one God. All is ascribed to One God."[4]

The Eight Million Gods are also explained as the various manifestations or the immanent side of the Sun Goddess, who is said to be both immanent and transcendental: "You can see in every drop of water an image of the moon, but the real moon is in the sky."[5] And: "For the sun, the moon, and our being all come out of the One-and-Whole Mind, they are not to be conceived of as alien things. The One-and-Whole Mind is the living spirit of the Universe, Amaterasu-o-mikami, and considering the Sun as the highest form of all things created, or as the supreme symbol, we worship Amaterasu-o-mikami through the sun."[6]

Man

Munetada worshipped the sun as the fountainhead of light, heat, and life, and he reached the conclusion that since the sun, or Amaterasu Omikami, is the origin of everything created, all creatures are sons of God. The main purpose of man accordingly must be to live in fellowship with his neighbors because they are all sons of the Supreme God, and to obtain harmony and happiness through oneness with God. The relationship of man and God is the same as that between son and father: "Oh, what a wonderful thing to think that there is no screen between Amaterasu-o-mikami and man, and that man is divine. Oh, children, brought forth by the Almighty God, do not annoy the heart of your Father God."[7]

One of the most important tasks of man is to give up his self-ishness. All sins and evils of this world are caused by man's false belief that his mind, body, and property are his own. Man must give up his small self and submit it to the great Self of God, and conceive of everything as belonging to the Supreme Being. Only then the non-self can be obtained. Munetada expressed this idea in the following poem:

> "This my being which I think to be my self
> is nothing but the Self of Heaven—
> there is not a single thing to be called mine.
> I have renounced my body, self, and mind
> for the sole Truth of the Universe."

As Munetada thought that the ultimate virtue of Amaterasu Omikami is *makoto* (sincerity), the ultimate goal for man must be to attain the same makoto during his life on earth. And all good qualities, such as loyalty, benevolence, filial piety, and mercy are manifestations of makoto and should also be cultivated by man. This is the basis of the Seven Commandments of Kurozumi-kyo:

1. Be on guard against infidelity, as your faith in God is yet immature.
2. Do not get angry or concerned with trifles.
3. Do not be proud or look down upon others.
4. Do not let the wrong of others increase your own wrongdoings.
5. Do not be idle when you are in good health.
6. Be sincere in thought since you have joined the religion of sincerity.
7. Be grateful every day.

Munetada exhorted his followers to live according to these commandments but always warned them against thinking too much of becoming imitations of him—the object of all must always be to get into direct contact with the Sun Goddess and thus become one with the universe: "Follow my example but go beyond me. The only way you should follow is to get into the great spirit of Amaterasu-o-mikami through the medium of your faith. So long as you have trivial human troubles in mind, you cannot escape from delusion and bewilderment. But if you burst open the cast in which you have enveloped yourself, you will find the truth of the universe crowned with the glory of the teachings of Amaterasu-o-mikami."[8]

Faith-healing

Kurozumikyo advocates that all evils and diseases will disappear when man is united with the Sun Goddess. To bring about this union various rites are performed, and even hypnotism is used. Therapeutic energy is supposedly transferred to ailing parts of the body by rubbing the part of the body in question. Healing occasionally is accomplished by the recitation of purification rituals, by offering consecrated water to the patient, or by water ejected from the mouth of a priest directly upon the patient or upon a piece of paper bearing the patient's name.

Life after Death

Confusion arises because certain writings seem to accept the idea of a hereafter while others seem to deny it. Kurozumikyo has devoted no specific arguments to prove or disprove the existence of life after death. They say that neither belief is at the center of Kurozumikyo doctrine—this is not the problem at hand. Emphasis is on this life:

"Kurozumikyo is a religion of life and optimism. It preaches the way of the present life and is unconcerned with the life hereafter."[9]

"If we acquire such belief of the oneness of God and man, there shall never be death, as Holy Munetada said, and again if you keep on in the true way, you will find that this way is life without end, the way of Amaterasu-o-mikami. Her spirit being one with our spirit, we are eternal provided only that we do not turn aside from the true way."[10]

Other Religions

Kurozumikyo is definitely of Shinto origin and has been a Shinto sect since its origin a century ago. Practically all of its practices and teachings are Shintoistic. However, it has apparently been under the influence of Christianity as well as Buddhism. Its tendency toward monotheism and its social work indicate the former, while the emphasis of non-self and the distinction between the small self of man and the great self of the supreme being apparently come from the latter. Kurozumikyo leaders are generally quite conscious of their indebtedness to Christianity and speak respectfully of it, whereas there seems to be a tendency to despise Buddhism as a "religion of pessimism which is unsuited to the Japanese mind" and as "a religion incapable of bringing about ultimate peace on earth."

Summary

Kurozumikyo has never been a really popular religion—its influence rarely extending beyond Kyoto and Okayama Prefecture. Its adherents have mostly been farming people. Claims to a membership of between 750,000 and one million are probably quite inaccurate. It seems probable that Kurozumikyo will remain a minor new religion, only keeping its following in Okayama Prefecture.

3

金光教 / Konkokyo

Konkokyo was listed among the thirteen Shinto Sects which were recognized by the Meiji government and is still registered under Shinto in the *Religious Yearbook* published by the Ministry of Education. However, while the form of Konkokyo is quite similar to Shinto, Konkokyo's interpretations are "new."

Konkokyo, like Tenrikyo, Kurozumikyo, and Omotokyo, is one of the "old" new religions. (The latter is covered separately as it is the "parent" of several other new religions.) It was founded by Kawate Bunjiro in 1859, the same year that saw the beginning of Protestant mission in Japan, and has recently held a grand-scale centennial celebration. Partly due to its long history, Konkokyo is one of the most stable of the new religions—a stability which is reflected in the constancy of number of members and amount of annual budget.

Its headquarters is situated in the city after which the religion is named: Konko city in Okayama Prefecture. The large temple compound centers on a main hall. Here, in front of the altar of this hall, the present leader of Konkokyo has spent twelve hours of each day for the past seventy years sitting, acting as the "mediator between God and man." Now there is another hall as well, a huge one completed in time for the centennial.

Founding and History

Konkokyo was started by a farmer named Kawate Bunjiro, now known by his posthumous honorary name of Konko Daijin. While **69** deeply religious all his life, until he was forty-five he lived the life of a farmer, devoting some time to Shinto activities. Religion was a refuge for him from all the misfortunes he met in his life, including a serious illness which lasted several years.

In 1859 he claimed to have had a revelation, which is described by Konkokyo in the following way: "After years of earnest seeking and praying he at last found God, Parent of all men, the Parent-God of the Universe, who revealed himself to Konko Daijin as Tenchi-Kane-no-kami. It was on November the 15th of 1859 that the words of God came upon the Founder, calling him to the sacred mission of saving men, and revealing at the same time that the prosperity of mankind is the ultimate purpose of the Parent-God of the Universe, and that without the realization of that purpose God Himself is morally imperfect."[1]

This revelation changed the life of Kawate Bunjiro. He gave up farming and turned his house into a meeting place, and for the next twenty-four years he acted as "mediator between man and God." During all these years every day without exception he sat in front of an altar in a small room from morning till night, praying for the people who came to him for help.

When Kawate Bunjiro died in 1883 at the age of sixty-nine, Konkokyo had already grown into a well-known religion with several hundred thousand followers. After the death of the founder his son acted as "mediator" (*toritsugi*) for ten years until 1893, and since then the grandson of the founder, Setsutane Konko, has been the leader of Konkokyo.

Konkokyo has at present 1,621 churches and forty-eight meeting places. Throughout the country various organizations are connected with these churches: Society of Believers, Young People's Association, Women's Association, Association of Boys and Girls, Boy Scouts, Girl Scouts, and Ministers' Association. The local groups of these associations have regular meetings in the church or, more frequently, at the homes of the members. Here serious problems are discussed, testimonies are given, and guidance is received. These small groups form the backbone of Konkokyo.

The believers were mostly farmers during the first decades of Konkokyo, but now there is also a large number of urban dwellers. They are divided into *shinto* (regular members), whose names are listed in a church record, and *kyoto,* people who attend Konkokyo services, express their willingness to conduct weddings and funerals by Konkokyo rules, and have the spirits of their ancestors enshrined in the main shrine at Konko. However this distinction is not so clear-cut now, and there is a tendency to abandon it.

According to the rules of Konkokyo, the leader is to be elected in democratic fashion by all the ministers of the religion, but it is emphasized that the patriarch must be a blood relative of the founder.

Education is an important part of the organization of Konkokyo. The founder taught that "man is the lord of all creation, and as the whole creation is rational, man's faith in God must also be rational. In accordance with this teaching, educational, and research activities are carried out by the various institutions of our religion."[2] The institutions include two junior high schools, two senior high schools, a training college for ministers, and an institute for advanced studies. Great emphasis is put on the training of lay members, and since 1947 there have been regular summer courses for young men and women to which famous religious scholars (not necessarily belonging to Konkokyo) are invited.

Ceremonies and Services

In form the worship of Konkokyo bears witness to the close connection with Shinto. Most of the ceremonies are Shintoistic, although a new meaning has been infused into most of them. The garbs of the officiants, the altar furnishings, the purification rites, and the food offerings are exactly like those of Shinto.

Konkokyo has advanced further than any of the other thirteen old Shinto sects in freeing itself from the many superstitions still so numerous in Shinto. Magic, divinations, and exorcism have no place in the worship of Konkokyo, where the emphasis is on piety, social concern, and self-criticism.

The center of the worship is a sermon which is related to the everyday problems of the believers. Konkokyo ministers always emphasize that faith is something which only exists in so far as it is manifested in daily life. The service usually takes place early

in the morning or in the evening, and in the largest congregations
there are three daily services—at six in the morning, two in the
afternoon, and at eight in the evening—to enable people of all
occupations to attend the service without breaking their daily
work routine. The simple and unelaborate service consists of prayers, usually chanted in unison, plus a few rites, and the sermon.

Writings and Doctrines

The central point in the teaching of Konkokyo is the principle of
jitsui teinei kami shinjin (absolute belief in God with sincerity
and thoroughness). All members are told to "believe in God (Tenchi-kane-no-kami), and through faith in Him love each other, pray
for peace in the world, and fulfill duties to self, family, and society in happiness and prosperity."[3]

The teaching of Konkokyo, which was slightly revised after the
war, is based upon the principles of the founder, Konko Daijin.
He left nothing written behind him, but his disciples compiled
scriptures from what he had said and preached. Although there
has been unusual freedom of criticism in Konkokyo, with numerous heated discussions and disputes on the doctrines, everything
is based on the thoughts and sayings of Konko Daijin. To enable
all the believers to read the words of the founder, Konkokyo scholars began to compile the biography of Konko Daijin just after
the war, the completion of which took them close to six years of
research.

The *Konkokyo Kyoten* is a compilation of admonitions and
precepts by the Founder. Here are some examples:

Pray earnestly this very day: God's blessing depends on your
own heart. Pour out your heart to God with absolute trust in
Him, at any time and at any place. Neither time nor space matter
to Him.

It is no miracle at all that God's blessing is given in answer
to prayer. It would indeed be a miracle if it were not given.

Faith polishes the jewel of your heart.

Give up your selfish desires and you will find the true path of
life.

1 ■ THE MAIN ENTRANCE TO TENRIKYO'S HEADQUARTERS IN
TENRI CITY NEAR NARA.

2 ■ HERE AT TENRIKYO HEADQUARTERS BELIEVERS PERFORM THEIR "FREE LABOR" AS A NEW PROJECT TAKES FORM.

TENRIKYO

3 ■ RELIGION AND DAILY LIFE MIX: THE PRESENT PATRIARCH, NAKAYAMA SHOZEN, AND HIS SON (AT LEFT) ENGAGE IN RICE PLANTING.

4 ■ A PORTRAIT OF KUROZUMIKYO'S FOUNDER, KUROZUMI MUNETADA, BY TAKEDA GOHO.

KUROZUMIKYO

5 ■ MUNETADA SHRINE, WHERE KUROZUMIKYO'S FOUNDER IS WORSHIPPED.

6 ■ A "WAKA" POEM EXECUTED BY MUNETADA'S OWN HAND.

7 ▪ INSIDE A LARGE WORSHIP HALL IN KONKOKYO'S HEAD-
QUARTERS.

8 ▪ KONKO SETSUTANE, THE PRESENT LEADER, GREETING
CHILDREN AFTER HIS DAY OF MEDITATION.

Pray for your physical health and build up a healthy body, which is the source of all the blessings of life.

In life or in death, know that the universe is your home.

The grace of God is always with you even after death and is also handed down to posterity. This grace of God is inexhaustible and everyone can have it if he has faith in Him.

Harmony in the home is the foundation of faith.

Do not be disrespectful toward your parents, in forgetfulness of the days of your childhood.

Since we are all children of God, no one is a stranger to us under the sun.

Many know the blessings of heaven, but few know the blessings of the earth.[4]

These few examples will suffice to give an impression of the simple faith of Konkokyo, centered around the love of God the Parent, the dependence of man upon God, and the brotherhood of men who are all the children of God.

God and Man

The conception of God in Konkokyo as the "Parent God of the Universe," the loving father who, in his concern for his children, sent Konko Daijin to enlighten them, is a monotheistic view that is different from the conceptions of deity in Shinto and Buddhism of Konko Daijin's time. It has been suggested that he was under the influence of some of the *kakure Kirishitan*. Other than the fact that some secret Christian communities once existed in the area, there has never been any conclusive proof of such influence.

The God of Konkokyo, Tenchi-kane-no-kami (The Great Father of the Universe), is not found in the writings of ancient Shinto even though Konkokyo started as a Shinto sect. Tenchi-kane-no-kami is a new deity introduced by Konko Daijin (as a manifestation of the Konko God on earth). Because of a decree of the Meiji government which stated that no sect could be recognized as official unless it had regular Shinto deities, three established Shinto gods were introduced into Konkokyo. These were all designated as "manifestations of Tenchi-kane-no-kami," but as soon as the government decree was cancelled in 1946 these three extraneous gods were dropped. Since 1946, Tenchi-kane-no-kami is the only deity listed by Konkokyo, and the religion may be called monotheistic, although the believers respect and acknowledge the deities of Shinto and other religions.

The relationship of God and man is regarded as similar to that of father and son:

"Our God, Tenchi-kane-no-kami, is the Father of all human beings. We are all *ujiko,* sons of our Father, and we are sustained by the grace of God. We cannot live without God. God, our Father, can only reveal his works through our service to society. The relationship between God and us, therefore, is interdependent. Our illusion comes from our ignorance of the nature of things; our affliction in this life lies in ignorance. *Our suffering is God's affliction too. Our salvation is God's joy.* [author's italics] To act as agent in propagating this doctrine, to pray to God for others, and to assist God in saving people were the tasks of the founder and are the tasks of each of us as well."[5]

As this quotation indicates, the most unique element in this conception of God is the dependence of God on man, without whose joy God cannot be happy.

If man forgets God, many sufferings and misfortunes will follow:

"Most of us are totally ignorant of the grace of God and of the fact that our life is sustained by the omnipotence of God, and feel that we live by our own strength alone—a state of mind which inevitably leads us to a life of uneasiness and loneliness. As a result unexpected sufferings and calamities befall us."[6] Again here we will see the dependence of God upon man: "These sufferings of man, God bears as his own. In this sense man's sorrow is God's sorrow."[7]

More than anything the father-son relationship of God and man is emphasized: "You will know God's love of His children through your love of your own children. A parent loves an unfilial child most; in the same manner God loves an unbeliever most. So have faith in Him and receive His blessings."[8]

The Act of the Mediator

The most characteristic feature of Konkokyo is the doctrine of *toritsugi,* the mediatorship of the patriarch according to which the patriarch is invoked and bears the sins and problems of the believers to God. In the same way the ministers in the local churches sit on a designated spot in their churches to receive the confessions of the believers and convey them to God on the believer's behalf. This reminds us somewhat of the confessional of the Catholic church, and might stimulate to further investigation those who subscribe to the theory that the Founder got his faith through contact with some of the Catholic kakure Kirishitan of his age. The unique appearance of toritsugi in the middle of the 19th century is among the most important material for the study of any possible relationship between the secret Christian groups and the older of the new religions that emerged a century ago. It seems plausible that the conception of God and several other doctrines and practices of religions like Tenrikyo, Omotokyo, and Konkokyo were due to the influence of hidden Christians, whose influence was never revealed or recorded as it would have meant death to them as well as to their protectors.

The mediatorship of Konko Daijin, as well as that of succeeding patriarchs, is based on several passages in the Scripture of Konkokyo—for example: "I have sent Konko Daijin to my children in order to enlighten them on the significant fact that your God deems as his own the happiness of his children. Many of My children in this world are in distress. Save them by your mediation. It will be a great relief to me, their Parent. As Parent and children we share one and the same prosperity which results from their salvation."[9] And again: "By this person, Konko Daijin, you have been enabled to receive my blessings, and through the same person I have come to be known to the world. You, and even I, Parent God of the Universe, are gratefully indebted to this person, Konko Daijin, and you must abide by his teachings and have faith in me. In time of emergency you may simply invoke the name of Konko Daijin instead of my name, and you shall have my help and blessings."[10]

The toritsugi, also defined as "an intermediary service through which man and God become indivisibly united, and the salvation of man is brought about," was transmitted from Konko Daijin to the succeeding patriarch, and the present patriarch is believed to have the same power. As mentioned, some of this power can be relayed to the ministers of the local churches, who, once authorized by the patriarch, can receive the confessions of the believers and transmit them before Tenchi-kane-no-kami.

Activities

Since its founding a century ago, Konkokyo has been very active in social welfare work along with the propagation of the religion. It maintains a large hospital, a public library, and two associations for providing scholarships on all grade levels for people who cannot afford the tuition. It has about a dozen kindergartens and nurseries, and works among lepers and prison inmates.

Konkokyo, like Tenrikyo, is one of the most active missionary religions in Japan and makes use of the radio, a good deal of published material, and audio-visual aids. During the period 1946–1952, when Tenrikyo published 152 books, Konkokyo published seventy-five, with other Shinto sects publishing an average of four books per sect.

Propagation has also been attempted in other countries. Konkokyo at one time had as many as sixty-five churches with 46,000 adherents. However, this was in Korea and Manchuria during the Japanese occupation and most of the believers were Japanese. At present Konkokyo has only about a dozen churches outside Japan.

Konkokyo and Other Religions

Konkokyo has taken a more active interest in other religions than have the majority of the new religions. In Konkokyo's literature there are numerous references to Christianity, Shinto, and Buddhism. The average teacher of Konkokyo is well acquainted with the Bible as well as with the writings of Buddhism and Shinto. They are studied comparatively—a method which enables Konkokyo to extract what they consider the best points and adapt them to their own religion. At present, the Pure Land sects of Buddhism, Tenrikyo, and the life of Christ are areas of concentration. Further, when the Ninth International Conference for the History of Religions was held in Tokyo in 1958, Konkokyo made a 300,000-yen contribution to the conference.

Konkokyo's attitude toward other religions is one of tolerance and understanding, but one which does not fail to emphasize the uniqueness of Konkokyo:

"Reverence toward our God should not lead to contempt of other Gods. Tenchi-kane-no-kami has no intolerance of other religions. You must not be narrow-minded in your faith. Think of the world with a broad mind, for the world exists in your mind."[11]

"The Konko religion is in no way related, doctrinally or otherwise, to any other religious faith, having its own teachings based on the unique experience of the Founder."[12]

Finally Konkokyo emphasizes the importance of working for world peace and recommends the teaching of the founder as a means of bringing this about:

"The principal aim of the movement is to make sustained efforts to bring the teachings of the Founder into practice in all the activities of our daily lives, and by doing so contribute towards the promotion of the welfare of all mankind and to the establishment of a true and everlasting peace in the world."[13]

Summary

Konko Daijin seems to have been a very sincere and admirable person whose personality and simple doctrines appealed to his fellow farmers. The idea of toritsugi probably struck a responsive chord in the hearts of many Japanese who make extensive use of a mediator, or go-between, in business and social activities. Further, Konkokyo arose in the formative years of the Meiji Restoration when the people were on the lookout for new ideas in religion as well as in other areas of life. Konkokyo's syncretic adaption of the main Shinto, Buddhist, and Christian thoughts gave the people something new without negating their past religious heritage. On the other hand, Konkokyo has never developed any strikingly new idea besides that of toritsugi, which may account for its lack of exceptional further growth.

I feel that it will probably not develop into one of the larger of the new religions, but its growth may increase some as a result of its penetration into the towns. Social work among the poor,

78 blind, and with orphans is certainly largely responsible for Konkokyo's growth from being mainly a religion of farming people. It has become a solid middle-size new religion and should remain so as long as it maintains its present approach and initiative.

II

The Nichiren Group

THE NEW religions described in this section are closely associated in one way or another with Nichiren Buddhism, the remarkable sect established by a monk named Nichiren (1222–1282) during the troubled times of the Kamakura period. Nichiren came to believe in himself as the only person who could save Japan from ruin, through his own interpretation of Buddhism. He taught that all the truth necessary to know was revealed in the Mahayana Buddhist sutra *Saddharma-pundarika*—The Sutra of the Lotus of the Good Law. Central among the beliefs of his sect was the importance of saying or chanting homage to the Lotus Sutra as an act of faith. The sutra is known as the Myoho Renge Kyo in Japanese, hence the often-heard invocation *Namu Myoho Renge Kyo* (referred to as the Daimoku). Recitation of the Daimoku plays an important role in Nichiren sects.

This crisis-born nationalistic and fanatical sect coincided with and played a major role during a turning point in Japanese history, and has continued to be a religious force till the present. Nichiren Buddhism is generally considered to be the culmination of the development of Japanese Buddhism—that is, Nichiren's teachings were a final Japanization of the Chinese Buddhist doctrines introduced in the 8th century.

Though the various sects of Nichiren Buddhism may each claim to be the exclusive bearer of Nichiren's "truth," they do not differ in doctrines to any great degree. This is also true of the three new religions that are considered under the heading, "The Nichiren Group."

Strictly speaking, Reiyukai and Rissho Kosei Kai were founded before Soka Gakkai; however, they are handled last in this section for two reasons. First, Soka Gakkai is a lay movement which is actually attached to one of the established Nichiren sects that date from the period following Nichiren's death, so any chronological **79** difference between it and the other two new religions is almost academic. Second, it is easier to see the establishment of all these groups in perspective if this more realistic historical treatment is used.

創価学会 / Soka Gakkai

A few years ago the name Soka Gakkai (Value-creating Association) would have meant little or nothing to the religious or political observer in Japan. Those who did know of Soka Gakkai would have dismissed it as a terrorist religion, or would have regarded it as just another of the mushrooming postwar new religions—perhaps a little sturdier than some, but still destined for an early death. Today there is no responsible observer who would dismiss Soka Gakkai so lightly.

Today religious groups, political parties, and news organs are putting Soka Gakkai under the microscope to see just what caused the phenomenal growth of this movement based upon the teachings of an established but, until recently, rather impotent Nichiren sect.

Beginning in 1930 as a lay movement of the centuries-old sect Nichiren Shoshu, Soka Gakkai got its second start in 1956 and grew at a fantastic rate under the able leadership of Toda Josei. 1962 has Soka Gakkai with a membership of 2.9 million families, which averages out to ten million individuals (according to S.G. statistics) making it the fastest growing religion in the world, with a monthly increase of close to 100,000 members. Furthermore, it has done what practically no other religion has been able to do in Japan: it has gained influence and power among the workers and trade unions. It won a memorable struggle with Tanro, the coal miners' trade union, and climaxed its growing political influence in 1959, when it succeeded in electing all of the six candidates it sponsored for the Upper House, giving it a total of nine members **81** in that chamber of the National Diet. The 1962 elections saw Soka Gakkai up this total to fifteen. Soka Gakkai now enjoys a singular position among religious movements, and the use of its potential and actual power poses many questions for the future.

Soka Gakkai's headquarters is located at the foot of Mt. Fuji in the temple compound known as Taiseki-ji. Here among ancient cedar trees is a group of 13th century temple buildings which are only a few yards from a towering six-story ferro-concrete structure completed in 1958. As the scene suggests, this lay movement of the modern age is closely interwoven with that dynamic "new" religion of the Kamakura period, Nichiren Buddhism, making it necessary to go back some seven hundred years for historical background.

Historical Background

The lifespan of Nichiren (1222–1282) covered one of the most eventful and dramatic periods of Japanese history. His conceiving and founding of the first distinctively Japanese Buddhist sect, one with such a direct and lasting appeal to the common man, was a major event of this era. The monk Nikko, an original disciple of Nichiren, later became the leader of one of the thirty-one branches that developed out of the original sect. This sect, Nichiren Shoshu (The Orthodox Sect of Nichiren), is the spiritual mother of Soka Gakkai.

Nichiren

Nichiren was a monk at the center of the Tendai sect (a Heian period development of Buddhism based on the continental sect T'ien-t'ai) on Mt. Hiei in the hills above Kyoto. He was dissatisfied with this and other forms of the Buddhism of his day, feeling that none met the needs of the common people. The result of his ten years of study at Mt. Hiei and his subsequent investigation was a firm conviction that he, and he alone, could help the Japanese people. He spent the rest of his life in fierce propagation of his teaching, the like of which has seldom been seen anywhere, especially in the religiously tolerant islands of Japan. After thirty turbulent years he died in 1282, leaving the propagation of his teachings in the hands of his six disciples and an indelible mark in the annals of Japanese religious history.

Nichiren's teaching was based on the Lotus Sutra, which Tendai Buddhism and other sects also used but which Nichiren declared to be the final and perfect revelation of truth. He claimed the Lotus Sutra made the use of other scriptures unnecessary or even harmful. Like Christianity and Islam, and in contrast to most Buddhist sects, Nichiren Buddhism may be called the religion of a book.

The main characteristics of his teaching were: identification of religion with national life; a ferocious intolerance of any but his own teachings; and an apocalyptic mysticism drawn from Mahayana Buddhism. These characteristics are continued in the teachings of Nichiren Shoshu, which was founded by one of Nichiren's disciples.

Nikko

Nichiren left the propagation of his doctrines to his six main disciples, one of whom was Nikko. Nikko was left in charge of the main temple of Nichiren Buddhism at Mt. Minobu while the other five went to another district. A quarrel broke out between Nikko and another disciple, and the latter (with the probable backing of the feudal lord of Minobu) won, causing Nikko to leave the temple. Nikko crossed the river into another fief and established a new temple, the Taiseki-ji, at the foot of Mt. Fuji. This was the beginning of Nichiren Shoshu, the Orthodox Sect as it pointedly was called.

Nikko's teaching has been changed slightly several times through the centuries but in the main represents the teaching of his master Nichiren. The present doctrinal structure of Nichiren Shoshu (and of Soka Gakkai) was formulated by Nikkan, who lived from 1665 to 1725. The basis of this teaching is as follows: The absoluteness of the power of the cosmic diagram (see below), a mandala drawn by Nichiren and known as the Gohonzon; the mystical oneness of Buddha, Nichiren, and the believer (*ninpo ikke*); a fanatical intolerance far exceeding that of other branches of Nichiren Buddhism.

This fanatical intolerance, always present, became further intensified through various struggles, especially with the main branch of Nichiren at Mt. Minobu. Though these two centers are only a few miles apart, their intense hostility toward each other has created a large gap between them. They are, figuratively as well as literally, on opposite sides of the river.

Through the centuries Nichiren-shu at Minobu had the upper hand in these conflicts. Figures indicate that at the end of the Second World War Nichiren-shu counted about ten million followers and more than five thousand temples, while Nichiren Shoshu had a mere 300,000 believers and only about two hundred temples. Even this latter figure was the result of the founding and development of the Soka Kyoiku Gakkai lay movement in the 1930's, but the postwar continuation of this movement (under its present shortened name) has seen drastic changes in the situation.

Founding

Makiguchi Tsunesaburo

Makiguchi Tsunesaburo, who was born in 1871 in Niigata Prefecture, was a former Tokyo elementary school principal before 1930, when he took some schoolteachers with him to Taiseki-ji and held the first training course on the teachings of Nichiren. This was the actual beginning of Soka Gakkai. The name at this time, however, was Soka Kyoiku Gakkai (Value-creating Education Association)—a reflection of Makiguchi's ideas as laid down in *Kachiron* (An Essay on Value). The word *kyoiku* (education) was dropped by later leaders when the goals of the organization became broader.

Makiguchi did not meet with much success at the start. From 1930 to 1937 the membership of the group only increased to sixty persons. However, as the war came, the fanaticism of Soka Kyoiku Gakkai spelled an end to even its modest beginnings. This was not because of any lack of nationalism on the part of the government—quite the opposite. The brand of nationalism favored by this Nichiren group was not the appropriate one in the eyes of the authorities. Makiguchi and his followers flew in the face of

State Shinto when they refused to worship Amaterasu-o-mikami, the Sun Goddess and "ancestor of the Emperor." A large number of Mikiguchi's followers joined him in prison on a charge of lèse majesté. Mikiguchi died behind bars.

Toda Josei

Soka Kyoiku Gakkai did not die with Makiguchi. It rose anew under the leadership of Toda Josei (1900–1958), who had been director general while Makiguchi was president. Now the name was changed to Soka Gakkai and the aims of the organization were broadened under the able leadership of Toda. Soon the group was up to prewar strength, and by 1951 five thousand members were gathered behind the new president, Toda Josei. The next year the membership increased to eleven thousand households. In 1956 the number had increased to four hundred thousand households, and at present a about three million households are claimed—this means a total reaching almost ten million, not including members of Nichiren Shoshu who are not in both organizations.

It must be emphasized that these are figures supplied by Soka Gakkai headquarters, and they are undoubltedly somewhat exaggerated, but if the results of the 1959 election are any indication, the figure may be closer to the official statistics than one might suppose otherwise. The rate of increase seems to be about 100,000 members per month, and it shows no indications at present of slowing down.

When Toda died on April 20, 1958, more than three hundred thousand people took part in the funeral procession. Many thought that this spectacle would be Soka Gakkai's last burst of activity, for Toda was a remarkable organizer, and his ability made it what it was. However, the movement is still going strong, and in a sense Toda is continuing his work. He had planned far in advance the election campaign that brought the six Soka Gakkai candidates into the Upper House; his tape-recorded voice still speaks to his followers on important occasions; and all important decisions and other noteworthy tidings are brought to his grave at Taiseki-ji.

Although Soka Gakkai speaks of Taiseki-ji as the center of the world, so far little effort has been made to carry Soka Gakkai's ideas to other countries. Meetings have been held for foreigners who happen to be in Japan, however, and a few of them have become believers. Thus most of the weekly papers commented at length on an American sailor who, having become a member of Soka Gakkai, apparently interpreted the doctrine of the "value of benefit" too literally and was caught by the police after having made off with a certain amount of cash.

Headquarters

Mt. Fuji has for many centuries been a holy place to the Japanese, and it is no accident that so many Buddhist temples and Shinto shrines have been built so near it. Nikko built Nichiren Shoshu's first temple here, and almost seven hundred years later, in 1958, the super-modern Grand Kodo was built there.

The Grand Kodo is a six-story ferro-concrete building with all modern equipment. It was erected at a price of 400,000,000 yen, and has a total floor space of about 9,900 square meters. There is a huge main hall that can accommodate about six thousand people, numerous offices and conference rooms for various uses, and on the top floor is an extraordinary roof garden with Mt. Fuji as a backdrop. Now construction has begun on a mammoth building that will dwarf the Grand Kodo.

This is the site of the almost seven-hundred-year-old *ushitora* service and of other religious activities. The Gohonzon (the mandala said to have come from the brush of Nichiren himself), relics of the founder, and other religious objects of importance are to be found enshrined and preserved here.

Taiseki-ji is always full of Soka Gakkai believers from all over Japan. Thus, in March, 1958, at the opening of the Grand Kodo more than 2,000,000 people gathered. They are not pilgrims in the strict sense of the word, as certain of them are undoubtedly brought there for pleasure, or out of curiosity. However, there is no mistaking their deep-rooted, almost fanatical conviction that Nichiren and Soka Gakkai are the answer for the future of the Japanese people.

Writings and Doctrines

Soka Gakkai, as such, has no teaching apart from that contained in Makiguchi's *An Essay on Value*. However, as a lay movement of Nichiren Shoshu, Soka Gakkai adheres to all the liturgy, doctrines, and philosophy of the parent sect, and thus goes back to the teachings of Nichiren himself. I shall first compare the application of Nichiren's teaching in Nichiren Shoshu and in Soka Gakkai, then add a few words on *An Essay on Value*.

The canonical writing of Nichiren Buddhism, and therefore of Soka Gakkai, is the Mahayana Buddhist sutra referred to in the introduction to this section. It is known as the Lotus Sutra, or the Lotus of the Good Law, and in Japanese as the Hokkekyo (favored over the formal title, Myoho Renge Kyo). Nichiren Buddhism may be termed "the religion of a book"—the Lotus Sutra. This sutra, which in some ways is similar to the Apocalypse, places the historical Buddha in an exuberant, supernatural setting as the center of the universe, surrounded by lesser Buddhas, Bodhisattvas, other deities, and countless hosts of believers. According to the sutra, the teachings imparted in it are the ultimate revelations of the Buddha, and their revelation on Vulture Peak was accompanied by all sorts of supernatural upheavals and other extraordinary phenomena. The Lotus Sutra played a major role in the development of the second phase of Buddhism, Mahayana, and in it is the basis for the Three Mystic Laws of Nichiren, which developed into the Three Fundamental Principles of Nichiren Shoshu.

Nichiren Shoshu divides the sutra into two parts, or rather, interpretations, and explains them in the following way: "The Hokkekyo is the highest doctrine of Buddhism. It consists of two parts: the *shamon* and the *honmon*. It is generally considered that the honmon is superior to the shamon in philosophical value; further, the time during which the shamon could be propagated has passed. In other words, the shamon interpretation is of no use in this age of the End of the Law [see below]. Hinayana Buddhism, provisional ["provisional" is a Nichiren term] Mahayana Buddhism, and the shamon of the Lotus Sutra are the teachings of Sakyamuni, the historical Buddha of India, but the honmon of the Lotus Sutra is the teaching that the Great Saint Nichiren, the True Buddha. We therefore practice the honmon alone, and this is the most remarkable characteristic of our sect."[1]

Beatification of Nichiren and Buddha

In chapter fourteen of the Lotus Sutra, Jogyo Bosatsu (*bosatsu* is Japanese for Bodhisattva) is mentioned as one of the four chiefs of the hosts of Bodhisattvas, and in chapter twenty he accepts the commission of the Buddha to preach and promulgate the teaching to coming generations.

It seems that Nichiren grew more and more convinced that he was a reincarnation of this Bodhisattva—that Jogyo and he were one and the same—so therefore it was his responsibility to promulgate the teachings of the Lotus Sutra.

Nichiren Shoshu goes still further, claiming that Jogyo was a reincarnation of the Eternal Buddha, that, in fact, Nichiren and the universe are one.[2]

From the conviction of Nichiren that he was Jogyo Bosatsu stems his tremendous self-assertion and belief in himself, which caused him to say: "One who would propagate the truth of Buddhism by convincing himself of the five principles is entitled to become the leader of the Japanese nation. One who knows that the Lotus of Truth is the King of all Scriptures, knows the truth of religion. If there were nobody who read the Lotus of Truth, there could be no leader of the nation. Without a leader the nation would simply be bewildered."[3] Or his famous words, that brought him a host of enemies: "I will be the pillar of Japan; I will be the eyes of Japan; I will be the great vessel of Japan."

From this belief of Nichiren, which Nichiren Shoshu developed further, comes also the absoluteness with which Nichiren Shoshu and Soka Gakkai regard Nichiren and Hokkekyo. Accordingly Soka Gakkai speaks of itself in terms of uncompromising absolute authority whereas most of the other new religions speak in terms of relative authority, recognizing the values in other religions.

The Three Mystic Laws

According to the *Main Doctrine of Nichiren Shoshu,* the Three
Mystic Laws or Three Mysteries are basic. These are: 1) the
Gohonzon, or chief object of worship; 2) the Daimoku, or invocation to the chief object of worship; 3) the Kaidan, or place
to receive proper instruction. These, says Nichiren Shoshu, are
implied in the chapter of the Lotus Sutra that is called the Juryo-
bon (one of the two chapters which members of Soka Gakkai
must learn by heart).

Gohonzon

The Gohonzon is a mandala, or graphic representation of the
universe organized in terms of the Buddhas: the Eternal Buddha
at the center and the various other Buddhas and Bodhisattvas ar-
ranged in a descending and expanding order as outlined in the
Lotus Sutra. In contrast to other Buddhist mandalas—such as those
of Tendai and Shingon Buddhism—the Nichiren mandalas contain neither pictures of the Buddhas and Bodhisattvas nor their
names in Sanskrit letters. All the names are written vertically in
kanji, the Chinese characters which are used by the Japanese as
well. In the center is the Daimoku.

The mandala of Nichiren is considered to contain the universal
power of all the Buddhas and Bodhisattvas whose names are written on it. And it is claimed that the *satori* (enlightenment) which
other schools of Buddhism endeavor to attain by profound meditation or strenuous training can be obtained just by gazing at the
mandala of Nichiren and repeating the Daimoku in front of it:
"The supreme law of Buddha is perceived by everyone in the
Gohonzon. People today, although they are not at all equal to
Sakyamuni in their penetration of mind or observation of rules,
will be able to attain the Buddha's power of faith, action, and
intellect, to attain enlightenment, get rid of delusion, and contribute towards the establishment of lasting world peace—all just
by earnest chanting of the fundamental prayer, the Daimoku,
before the Gohonzon."[4]

Nichiren Shoshu claims that the mandala kept at Taiseki-ji
is a genuine one, drawn by Nichiren himself, and regards the

mandala as a proof of the sect's orthodoxy. However, this has been a bone of contention for centuries between Taiseki-ji and Minobu-san, the latter claiming that the mandala at Taiseki-ji was written by one of the disciples of Nichiren. Professional calligraphers have wanted to compare the handwriting of the mandala at Taiseki-ji with other authentic specimens written by Nichiren but have not been allowed to do so as Nichiren Shoshu does not want to show the mandala to non-believers. Whether this is out of reverence for the holy object or for other reasons is a question.

Whereas the power of the mandala has been part of the teaching of Nichiren Shoshu for centuries, the modern application of this power to heal sickness, create wealth, and bring about world peace is due to Soka Gakkai, which strongly emphasizes that acquisition of right faith must be proved by visible facts. Every issue of the *Seikyo Shimbun,* the weekly Organ of Soka Gakkai, records stories of miraculous cures by the power of the Gohonzon. These range from claiming the credit for cures of breast cancer and polio to the doubling of rice sales by a dealer who just joined the organization and the awarding of a patent to a Soka Gakkai inventor.

Soka Gakkai has become well known for its emphasis on faith-healing, the practice of which they carry further than most other new religions. Where most only teach the therapeutic side of faith-healing, that is, how to get well again, Soka Gakkai goes one step further and recommends faith in Soka Gakkai as a means of *preventing* disease. They say, "If you join us, you will not become sick," or they go so far as to say that "if you do not join us, you will certainly *get* sick."

It is obvious that the promise of faith-healing from all kinds of diseases will be an extremely effective means of propaganda for some time. Many people will listen to the slogan "Don't waste your money on medicine and doctors, join Soka Gakkai!" And the successful cases of healing, especially from nervous or imaginary diseases, will draw a lot of other people to the Soka Gakkai camp. However, it is equally obvious that if the expected healing does not occur, the promises may boomerang with unpleasant results. In this connection it is interesting to see that the idea of not going to the doctor at all is on the wane and is gradually being replaced by the safer "Consult the doctor first, and if it doesn't help, then come to Soka Gakkai!"

Daimoku

The recitation of the Daimoku is in many ways a parallel to the *nembutsu* of the Pure Land Buddhist sects. This was an act of faith that simply involved calling on the Amida (Amitabha) Buddha by uttering the phrase *Namu Amida Butsu* (Adoration be to Amida Buddha). The Daimoku is regarded as a rallying cry, a prayer containing unlimited power, a way toward the salvation of non-believers, and an expression of firm belief in the doctrines and mysteries taught by the Lotus Sutra.

The effectiveness of this invocation was mentioned above. Suffice it to quote a passage by Nichiren in his essay *The Sole Great Thing Concerning Life and Death:* "To utter the sacred Daimoku with the conviction that the three are one, the three being Buddha Sakyamuni, the Lotus of the Truth, and we beings in all realms of existence. To utter the sacred Daimoku is the heritage of the sole great thing concerning life and death. This is the essence of what is promulgated by Nichiren. If it should be fulfilled, the great vow of propagating the Truth all over the world would be fulfilled."[5]

Kaidan

The Kaidan, or the place for instruction and ordination, is also where the mandala is located. It is regarded as the center of the country and of the universe, and is often compared to Vulture Peak, the place where the Buddha is said to have revealed the Lotus Sutra. Nichiren spoke of it in apocalyptic terms: "When the law of Kings shall merge with the Law of Buddha, when ruler and people alike shall hold to the Three Great Mysteries, then the Holy See shall be established in a place as excellent as the Vulture Peak. Thus the moral law will be established in actual life. In this sanctuary men of all countries in the world will receive the precepts of repentance and expiation, and thither also great gods like Brahma and Indra will descend."[6] Nichiren usually has Mt. Minobu in mind when he speaks of the Kaidan, but sometimes he identifies the Kaidan with himself: "I live in a lonely mountain retreat. But in Nichiren's bosom, in his body of the flesh, is secretly enshrined the great mystery, which the Lord Sakyamuni transmitted to me on the Vulture Peak. Therefore it is in my breast that all Buddhas are immersed in contemplation, on my tongue that they turn the Wheel of the Law, in my throat that they are born, and in my mouth that they attain enlightenment. This place being the abode of such a man mysteriously realizing the Lotus of Truth, how can it be less noble than the Vulture Peak?"7

The apocalyptic character of Nichiren's thinking is evident in his elaboration on the Mahayana Buddhist prediction of the division of the history of the world into three periods of a millennium each, starting from the death of the Buddha set at 947 A.D. after the chronology of Chinese Buddhism. The first division is called *Shobo,* the period of the "true law," and this roughly covers the Hinayana period of Buddhism, which was more or less based on the teachings of the historical Buddha. The second division, *Zobo,* or period of the "image law," covers the period that saw the development of Mahayana Buddhism with its pantheon of deities centered around the Eternal Buddha—this period roughly began at the same time as Christianity. The last division is *Mappo,* the period of the "destruction of the law," which, according to Nichiren, started about the year 1000. This was to be a period where the laws of Buddhism were to become corrupted, and Nichiren took advantage of the religious and political turmoil of his time, claiming that these were indeed the evil days of Mappo that had been predicted. Nichiren taught that at the end of Mappo the Kaidan would become the center of the world, and all beings would be saved by the power of the Gohonzon.

Nichiren Shoshu and Soka Gakkai are not so interested in the apocalyptic and mystic interpretations of the Kaidan. To them the Kaidan is Taiseki-ji, where the Gohonzon is located. According to their teaching, Taiseki-ji will become the "national tabernacle" of Japan when Mappo comes to an end, and a bright future under the leadership of Nichiren Shoshu and Soka Gakkai will ensue.

An Essay on Value

The ideas of Makiguchi Tsunesaburo as recorded in *Kachiron* (An Essay on Value) are the only doctrinal writings of Soka Gakkai itself. The following is from an introduction to the essay and shows the importance attached to it.

"The fallacies inherent in the usually quoted conceptions of truth, goodness, and beauty as the substance of value that have existed since the philosophy of Kant are refuted in the *Kachiron,* an epochal philosophical work that explains the difference between truth and value, and advocates a system of value based on new concepts of goodness, beauty, and benefit. It dissolves the confusion existing in the contemporary world and closely examines the sources of happiness."

Makiguchi contrasts the three values of goodness, beauty, and benefit with the three anti-values of evil, ugliness, and harm. There is a deep significance in the substitution of benefit for truth, part of it being the potential popular appeal of a system worked out on this basis. For the man in the street or on the farm, "benefit" has a far better sound than "truth"—a practical, down-to-earth sound without the vagueness or troublesome overtones of abstractions. Later in the essay, Makiguchi points out that what is truthful does not necessarily bring happiness. On the whole it can be said that the *Kachiron* is an attempt to find a new religious philosophy based on man's self-assertion and on popular appeal, not on abstract thinking about truth.

Worship

Taiseki-ji is the scene of the strange service known as the *ushitora,* which takes place from 12:00 a.m. to 1:30 a.m. This service has been carried on for 670 years and has never been cancelled. The Taiseki-ji "police," young men with special armbands, direct the crowds to the worship hall. Worship starts with continuous repeatings of the Daimoku for about twenty minutes. The amplified voices of several thousand people create a mood that must be almost hypnotic in its effect on the assembled. After the recitation of the Daimoku, part of the lotus Sutra is read by the chief priest, whose far-off voice is accompanied by the peculiar dry sound of the rustling of thousands of rosaries. Ear-splitting beats on the drums usher in another twenty minutes of the Dai-moku. This ends the service, and the "police" direct the people to their respective sleeping quarters.

There can be no doubt that the ushitora service gives the be-lievers a strong sense of fellowship, increases discipline, and gives a deep impression of power and strength. Believers returning from this moving experience are unshakably convinced that Taiseki-ji is the future center of Japan and the world.

Homage is paid to the Gohonzon and to other objects, among them some relics of Nichiren. There is a statue of Nichiren which was carved by one of his disciples, but of more significance is the *onikuge,* the tooth of the great founder, about which Nichiren Shoshu teaches the following:

"Records show that when the Great Saint Nichiren was past the age of fifty, he himself pulled out a tooth that had become loose and handed it to Nikko, his favorite disciple, with the words: 'Take this and use it as a testimony in propagating the religion among all mankind in the future.' Since then more than 610 years have passed, but the tiny bit of flesh that was attached to the root of the tooth when Nichiren gave it to Nikko, began to grow and by now it covers practically the whole tooth. It has been said that when the entire tooth is covered with flesh, the time will have come when our religion has reached its zenith. The growth of the flesh attached to the tooth has therefore been watched in every age with the closest attention. It is carefully kept in a three-layer crystal case, and customarily never shown to peo-ple. An exception was made on the occasion of the seven-hun-dredth anniversary of Nichiren Shoshu in 1952, when it was displayed. Also now, at the inauguration of the Grand Kodo, it will be shown to a multitude of 100,000 people. The flesh looks alive and shines with a pearl-like color. It has increased in size so as to cover almost the whole tooth. For more than 610 years the tooth of the Great Saint Nichiren has remained alive. This is a phenomenon of unparalleled strangeness that will surely challenge the medical, biological, and other learned circles when it becomes widely known. We believe that the onikuge testifies to the unique power of the Great Saint Nichiren."[8]

Religion and National Life

Although Soka Gakkai had become fairly well-known as a religion, or a religious movement, by 1954, it was not until 1955, when it entered into the political arena of Japan, that nationwide attention was focused on it. The potential strength of Soka Gakkai has nowhere been demonstrated so clearly as in politics. The local elections in 1955, the Upper House elections in 1956, the clash with Tanro (the Coal Miners' Labor Union) in 1957, the local and Upper House elections in 1959, and the Upper House elections in 1962 have all been unmistakeable demonstrations of what Soka Gakkai may develop into.

To understand the rather unusual marriage of religion with politics which Soka Gakkai represents, it must be pointed out that this is part of the heritage from Nichiren, who identified religion with national life and claimed that the two are one in health or disease. The close connection between state and religion is emphasized again and again in the writings of Nichiren, e.g.: "If those who preach false doctrines are suppressed, and those who hold the true faith are respected, then there will be tranquility throughout the land, and the country will be at peace."[9]

Soka Gakkai and Tanro

The battle between Soka Gakkai and Tanro, the giant coal miners' union, started out like the fight between David and Goliath, but the result was that Goliath was hamstrung not by David himself but by the law, which prohibited any act infringing upon the freedom of religious belief guaranteed in the postwar Japanese Constitution. David won the first round by default.

The battleground of the conflict was Hokkaido, one of the traditional strongholds of Tanro. In this northern island, Tanro held undisputed power among the coal miners until 1955, when

Soka Gakkai gradually began infiltrating the ranks of the coal miners. In 1953 Soka Gakkai had only one hundred member families on Hokkaido, but the members increased rapidly. In 1954 there were 1,500 families; in 1955, 3,880 families; in 1956, 11,500 families; in 1957, 38,000 families, and in 1958, 54,000 families or close to 200,000 individuals. Out of the present number of 250,000 believers in Hokkaido approximately half are coal miners and their families. One of the aims of Soka Gakkai was to establish a branch in every place where there was a Tanro chapter, a task that was already completed in 1958.

One of the reasons behind the penetration of Soka Gakkai into the coal mine areas is that the livelihood of the coal miners is fraught with danger and uneasiness. This situation has left the coal miners with a strong spiritual need, which Tanro in its contempt for religion has been unable to meet. Soka Gakkai has capitalized on this in their campaign by making all kinds of promises to the coal miners who are willing to enter Soka Gakkai. Among their promises are automatic rise of wages without resort to strikes, cessation of mine accidents, end of diseases, and a life of physical and spiritual happiness through the power of the Gohonzon.

Although Tanro seems to have recovered during the past years, the crisis was so acute that the matter was taken up for special action by the National Convention of Tanro in Tokyo on May 18, 1957. The following plan of action was adopted after much discussion: "Social science teaches that when a society is unhealthy, new religions are born, and *jakyo* (heretical teachings) become powerful. Among the religions that recently encroached upon the mining districts there are some violent fake religions. They teach that if only there is faith, salaries will be raised and life will become easier without strikes, that nobody will be injured in the mines, that nobody will become sick, and that even if man dies he will return to life, etc. We, representing the mining society, studying the reasons why these religions gained their position among the members of the union, are in favor of the following directives:

1. To struggle resolutely against all religious activities that undermine class solidarity.

2. To strengthen propaganda activity in order to educate believers in the new religions because the union should care for the education of its members, and help them realize the nature of Soka Gakkai, and the fact that this kind of religion is harmful to the workers.

3. To advise believers in the new religions who obstruct union activities to cooperate. The union should not immediately exert its power of control to exclude such members.

4. To reflect upon the fact that the weakness of union activities is caused by the membership of such believers, that the union itself should become good advisers to its members suffering from the hardships of life, and should work for the establishment of deepening mutual understanding.

"In this movement not only Tanro should participate, but all other labor movements must help."[10]

The vigorous campaign of Tanro and other labor organizations seems to have curbed the increase of Soka Gakkai members in the coal mines of Hokkaido and elsewhere in the nation. Their main daily counter activities have been to point out the fallacies and dangers of Soka Gakkai teachings, mention Soka Gakkai members who are neither healthy nor wealthy, and to ask miners who are fanatic members of Soka Gakkai to volunteer for especially dangerous mining work. This has been rather effective in reducing Soka Gakkai's power.

Soka Gakkai and Elections

In 1955 and 1956 Soka Gakkai had taken part in the national elections with a fair amount of success, but the first occasion on which the whole nation was shocked into overnight recognition of Soka Gakkai as a force to reckon with was the local and Upper House elections in the spring and summer of 1959.

In the local election, on April 30, 1959, *all* seventy-six of the Soka Gakkai candidates in the Tokyo area were elected to the twenty-three town assemblies, and 261 out of the 287 Soka Gakkai candidates throughout the nation were successful.

In the Upper House election on June 2, 1959, *all* Soka Gakkai candidates were elected: five in the national constituency and one in the local constituency of Tokyo. The total poll for Soka Gakkai candidates was 2,490,000 votes, or an increase of almost three hundred percent from their poll in the Upper House elections three years earlier. The woman who was a Soka Gakkai candidate in Tokyo, Kashiwabara Yasu, polled the largest vote of any candidate in Tokyo (including the candidates of the leading Liberal Democratic Party) with a total of 470,000 votes. With three previous members in the House of Councillors this gave Soka Gakkai a total of nine representatives in the 250 seats in House, and made it the fourth largest group after the Liberal Democratic Party, the Socialist Party, and the eleven-man Ryokufukai Party. The Soka Gakkai members were not listed as a group but only as "independents."

Political and religious observers were busy trying to find out just what happened. Many observers felt that the votes for Soka Gakkai reflected a reaction to the old political parties and a wish to see a new party with religious affiliation. Others attributed the victory of Soka Gakkai to the rigid discipline and the tight unity of the sect. Again others claimed that the election tactics of Soka Gakkai should be considered the backbone of its success. Undoubtedly the tremendously successful debut of Soka Gakkai in the political arena must be seen as a combination of all three reasons mentioned above, and of still more reasons, more difficult to define, such as the peculiar confidence Soka Gakkai inspires in its members.

The election campaign in 1956 was carried out by Soka Gakkai with no regard for election laws, and many members were arrested. One of them said: "To win we had to carry out the most effective election campaign. We therefore simply had to disregard the election laws. But we cannot have committed anything wrong, for all we have done is only for the good of our Gakkai!" Again we are reminded of Makiguchi's three principles and his substitution of benefit for "truth." The 1959 election campaign saw many fewer violations from Soka Gakkai believers—in fact only thirteen cases were reported to the Metropolitan Police—and Soka Gakkai seems to have changed to more indirect campaigning methods. Instead of threatening people to vote for their candidates or throwing packets of cigarettes on the street bearing a candidate's name as they did in 1956, the main emphasis has been put on letter campaigning, whisper campaigns, and house-to-house visits. One of their favorite tactics was to arrange meetings which appeared to be religious gatherings, but where the Soka Gakkai candidate delivered the main speech. Thus 100,000 people gathered on May 17, 1959, just two weeks before the election, at Osaka Baseball Stadium for a Kansai Convention Meeting of Soka Gakkai. To all intents and purposes it was a religious meeting, with the one exception that the election candidate for the Kansai area, Nakao Tatsuyoshi, was one of the speakers, and incidentally, the most applauded one. There is no doubt that the clever indirect campaigning methods have been responsible for much of Soka Gakkai's success.

Their successes have continued, and in the 1962 Upper House election Soka Gakkai members, running as candidates of an organization known as the Komei Seiji Remmei, increased the number of seats held in the Upper House from six to fifteen. The election of these additional nine representatives, which attracted international notice, was followed by the organization of a party known as the Komei Kai, the third largest in the upper house.

Soka Gakkai and Nationalism

The main question in the wake of the elections is towards what ultimate objective will Soka Gakkai use its political power? Many troubled eyes are looking towards Ise, fearing to see the specter of ultra-nationalism rear its head again from the center of Shintoism, but perhaps instead they should turn their eyes towards Taiseki-ji, the center of Soka Gakkai. Ultra-nationalism, which once wore the garb of Shinto, may return in the new robes of Soka Gakkai.

There is undoubtedly much in the military structure of Soka Gakkai, which might lead it in the direction of extreme nationalism: its strict discipline, the fanatic campaigning, the belief that the Kaidan at Taiseki-ji shall become a national tabernacle. Furthermore Soka Gakkai openly avows that its political intention is to win the majority of the seats in both houses within a span of two decades. It is also a disturbing fact that when he was

Prime Minister, Mr. Kishi and his Education Minister, Matsunaga, came to Toda's funeral and paid their homage in front of the Gohonzon at the headquarters of Soka Gakkai, although the intention of the two visitors, who do not belong to Soka Gakkai, was to "bow to some two million votes behind the altar," as one newspaper put it.

Iichi Oguchi, one of the greatest authorities on the new religions in Japan, expresses his opinion thus: "Just because Soka Gakkai is organized in military fashion and sings military songs, we need not worry that it will grow into fascism. The only problem is how the Gakkai hereafter will develop their main idea of establishing 'the national ordinational seat,' regarding which, of course, they do not use the words 'national religion,' but. . ."[11]

Will Soka Gakkai keep religious and political activity apart, or will they use their political power towards establishing Soka Gakkai as a national religion? The *Seikyo Shimbun,* the weekly newspaper of Soka Gakkai, three years ago carried an editorial calling for the building of a national tabernacle at the foot of Mt. Fuji and turning Soka Gakkai into the state religion. Toda, when asked to comment upon this, answered in seeming innocence, "How can such a thing be done?" This answer can be interpreted in several ways, which apparently was Toda's intention. Ikeda Daisaku, one of the leaders of Soka Gakkai, declared after the 1959 elections, "Our Gakkai is not a political party, but it is the *king* of the religious world. We wish to go forward without being partial to any of the political parties, only for the happiness of the nation."[12]

Neither Toda's words nor those of Ikeda are reassuring, especially in the light of the fact that the heritage of Nichiren concerning the importance of the union of religious and national life for the well-being of the nation has been part and parcel of the teaching of all Nichiren sects, incuding Nichiren Shoshu, for the past seven centuries. Until now no Nichiren sect has been in a position where it was able to carry out this union. But many believers of Soka Gakkai believe that they will be able to do so during the next two decades, or even earlier.

Propagation

The relationship between Soka Gakkai and other religions is based on the *shakufuku* principle. Shakufuku literally means "to break and subdue" (the evil spirits, and make straight the true teaching of Buddha). And the shakufuku principle is the missionary method adopted by Soka Gakkai: to attack every other religion ferociously, using logical reasoning along with simple abuse.

The shakufuku method was originated by Nichiren himself, and the fanatical intolerance of Soka Gakkai and Nichiren Shoshu can be traced back directly to him. Nichiren maintained that to kill heretics is not murder, and that it is the duty of the government to extirpate heresy with the sword. His invective brought him into numerous conflicts with the government and with other religious groups. Some examples of his strong language and firm self-assurance follow: "If Nichiren had not appeared in the period of Mappo, then Sakyamuni would have been a great liar, and all the Buddhas would have been great cheats."[13]

He claimed that every repetition of the nembutsu of the Pure Land Sects would cost those who uttered it ages in hell. And he called Kobo Daishi, the founder of Shingon Buddhism and one of the most revered Buddhist patriarchs, the biggest liar in Japan. He summarily disposed of all existing religions in his country in the following: "The nembutsu is hell, Zen is a religion of devils, Shingon is national ruin, and Risshu people are traitors to the country!"[14]

The shakufuku of Soka Gakkai is no less violent than that of Nichiren, but it is couched in pseudo-scientific wording. The idea is not only to vituperate but to prove the other religions wrong. The teaching of Soka Gakkai on other religions is contained in the book called *Shakufuku Kyoten* (The Book of Purgation), a book that all Soka Gakkai believers must study before they become members. There is a short chapter on each of the main religions of Japan: the main Buddhist sects, various new religions, Shintoism, and Christianity. As the shakufuku conception is vital to the understanding of Soka Gakkai, excerpts of this book will be quoted, most of them on Christianity:

"Since Christ had a physical body, he must have been heavier than air according to the law of gravity. If a heavy body had arisen into light air, it would be contrary to Archimedes' principles. And if you believe this to be a fact and so break one of the laws of the universe, you will have to deny all rules and laws."[15]

"At first the pure teaching of Christianity consisted only of the Sermon on the Mount. The other ninety percent of the Bible is no more than the dogmas of the disciples. Let us first inquire into the words of Jesus: 'My Father in Heaven makes his sun rise on the evil as well as on the good. For if you love those who love you, what reward have you? Do not even the tax collectors do the same? You should be as perfect as your Father in heaven.' The word 'perfect' means perfect love, and in Christianity the Crucifixion is regarded as perfect love, the love of redemption. According to the words of Jesus, love is indispensable for the practice of Christianity. You see how much more demanding and full of conditions Christianity is, when you compare this with Buddhism, where you have only one condition: to believe. It shows the difficulty of practice and the inferiority of the teachings of Christianity. In the second place, regarding 'for if you love those who love you, what reward have you?' and 'you must become perfect as your Father in heaven,' we see ideas that are completely in opposition to the law of cause and effect. There is an effect wherever there is a cause. Even if you love those who love you, the effect of your love never fails to come out. Furthermore, you have in your mind both the nature to love and the tendency to abhor—to love alone is therefore not possible, except in words. In the third place, their claim that they can atone for the sins of others and expiate the sins committed by themselves as well as others is erroneous. The sins of other people belong to them exclusively and even if you forgive them their sin, it is impossible that their sin thereby will be erased. On the contrary, the very Christians who insist that Jesus was crucified for them for the sake of redemption always commit sin, and confess, and sin again—sin does not at all diminish but increases all over the world. In the fourth place the paragraph 'so perfect as the Father in Heaven' is built on the premise that the perfect Father in Heaven exists. There is no explanation of the substance, the nature, and the faculty of this Father in Heaven. There is no cause, by which this Father has been born, and there can be no effect without cause."[16]

"Jesus worked miracles. They say that forty-six miracles have been put on record. However, posterity could have invented these miracles; they cannot be proven just by the fact that they are written in the Bible. Even nowadays Christians call all sorts of unusual phenomena miracles. It betrays their inferiority that they are ignorant of the reason behind these phenomena."[17]

"Christianity overestimates sin. They talk of original sin, a sin that nobody can escape. Hence they regard all human beings as criminals. A true religion must give strong vitality to man and not reduce him to a criminal."[18]

"God is not the Creator. Living things as well as non-living things of the universe are not given birth by other things, but by themselves. Our life is not given to us by our parents, and is not either given by God or Buddha."[19]

"Jesus died on the Cross. This fact shows that he was defeated by opposition, whatever interpretation posterity may have given to this fact. The great Saint Nichiren shouted to his executor when he was about to be beheaded: 'The time is passing. Be quick; cut off my head.' And as soon as he said so, the gods of the universe gave him all the power of their protection, and meteors shot across the heavens. *He* defeated his opposition. Comparing this vitality with the fate of Jesus we see that Christianity has no power."[20]

Nor is Soka Gakkai silent on the subject of Shinto: "Saint Nichiren preached that if you revolt against the true and orthodox religion, and if heretical opinions prevail, then the gods will disappear from us, the saints will stay away, and the demons will come into the vacant house. Shinto obstructs the spread of orthodox and true Buddhism, and therefore demons have come and live in the Shinto shrines as well as in society. Shinto is a heretical religion that we must destroy."[21]

There are indictments of many of the other new religions: "[Tenrikyo believers] pray to a Father God who created our world, gave life to all beings, and is the source of everything. It is natural that people whose intelligence is at the same [low] level as Christians should believe such a thing."[22]

"Why does this absurd and good-for-nothing religion have so many believers? The reasons are the same as with other perverse religions: 1) people's ignorance of religion; 2) the psychological reason that a drowning man will catch at a straw; 3) diseases are often cured by accident by the Tenri leaders; 4) they say that you will be cursed if you revolt against *tenshaku* (God's will) as revealed through Tenrikyo."[23]

On Reiyukai: "In the Taisho period, Nishida Toshizo, whose two children were one a mute and the other a cripple, was unhappy in Yokohama. He took to copying posthumous Buddhist names from tombs and worshipped them, reciting the Daimoku in front of them. He established the Bussho Gonen Kai, and together with Kotani Yasukichi, Kotani Kimi, and Kubo Kakutaro, he created Reiyukai."[24]

On Rissho Kosei Kai: "Niwano Shikazo, who was working in a pickles shop, learned onomancy from his master, who was fond of fortune-telling. He later opened a milk-shop and became a believer of Reiyukai. However, together with Mrs. Naganuma, he broke away from Reiyukai and started Rissho Kosei Kai. Their mother church was a small house in burnt-down Tokyo; however, thanks to the decayed morality in postwar Japan it spread like a pest, many people entering this worthless fake religion without knowing what they were doing."[25]

We can see that the shakufuku, the devastating propaganda of Soka Gakkai, consists of a mixture of pseudo-scientific "proofs" and venomous attacks against all other religions, coupled with fanatic self-assurance and belief in the doctrines of the sect and the lay movement.

All members of Soka Gakkai are expected to practice shakufuku among their family, friends, and neighbors. Sometimes, although perhaps not so often as would appear from the newspapers, the propaganda is accompanied by physical violence. Here are two examples as they appeared in the newspapers:

"Omisawa, Aomori Prefecture, June 20. A few fanatics of the Soka Gakkai group stormed into a local Christian church, turning it into a shambles in a mad attempt to solicit membership from the church minister. The incident occurred on the night of June 14, when the group stormed the local Holiness Church. They woke up the minister, Murakami Suekichi, and his wife and urged them to become Soka Gakkai members, asking Murakami to become leader of their local organization. When the minister turned down their request the fanatics suddenly became wild and began hurling about chairs, tables, and a few volumes of the Bible. Local police today launched an investigation. According to police investigations there are about five hundred members of the Soka Gakkai in Omisawa town. It is said to be an open secret that the members, including street toughs, racketeers, and even prostitutes, frequently give trouble to households in the locality by soliciting membership through extortion and blackmail."[26]

"Eihachi Sato, 43, in Nakase-cho, Shiba, Minato Ward, Tokyo, entered the Soka Gakkai three years ago but had lost his enthusiasm. A friend of his, Tomizo Fujisawa, a devout believer in Soka Gakkai, came to Mr. Sato about two weeks before the election in June 1959. He showed Mr. Sato a piece of paper on which the names of the two Soka Gakkai candidates were written and asked Mr. Sato to write these names on the ballot on election day. Mr. Sato, however, turned down his request, saying he was free to decide whom he would vote for. Mr. Fujisawa flared up, took a wooden divine tablet from a Shinto shrine that he saw on the table, and tried to burn it, saying: 'It is this kind of thing that will bring you misfortunes. Where did you get this?' Mr. Sato answered: 'It is my concern where I got that, not yours.' Still Mr. Fujisawa tried to burn the tablet, but in vain, whereupon he left with the final words: 'Soon you will see that something terrible will happen to you.' But this was not the end of it. Mr. Fujisawa came back every day until the election was over and pestered Mr. Sato to give his vote to the Soka Gakkai candidates. Finally this was too much for Mr. Sato. He got a violent neurosis and at last confided his troubles to the boss at his office, who complained to the police, whereupon Mr. Fujisawa was arrested for violation of the election law."[27]

The organization of Soka Gakkai has undoubtedly contributed towards its success, and several religions as well as political parties are busily studying it, among them the Gokokudan rightist group and the Communist Party.

The Soka Gakkai organization has a strong military color. Fifteen families constitute a squad, six squads form a company, ten companies a local district, and thirty districts a regional chapter. The latter is directly responsible to the Tokyo headquarters. At present the five regional chapters are: East Japan, Central Japan, Kansai, Kyushu, and Hokkaido. A, B, and C grades are given to the various branches on promotion after successful shakufuku.

An outstanding characteristic of Soka Gakkai is the extraordinarily large number of young people enrolled in the Youth Corps. This group, also using a military organization as described above, consists of people under thirty years of age and has a men's and women's section. The former has a membership of 450,000 and the latter 300,000. Each is divided into 109 corps with detachments all over the country.

Each detachment has its own banner, which is carried (as a military banner would be) to all ceremonies. The highly revered banner of the headquarters is also in evidence. The whole program—the singing of the corps song, the flute and drum band, group exercise and physical conditioning—is imbued with a military look that apparently has much appeal to a large number of young people.

There is no doubt that the youth corps is the backbone of Soka Gakkai. The members are very proud of the large number of young people who join, and they proudly say that "a religion that can only gather old people on the verge of dying is a weak religion—only a powerful religion can gather the youth of Japan."

Soka Gakkai's organization and uncomplicated doctrines have made it possible to penetrate into groups until now considered as extremely poor ground for religious activities—such as, among coal miners, schoolteachers, policemen, and in all kinds of trade unions.

The reasons for the stunning success of Soka Gakkai have already become apparent. Besides its historical nationalistic appeal, its easy doctrines, its able leadership, its pointed entry into the fields of politics and trade unionism, and its zeal, there may be at least one emotional factor behind this that demands further explanation: that of its being a crisis religion.

There is a curious parallel between the situation Nichiren found himself in seven hundred years ago and the situation many Japanese found themselves in during the first few postwar years. Both eras were times of crisis. The Japan of Nichiren's time was threatened by invasion from the hordes of Mongols and allied armies under Genghis Khan. Nichiren himself claimed no small amount of the credit for the thwarting of these overwhelming enemy forces. The Japan that saw a rebirth of Soka Gakkai under the leadership of Toda Josei was that of the time of the recent U.N. action in Korea, when (on the heels of World War II) many Japanese feared an invasion by the Chinese Communist forces from the mainland. In both cases, large numbers of Japanese sought a national and religious place of refuge, and in both cases the strong personality of Nichiren—amplified by Toda in the later period—was available for them. Toda was, no less than Nichiren, one who could use the political and social conditions of the time to his advantage.

Once Soka Gakkai got on its feet, its phenomenal organization seemed to be a concrete factor in its mushrooming membership. Every person who becomes a member of Soka Gakkai must promise to bring three new members, and this is a promise that seems to be more than words if one studies the membership statistics of the organization for the past few years. If the vigorous shakufuku of the lay members continues in earnest at it has in the past, a future as one of the strongest religions in Japan is assured. In May, 1960, when Ikeda spoke after his inauguration as the third president of Soka Gakkai, he said: "By 1964 we will be three million households." So far, nothing has cast any shadows on his prediction.

One of the main questions in connection with the future of Soka Gakkai is the large number of strong personalities who are found here in larger numbers than in other new religions. Ikeda, Ishida, Koizumi, Harajima, and Kashiwabara are just a few of them. In other new religions, the concentration of so many strong personalities has been the signal for a series of secessions, a splintering-off process that spells the end of a once-strong group. Under Toda's strong leadership there was little chance of this, but now that he is dead it seems likely that there will be internal disputes and quarrels—and this could result in secession by discontented members. If this happens the impetus of Soka Gakkai will be weakened considerably, but if these strong personalities continue to cooperate, Soka Gakkai seems destined to play a very important role in the religious life of Japan, not to mention the other fields of influence to which this organization aspires.

2

霊友会 / Reiyukai

Reiyukai, the Association of the Friends of the Spirit, was founded in 1925 and claims to have more than three million members at present. It is one of the new religions which have sprung from Nichiren Buddhism, although it is not characterized by the fanatic intolerance usually associated with the Nichiren sects.

Reiyukai has been a striking victim of the branching-off process. The following new religions have all sprung from Reiyukai: Rissho Kosei Kai (separated in 1938), Myochi Kai Kyodan (1950), Busshogonen Kai Kodan (1950), Myodo Kai Kyodan (1951), Hosshi Kai Kyodan (1950), Seigi Kai Kyodan (1950), Shinshin Kai (1938), and Daie Kai Kyodan (1951). Of these splinter groups, the first two are the only ones which have been successful—and only one successful enough to warrant coverage in this book. The others are rather insignificant. One of the main reasons for their splitting off was a dissatisfaction with Reiyukai's leadership. They do not owe allegiance to the parent religion, though their doctrinal systems, worship, and organization show a general resemblance.

From its founding in 1925, Reiyukai expanded continuously through prewar days, wartime, and the five postwar years. Until 1950 and 1951, when the six groups separated from it, Reiyukai was one of the most active and popular of the new religions. Now Rissho Kosei Kai, an earlier offshoot, and others of the various new religions have apparently taken the initiative.

The founder and organizer was Kubo Kakutaro, who was a carpenter. Kubo, born in 1890, in later life became a friend of Baron Sengoku, who was impressed with the sincere and friendly personality of the carpenter and had him adopted into the family of one of his friends. The members of this family were all fanatic adherents of Nichiren Buddhism, and Kubo gradually became interested in the teachings of Nichiren. Finally, together with a woman by the name of Kotani Kimi, he started Reiyukai. Kotani Kimi, born in 1901 in Kanagawa prefecture, took over the leadership of Reiyukai in 1944 on the death of Kubo.

The years before the start of Reiyukai were the years of World War I and the Tokyo earthquake with the accompanying economic panic, unemployment, inflation, and rice riots. It was an age of pessimism and despair, and many Japanese saw in this state of affairs a fulfillment of Nichiren's words about the "Days of Destruction."

Reiyukai fitted superbly into the contemporary social and religious situation, with its inherent optimism and its fanatic belief in the unique future of the Japanese people. Also the emphasis of Reiyukai on ancestor worship, through the medium of which people were brought in connection with the former Golden Age of Japan, contributed to the success of the sect. Finally the growing nationalism, so often coinciding with the popularity and expansion of the Nichiren sects in the history of Japan, gave further impetus to the development of Reiyukai, especially during and after the Manchurian Incident.

Until the beginning of World War II the majority of the believers lived in the Tokyo area, but during the war many of them were evacuated from the metropolitan area, and Reiyukai spread into the rural areas all over the country, at the same time losing much of its strength and influence in the capital.

Kubo, who had contributed much to the success of Reiyukai with his sincere and charming personality, died in 1944. Kotani Kimi does not have the personality of Kubo, and she has been involved in financial scandals which have hurt the reputation of Reiyukai. The first of the scandals took place in 1950, and it is not a chance coincidence that the many secessions from Reiyukai took place during that year and the following one. Many of the leaders of the religion look forward to the time when Kubo's son, Tsuginari, who in many ways has the charming personality of his father, will succeed to the leadership of his religion.

Worship and Practices

The "mecca" of Reiyukai is the main hall of the headquarters in Tokyo—a small and unpretentious building in contrast with the magnificent centers of some other new religions. The center of the tatami-floor hall is the altar, called *gohoza* in Reiyukai terminology. In front of the altar are the usual offerings of fruits and vegetables, and above it is the crest of Nichiren, the *tachibana* (wild orange). The main objects at the altar are a wooden board with the posthumous name of Kubo, a mandala written by Kubo, and a copy of one of the mandalas of Nichiren.

The mandala is the center of worship in Reiyukai, and it is claimed that the believers through it can get into direct connection with all Buddhas and Bodhisattvas of the past, present,, and future. The mandala is a graphic illustration of the teachings of Nichiren, with the words *Namu Myoho Renge Kyo* in the center, and the names of various Buddhas and Bodhisattvas, as well as those of some Shinto deities, grouped around it. Since all Buddhas and deities of the past, present, and future are concentrated in the mandala, the believers find it unnecessary to worship any others. Reiyukai is one of the few religions in Japan which do not have a distinct doctrine of a Supreme Being—only the mandala with its concentration of deities is worshipped. In contrast to Rissho Kosei Kai, which teaches that the mandala does not have any special power and only is an illustration of faith, Reiyukai believes that all power in the universe is concentrated in the mandala, which accordingly is the center of all worship and the place from which all power begins. According to Reiyukai, however, the power of the mandala alone cannot bring salvation: it must be combined with faith on the part of the believer, and this to be manifested in words and deeds.

Besides the headquarters there exist only three other Reiyukai temples in Japan, but the organization is divided into small local groups (*hoza*) which meet in the homes of the believers.

All believers must abide by the Six Rules of Conduct, the *Rokuseigyo*, which are listed below. They must read selected parts of the Lotus Sutra every day, have a rosary, shoulder band, sutra, a copy of the mandala, and they must have an altar in their homes similar to the one in headquarters, in front of which they are supposed to worship their ancestors. The latter point is strongly emphasized, and the believers are told that neglect of the ancestors may cause diseases and all kinds of disasters, just as the nation never will reach its glorious destination if the ancestors are not dutifully worshipped. All believers upon entering Reiyukai must submit a list of their ancestors as far back as possible. The names are registered at headquarters, and posthumous names are given to all by Reiyukai officials. Despite the emphasis on the ancestor cult, Reiyukai has no graveyards, and permits its believers to be buried in the cemeteries of other Buddhist sects or new religions.

The official prayer used when the ancestors are worshipped runs as follows: "Forgive all the spirits of my ancestors and all my family for their mistakes and misunderstandings, and for all the sins and faults they unintentionally have committed. I read respectfully the holy sutra, not through my own ability, but through the merits of Buddhas and Devas. As they (the ancestors) now hear this sutra, make their spirits vow to devote themselves to Bodhi. Adoration be to the Lotus Sutra." The prayer is called "The Prayer of Transferring Merit."

Doctrines and Writings

There is much similarity in the worship and doctrines of all the Nichiren group of the new religions, including those that have branched off from Reiyukai. They are all based on the teaching of Nichiren, their main sutra is the Lotus Sutra, they use the mandala as the central object of worship, and they all use the invocation *Namu Myoho Renge Kyo*. They all emphasize the importance of the ancestor cult, the necessity of memorial services and special posthumous religious names for the departed ancestors, and the inevitability of earthly rewards for exact observation of these rules.

The teaching of Reiyukai is expressed as follows by Kotani Kimi, the present leader: "The center in our religion is to follow the doctrine of the Lotus Sutra, and the principal object of our practice is to do the ancestor service of the mysteries of the Sutra, moreover to lead a life of goodness in social service. Our canonical text is taken from the Lotus Sutra, which consists of the following three portions: 1) the prolegomena to the Lotus Sutra, the *Muryogikyo* (Measureless Meaning Sutra); 2) the Loutus Sutra proper; 3) the end, the *Kan Fugenkyo* (Meditation on the Bodhisattva Fugen). As our rule for daily life we have the Six Rules of Goodness. Transmigration and transformation through past, present, and future, and the law of causality are also part of our belief. What Buddha has taught makes us realize that all human beings are friends of the spirit throughout the Three Worlds. This we express in our name Reiyukai, which means the Society of Fellowship of Spirit. Our service for the ancestors is based on the belief that faith and the effect of its merit can be extended from one to another, to all beings, and at last will contribute to the welfare and peace of the whole world."[1] The teaching of Reiyukai is practically identical with that of Nichiren Buddhism, and among the new religions Reiyukai is probably the one which is most deeply imbedded in Buddhist doctrine and least interested in the doctrines of Christianity and other religions.

The first part of the canon of Reiyukai is the Measureless Meaning Sutra (*Muryogikyo*), which promises all kinds of merits and virtues to those who read it: it shall make the greedy charitable, the angry patient, the ignorant enlightened.

The next part is chapter eleven of the Lotus Sutra, in which the "wonderful law of Buddha is explained as it has been expounded through countless ages."

Then follows chapter twelve of the Lotus Sutra: "The Buddha addressed the assembly of monks: whosoever, in future, man or woman, hears the chapter of Devadatta of the Lotus Sutra, and by doing so is relieved from doubt and puts his reliance on the pure mind, he shall not fall so low as to be born in hell, or in the world of hungry demons, or in the world of beasts, but he shall be born before the face of Buddha in the ten quarters ..."

After this chapter comes chapter sixteen of the Lotus Sutra, which tells about the duration of the life of the Eternal Buddha. It is followed by chapter twenty, the *jofukyo*, one of the most important chapters in the worship of Nichiren Buddhism. It states that the only sutra which has been preached from eternity by all the Buddhas is the Lotus Sutra, and that those who have heard and promulgated this sutra will meet Buddha in every existence and soon be able to accomplish the Way of Buddha.

Chapter twenty-one of the Lotus Sutra tells about the mysterious power of the Tathagata. Chapter twenty-three promises all who read the sutra deliverance from pain and fulfilment of every wish. Chapter twenty-six reveals the mercy and compassion of the Bodhisattvas, and finally chapter twenty-eight tells of the blessings waiting for those who follow the Lotus Sutra, and the terrible things that will happen to those who scoff at the sutra: "One who, after my entering into Nirvana, keeps, reads, and recites this sutra will not be greedy, nor covetous of clothing, couches, food, drink, and the other necessaries of life. His desires will not be void, and he shall meet with happy rewards also in the present existence. If one happens to defame a devotee of this sutra by saying to him, 'You are just mad. You will get nothing at the end of you life. All you do is in vain, that man shall be reborn as a blind man in every existence in return for his defamation. While one who presents his services and praises the devotees of this sutra shall get his wishes fulfilled in this existence. The man who brings out the faults and criticizes the devotees of this sutra shall contract leprosy in this existence. He who scoffs at the devotee of this sutra shall in every existence have his teeth broken and separated, his lips shall be ugly, his nose flat, his feet and hands contorted, his eyes squinting, his body disgusting; he shall have ulcers, pus, and blood shall come from his body, his belly shall swell up from water, he shall be short of breath and suffer from all kinds of malignant and serious diseases. Therefore, if one should see—even from afar—a man who is keeping this sutra, one should rise and show him the same reverence as to the Buddha."

The latter part of the Reiyukai scripture is the Meditation on

9 ■ SOKA GAKKAI'S LARGE FIVE-STORY CENTER AT TAISEKI-JI, NEAR MT. FUJI.

SOKA GAKKAI

10 ■ THE OLD PAGODA OF THE NICHIREN SHOSHU SECT AT TAISEKI-JI. SOKA GAKKAI HAS GIVEN THIS CENTURIES-OLD SECT A NEW IMPETUS.

SOKA GAKKAI

11 ■ THE HOAN-DEN AT TAISEKI-JI, WHERE RELICS SACRED
TO SOKA GAKKAI AND NICHIREN SHOSHU ARE KEPT.

REIYUKAI

12 ■ THE ALTAR AT THE HEADQUARTERS OF THE ONCE-
POWERFUL REIYUKAI. THE CHARACTERS READ "REI YU."

RISSHO KOSEI KAI

13 ■ THE NEARLY COMPLETED MAMMOTH TOKYO HEADQUAR-
TERS OF RISSHO KOSEI KAI, A RELIGION THAT SECEDED FROM
REIYUKAI AND HAS SINCE GROWN RAPIDLY.

14 ■ THE "HOZA" SOCIAL COUNSELLING, A FEATURE OF REIYU-
KAI THAT RISSHO KOSEI KAI HAS USED EFFECTIVELY. EACH
MEMBER TELLS HIS PROBLEMS TO THE GROUP LEADER.

RISSHO KOSEI KAI

15 ■ THE OESHIKI FESTIVAL, A PICTURESQUE CELEBRATION HELD EACH OCTOBER 12 ON THE EVE OF THE MEMORIAL DAY OF NICHIREN.

16 ■ PART OF THE 10,000 FOLLOWERS WHO COME TO THE GIANT HEADQUARTERS DAILY FOR WORSHIP AND THE "HOZA."

the Bodhisattva Fugen Sutra. This sutra states how the recital of the Lotus Sutra and devotion to the Bodhisattva Kannon, (the Goddess of Mercy), will destroy all the evil created by the six sense organs.

All the doctrines of Reiyukai have been extracted from the canonical writings above, and no other sutras are recognized.

Activities

Reiyukai is not so intolerant or fanatic as most other Nichiren sects. Its term for religious propaganda or mission is *michibiku*, which means to guide along the Way, whereas the term for mission used by Soka Gakkai, another new religion from Nichiren Buddhism, is *shakufuku*, to break asunder. Reiyukai believers are allowed to have contact with other religions and may even go to the Shinto shrines and attend religious services of other religions.

Rather than for participating actively in missionary endeavors, Reiyukai is best known for its social services, which are reflected in the Six Rules of Conduct (the above-mentioned *Rokuseigyo*, which literally means "six prayers of goodness"). They are:

1. We swear that we through the religious service for our ancestors will help and respect each other, and that we will learn with gratefulness and deep reflection what the Gracious Guru (Kubo) and the Present Head (Kimi Kotani) teach us.

2. It is a sin of the organ of taste that one perplexes others with personal attacks, evil words or lying. We should always be aware of sin, as it cuts off the root of the plant of virtue.

3. The central faith of our religion is to do religious services for our own ancestors with a mind of sincerity. We should never force other persons or associations to join us.

4. Some people say, "If you join our reiigion you will recover from illness and you will be prosperous, and if you lead a certain number of other persons into this faith you shall be rewarded." We should take care never to make persons join us with such honey-sweet flattering persuasions.[2]

5. We should take diligent care not to bring business into our religion, not to take loans from other believers nor force people to bring money or offerings.

6. We, the members of this religion, should cultivate our own minds, do goodness, and practice the elevation of our characters and do everything sincerely, with gratitude and thankfulness towards this our religion.

All kinds of social activity are carried out by Reiyukai, mostly by its two organizations: the Kunimoto Ladies Society and the Reiyukai Youth Society. Such things as pianos, television sets, recorders, and projectors are donated to welfare groups such as rehabilitation centers for the physically handicapped. Funds are provided for nurseries, campaigns are waged against the use of narcotics, books written in braille are given to the blind, and Community Chest campaigns as well as Red Cross campaigns are carried out. The social activity of Reiyukai culminated in the construction of a huge social hall at a cost of 200,000,000 yen, which was donated to the city of Tokyo for welfare work.

Summary and Future

Reiyukai, which was one of the most popular new religions before and in the first five years after World War II, has been gradually losing its position. A series of setbacks—the death of its talented leader, Kubo Kakutaro, in 1944; the secession of various groups; the charges of financial corruption against the present leader, Kotani Kimi—almost spelled the end of the religion. Further, the hoza organization, which was one of the main reasons for the initial success of Reiyukai, has come to be associated with Rissho Kosei Kai in the popular mind. However, there is reason to believe that Reiyukai has reached the bottom of its decline and will become somewhat stronger under the future leadership of Kubo's son—the youth movement is already growing in numbers and influence. Still, it would be unrealistic to expect Reiyukai to be counted among the stronger new religions in the near future.

One indication of its growing strength, however, is a tremendous center planned for the city of Ito on the Izu Peninsula. The estimated cost of this project is about 1,500,000,000 yen.

3

立正佼成会 / **Rissho Kosei Kai**

The Society for the Establishment of Righteousness and Friendly Intercourse, or Rissho Kosei Kai, is one of the most active and successful of the new religions. After a comparatively slow start during the years 1938–46, it has developed rapidly and at present has over two million believers. Rissho Kosei Kai still has some serious drawbacks to overcome—especially the lack of an institution where teachers and ministers can be trained—but in spite of this the religion shows every sign of developing into one of the strongest religions in Japan. With the exception of Soka Gakkai, Rissho Kosei Kai is practically the only religion in Japan today which has been able to penetrate deep into the working classes—a clear indication of its potential strength. It is a layman's religion, without emphasis on an organized clergy.

Founding and History

Rissho Kosei Kai has two founders: Niwano Shikazo, the son of a farmer of Tokamachi in Niigata Prefecture, and Naganuma Masa, from Saitama Prefecture. They are now known by the names they adopted after founding the religion: Niwano Nikkyo and Naganuma Myoko.

Niwano was born in 1906. As a young man he went to Tokyo and eventually became a milk dealer. He had no higher education, but intensely studied subjects on his own—especially *hoigaku,* a kind of divination. Niwano gets along well with people, has a pleasant personality but is not an especially good speaker. His **117** leadership of Rissho Kosei Kai is a democratic leadership compared to that of most new religions. He does not take on an air of superiority and can be approached by people from any class or occupation.

Naganuma Myoko, born in 1899, was also of a farming family. She came to Tokyo from Saitama Prefecture and got a job in a factory. Later she married a man in the ice business. She suffered for many years from a serious disease and as a result was obliged to drink a good deal of milk. Niwano, then a member of Reiyukai, was working as the local milkman. He invited her to join Reiyukai and be cured of her disease. Shortly after following this advice her trouble disappeared. She became a close friend of Niwano and remained a member of Reiyukai until they finally seceded from it and, on March 5, 1938, they started their own religion. The reason for the secession was not a profound doctrinal difference, but rather Niwano had become conscious of his abilities as a leader and wanted to become independent.

Niwano is now the sole leader as Mrs. Naganuma died in September, 1957.

Headquarters

The headquarters of Rissho Kosei Kai is located in Suginami Ward of Tokyo and is one of the most interesting and impressive of all the various headquarters we have discussed. Various religious activities are carried on from early morning to late evening. The morning service attendance runs on an average around ten thousand total, and about twenty-five thousand visitors come to the headquarters every day.

Outside the entrance to the main worship hall "traffic police" are at work every day. These are members of the religion who work voluntarily without remuneration. Equipped with armbands, flags, and whistles, they insure that the traffic around the headquarters is orderly.

This is another instance of the order and discipline, often tending towards the semi-military forms which is so characteristic of many new religions, particularly those with Nichiren Buddhist backgrounds.

The main hall is dedicated to Sakyamuni and is regarded as the most sacred place at the headquarters. All members of Rissho Kosei Kai who pass the headquarters pay homage here. This hall, always crowded with people, is also the place where the posthumous names are awarded.

Among numerous other buildings are the two instruction halls, the *shuyodojo*, where both worship and instruction take place, and the *gyogakuen*, or administration building, with a public library, offices, and meeting rooms. There are also a wedding ceremony hall, facilities for sports, especially baseball and judo (in both of which Rissho Kosei Kai ranks high in Japan), and a garage for official vehicles.

Most impressive of all is the gigantic Grand Temple (*Daiseido*), which was begun in 1956 and will be completed in 1964. It is a huge edifice which will accommodate more than fifty thousand people and has a total floor space of 22,840 square meters. A seven-story ferro-concrete building, it has an interesting top floor with ancient Indian-style temple domes. This impressive building, which is costing Rissho Kosei Kai at first estimate some 1,600,000,000 yen, will be the largest building for religious use in the East, and there is no doubt that it will boost the even now considerable success of Rissho Kosei Kai.

It should be noted that al the buidings are pink, the favorite color of the late Naganuma Myoko.

Worship and Practices

At present worship takes place in the Instruction Hall at headquarters for those who can come there, or in the instruction halls of the local branches throughout the country. The former is called *Hombu Shuyo Dojo*, the latter *Chiho Dojo*. These instruction halls take the place of temples and shrines, and in them the two main types of Rissho Kosei Kai activities, morning service and group counseling, are carried out.

Morning Worship

The morning service starts at nine o'clock and lasts about an hour. The service at the instruction hall at the Tokyo headquarters is attended by up to ten thousand people. They crowd into three halls, each one on a different floor, directly above the other. Above the altar in each hall is the Rissho Kosei Kai mandala, a diagram-illustration of the teachings of this religion. It is a *kakemono,* or oblong wall-hanging, with the words *Namu Myoho Renge Kyo* in the center. Grouped around this invocation are the names of various Buddhas and Bodhisattvas, as well as the names of assorted Shinto deities—among them Amaterasu-o-mikami, the Sun Goddess.

The service consists in the unison chanting of the Lotus Sutra, interspersed with three repetitions of the Daimoku (the above-mentioned invocation) for each chapter and ten Daimoku at the end. A loudspeaker gives the numbers of the chapters, and at the end of the recitation there is a short sermon, also through the loudspeaker, usually illustrated with stories from the life of Buddha. At the end of the devotion all exclaim in unison, *"Kaicho-sensei ohayo gozaimasu"* ("Good morning, Leader"). This greeting is intended for the present leader Niwano Nikkyo.

Those who are unable to attend morning service because of work try to pass by the headquarters, where they go to the main sanctuary and recite the Daimoku, making three deep bows for all the gods and Buddhas in the world, once in the direction of the mandala in the main sanctuary, once towards the east, and once towards the west.

Group Counseling

After the morning service the important hoza, or group counseling begins, and this continues until three o'clock in the afternoon, every day all year round. The hoza system is unique in the religious world of Japan and undoubtedly accounts for much of the success of Rissho Kosei Kai.

The believers of Rissho Kosei Kai, mostly women, attend as often as possible—many of them every day—whether in Tokyo or in the local branch temples. In the case of the headquarters in Tokyo they claim that up to ten thousand people by the end of day have come for this event and participate in part or all of it. When the morning service is over, they all sit on the mat floor of the three big instruction halls. At any one time there are about two hundred groups of ten to twenty participants, each group presided over by a teacher or counselor, who leads the discussion.

Each one is a study group with a leader who instructs them and tries to answer their questions. The leader stresses the close relationship between deep faith and daily life. The questions are not abstract ones on philosophy and dogma, but ones springing from everyday problems. The members talk of their needs, wanting to know what they must do to raise their children better, to lead a better life, or to be happy. The amazing frankness of these sessions may seem rather un-Japanese to foreign observers who are used to traditional Japanese reserve. Here are two actual examples: Question: "I am a flower-arrangement teacher. One of my students stole a vase when I was away for some time. What can I do to help her to repent?" Answer: "Give her another vase and be very kind to her. Then she will return both vases, repent and become saved." Or; "I always seem to have a bad cold. What can I do to get rid of it so that I can do more efficient work and be more happy?" Answer: "You believe in Buddha, but you are thinking too much of yourself. If you try every day to do your utmost to bring our religion to others, your cold will disappear. Your egoism is the cause of your sickness, and when the cause disappears, the result will also disappear."

It is an amazing experience to sit and listen to the deluge of questions that are asked at the hoza. One cannot help wondering if this is the result of centuries of Japanese reservation and suppression of thoughts and feelings. Is it possible that the success of Rissho Kosei Kai, and a few other new religions, is mainly due to their ability to meet this tremendous urge and need for the Japanese people to speak openly of all the problems that could not be discussed before, because of centuries of traditional Japanese reserve?

Risho Kosei Kai has often been accused of making use of divination, mystical oracular transactions, and other shamanistic elements. There is some truth in these accusations, although not at all to the extent that most articles written by outsiders would lead one to believe. The only two shamanistic practices widely followed by Rissho Kosei Kai believers are the *seimei handan,* according to which the future of a person can be told from his name; and the *hoigaku,* or aspect divination, which makes use of the sun, moon, and stars for the same divinational purpose.

Finally it should be added that Rissho Kosei Kai has three yearly festivals: the Foundation Festival on March 5, the Flower Festival on Buddha's Birthday, April 8, and the stupendous Grand Festival on October 13.

Doctrines and Writings

Rissho Kosei Kai broke away from Reiyukai in 1938, and in its doctrines is quite similar, both being built on the teachings of Buddhism as interpreted by Nichiren. It might thus be defined as a sect of Nichiren Buddhism, but Rissho Kosei Kai people prefer to call their religion a "revival movement of original Buddhism as transmitted through Nichiren." There can be no denying the fact that the doctrines of Rissho Kosei Kai are very close to those of Nichiren, but the interpretation and application of the doctrines shows influence from the modern age and the doctrines of other religions. The teaching of Rissho Kosei Kai is explained in the following way:

"The doctrine of our faith is based upon the Three Hokke Sutras [the Muryogi Sutra, the Lotus Sutra and the Kanfugen Sutra], which express the original intent of Sakyamuni Buddha. We follow Saint Nichiren's tenets, revere the Mandala, and worship the primordial Sakyamuni Buddha, who was enlightened in the far distant past and is the most excellent Dharma [the Eternal Buddha or Truth]. Our goal is the attainment of a perfect personality, that is Buddhahood, through practice of the way of the Bodhisattva. It is a faith for all mankind as it is a religion of the laity."[1]

The doctrines of Rissho Kosei Kai may be divided into the following subjects: faith in Buddha and Nichiren; expression of this faith through the Lotus Sutra, the Daimoku, and the mandala; belief that man is bound by the law of transmigration and causality; and the teaching that these two laws can be broken through repentance and perfect living by the believers.

Faith in Buddha and Nichiren

Rissho Kosei Kai believes that Buddha is the ultimate truth, and that Nichiren alone represents the true tradition of the historical Buddha. Nichiren is regarded as an incarnation of the Eternal Buddha. According to Rissho Kosei Kai, the true tradition of Buddhism through Nichiren continues through them only, and they have come to regard other Japanese Nichiren sects as unauthorized. As far as doctrines are concerned, however, there is little to differentiate them.

Hokkekyo, Daimoku and Mandala

According to Rissho Kosei Kai the true teaching of Buddha has been given in the three sutras mentioned above, out of which the most important is the Hokkekyo, or the Lotus Sutra.

The Daimoku, or intonation of the words *Namu Myoho Renge Kyo* (Adoration be to the Lotus Sutra) is used on all occasions as in the other Nichiren sects. However, there is some difference in the interpretation of the Daimoku in Rissho Kosei Kai.

In Soka Gakkai, for example, the Daimoku is considered to have unlimited power, so that the intonation of the Daimoku alone could even cure diseases. In Rissho Kosei Kai the Daimoku is not thought of as possessing power in itself. Thus the law of causality cannot be broken by the Daimoku, but only through repentance (see below), after which the Daimoku is used chiefly as an expression of gratitude and faith.

The mandala is only a graphic illustration of the teachings of Nichiren, drawn by Niwano. Again in contrast with Soka Gakkai and Reiyukai, it is not considered to be a "powerful concentration of saving grace." The mandala is only regarded as the liturgical center and an illustration to the layman, who has no time to enter into the depths of Nichiren philosophy, of the mysteries of the faith he is proclaiming.[2] Mandalas of all Nichiren sects resemble each other. Chinese characters replace graphic images.

Laws of Transmigration and Causality

One of the basic doctrines of all Buddhist sects, including Rissho Kosei Kai, is that man because of ignorance is bound by the laws of karma (the law that every good cause will have a good effect). Man is bound by this law of karma through endless existences of transmigration until at last ignorance has been dispelled, the cycle is ended, and he can enter into Buddhahood.

Rissho Kosei Kai expresses this in terms of the three words: *myo, tai* and *furi*. Myo is the invisible world of the Buddhas, tai is the actualization of myo, and furi is the action (faith) which effects the actualization of myo in tai. In other words, by faith (and repentance) man can become united with Buddha.

Breaking the Chain of Causality

Rissho Kosei Kai teaches that this ignorance which keeps man in the chain of karma and is the cause of all our diseases and misfortunes, often is ignorance of our ancestors. When the ancestors are correctly worshipped, one of the two conditions for happiness and health has been fulfilled. The second condition, without which the karma of the individual cannot be broken, is his repentance (*zange*), which must include efforts to live a perfect life in service of his neighbor. Stated more simply, in order to break the chain of karma caused by man's ignorance, man must first understand on which points he has been ignorant (forgetfulness of his ancestors and neighbors). Then he must repent before Buddha as well as before Rissho Kosei Kai, and from that moment he must try to live a perfect life in service of his neighbor. Finally, after numerous transmigrations through which be gradually grows into perfectness, he will enter into Buddhahood— he will have ended the karma cycle as a result of his own efforts *and* the mercy of Buddha.

Propagation and Activities

The success of Rissho Kosei Kai's propaganda is to some extent due to the membership system which, more than in other Japanese religions, is built entirely on the family. The name of the applicant is not enough for membership—the names of his parents, of his wife's parents, and a list of the posthumous names of the deceased members of the family must be submitted. The whole procedure of registration is designed such as to put emphasis on the family and not upon the individual, and reminds one somewhat of the *danka,* a system of controls on the populace exercised by the Tokugawa shogunate through the local temple. This emphasis upon the family, adhered to in all phases of the organizational and devotional life of Rissho Kosei Kai, has turned out to be one of the strong points of this religion. Although the Japanese try to become modern and democratic, they have not yet emerged from the feudal family system and still continue to favor the group at the expense of the individual.

Rissho Kosei Kai is carrying on many kinds of activities for its members, who in turn are urged to carry on missionary activity as laymen—that is, all believers should become missionaries.

The various activities include social service—especially the cleaning of public places by groups of young people—and such other activities as band and choral concerts, group pilgrimages, and festivals. The watchword is that Rissho Kosei Kai takes care of the individual from the cradle to the grave. There are Rissho Kosei Kai nurseries and kindergartens, middle schools and high schools for boys and girls, a hospital (the most modern in Tokyo, completed in the summer of 1959 for 400,000,000 yen), old people's homes, and cemeteries.

Summary and Future

Rissho Kosei Kai has had a phenomenal growth and shows no signs of stagnation. The rate of its growth increased rapidly from a thousand members in 1945 to over a million in 1959. It now claims to have more than two million. It is well represented all over the country, but its stronghold is the area including Tokyo and the prefectures that surround the metropolis. Its leadership and organization seem to be functioning well, and it has penetrated the working classes as well as the agricultural classes. Furthermore, its initiative and activity in social welfare is most remarkable.

Rissho Kosei Kai is one of the strongest and most successful new religions today, and indications are that its future is going to be even more spectacular after the gigantic headquarters is finished in 1964. The main problem that the religion faces is the lack of teachers and ministers, which is greater than in most other religions. At present no facilities for the training of these exist at all. This seems to be the only obstacle to becoming as strong and influential as Tenrikyo and Soka Gakkai in a few years.[3]

III

The Omoto Group

The Omoto group consists of Omotokyo and several other new religions which, whether they acknowledge it or not, are offshoots or adaptions of Omotokyo. The offshoots emphasize various doctrines of Omoto, mainly because the founders were followers of Omoto's founder, Deguchi Onisaburo, or were greatly influenced by him. One main stream of thought begins with a spiritualist known as Master Honda, author of *Kami no Mokuji* (Divine Revelation), in which many ideas now popular among Japanese spiritualists are written. His disciple, Nagasawa Katsutate, was the teacher of Deguchi Onisaburo and others who eventually founded new religions. The striking personality of Onisaburo dominates his own religion, but his ideas are merged with those of his former teacher and are further molded in the hands of the founders of the various religions of the Omoto group.

1

大本教 / Omoto

Omoto, or Omotokyo, means "The Teaching of the Great Origin," and is another new religion of 19th-century origin. It started in 1892 and reached its climax between the two world wars when it counted about two million followers. At present it **127**

has only around 200,000 believers, and cannot be called one of the larger new religions. However, it is extremely important for the study of the new religions, as it is the mother religion of a whole group of newer ones, which together have more than two million adherents: Ananaikyo, Seicho no Ie, Sekai Kyusei Kyo, Ishin-kai, Sekishinkai, and Shinto Tenkokyo.

Omoto defines itself as a religion and yet more than a religion, because it is the "truth" that throws light upon politics, economy, culture, education, art, and science as well as other branches of human activity."[1] Omoto, like so many other new religions, greatly emphasizes the teaching that religion in itself has no value if it is not closely bound with life in all its phases. Often repeated Omoto bywords are: Man must live in religion; not one thing that man does is outside the sphere of true religion.

Founding and History

Deguchi Nao

The foundress of Omoto was a farmer woman by the name Deguchi Nao who was born in 1836 in the town of Fukuchiyama near Kyoto. Her life seems to have been nothing but suffering and ill fortune. She was the daughter of one of the poorest farmers of her village, and she had to become a housemaid at the age of eleven. Her marriage sent her to a poorer home where even food was scarce. She had eight children, but two girls went mad, two boys ran away from home, and three children died soon after they were born. Then,, when she was thirty years old, her husband died, and she had to earn her living by selling rags.

Her sufferings constantly had her on the brink of despair, and when her favorite daughter went mad in 1892, she had come to the limit of her strength. While in this state she claimed to have had a vision in which she was told by God (Tenchi-kane-no-kami, the Konkokyo deity) that the final destruction of the world was at hand, that God would send a messiah to save the world, and that the Kingdom of Heaven would be constructed upon the earth after the day of judgment. The same doctrinal combination of destruction, messiah, and the earthly heaven is found in all the above-mentioned Omoto group. This revelation is described in *Scripture of Omoto:* "Through the manifestation of Divine Power, the Greater World shall be reconstructed and transformed into an entirely new world. After going through a complete cleaning-up, the Greater World shall be changed into the Kingdom of Heaven, where peace reigns through all eternity. Be prepared for it! The Word of God given through Deguchi Nao shall never fail."[2]

Deguchi Onisaburo

Nao was a farmer's daughter without any education; therefore it was not within her ability to give Omoto an organizational and doctrinal form. This task was performed by Deguchi Onisaburo, one of the most interesting and colorful personalities in the religious history of Japan.

Deguchi Onisaburo, whose former name was Ueda Kisaburo, was born at Anao in Kyoto Prefecture. He was a precocious child, becoming an assistant teacher at a primary school at the age of twelve, a student of Chinese classics from the age of seventeen, and winner of all literary contests he cared to enter.

After the death of his father, Kisaburo went to the mountains of Takakuma and underwent various ascetic practices. He claims that he left his physical body behind in a cave on the mountain, while his soul soared into the spiritual world, where he was shown heaven and hell, gained complete knowledge of the mysteries of the universe, and became conscious of his mission as a saviour of mankind.

After studying for some years under the famous spiritualist Nagasawa Katsutake, he went to the village of Ayabe in 1898, where he met Nao. She claimed that he was the messiah God promised to send. Ueda was adopted into the Deguchi family, taking the name of Deguchi Kisaburo. Shortly afterwards he married Nao's youngest daughter Sumiko.

Together Nao and Kisaburo started a religious sect, which in the beginning was called Kinmei Reigaku Kai, and later developed into Omoto. Based on Nao's revelations, the sect's main activities were shamanistic ceremonies, including the healing of diseases by mystical power. Kisaburo transmitted these powers to the various churches of the sect in the form of a large wooden spoon on which he had written some words.

The "First Incident"

New sects in Japan had to lead a precarious and insecure existence in the beginning of the twentieth century. Omoto was no exception, especially as Kisaburo often criticized the government. The following words, which were written just after the Russo-Japanese war, show one reason why he was a thorn in the government's side: "Armament and war are the means by which landlords and capitalists make their profit, while the poor must suffer. There is nothing in the world more harmful than war and more foolish than armament."[3] No wonder that the government gradually became afraid that the dissatisfied classes, particularly the revolutionary-minded farmers, would gather around Kisaburo's banner. Simultaneously, Kisaburo got the idea that he himself must take over the throne to reverse the social order of the country and re-establish Japan as the Kingdom of God. This idea was manifested when he changed his name from Kisaburo to Onisaburo, using characters that had been exclusively used by emperors and princes. Sometimes he signed his name simply "Kimihito," which gave the impression that he belonged to the Imperial Family.

All of this led to Onisaburo's arrest in 1921, the destruction of Omoto's temples, and the prohibition of pilgrimages to Ayabe. Onisaburo was imprisoned for four months but was released as a result of the amnesty issued at the death of Emperor Taisho.

During the next years Omoto witnessed an amazing expansion. The new religion became known throughout the world, and Onisaburo published his *Reikai Monogatari* (Stories from the Spiritual World), the eighty-one volume Bible of Omoto. In 1923 Esperanto was introduced into the religion, followed by the establishment of the Esperanto Propaganda Association and publication of a monthly magazine in Esperanto. Onisaburo gradually expanded his international relations, obtained close contacts with other Asiatic religious groups, such as the Taoists, as well as with the syncretic Red Swastika Society of China and the well-known Bahai religion. This led to the establishment of ULBA (Universal

Love and Brotherhood Association) by means of which Omoto became known throughout the world. This was an Omoto organization, but one consisting of individuals interested in the universal aspects of religion.

There were probably between two and three million Japanese, mostly farmers, who were adherents of Omotokyo in 1934, but even before the religion's popularity had reached this point, the government had a long list of grievances against Onisaburo. In 1924 he went to Mongolia, where he brought down the wrath of the local war lord by letting it be known that he was the "Saviour of the World." The Japanese consul saved him at the last minute as the "Saviour" stood facing a machine gun. About the same time Onisaburo began to ride a white horse in front of people, a privilege usually reserved for the emperor. Back in Japan, and again in imitation of his sovereign, on leaving his headquarters he would be escorted by several motorcycles. He even went so far as to change the names of the rooms in his headquarters to names used in the Imperial Palace. The government once again took strong action.

In 1935, Onisaburo, his wife, and fifty of his chief followers were arrested, and all the buildings of Omoto completely destroyed by dynamite. The court prosecution took place amid all kinds of rumors that bombs, bamboo spears, and dynamite had been found in the headquarters. Onisaburo was convicted of lèse majesté and sentenced to life imprisonment. In 1942, however, he was released on bail, and went back to his home, to spend the rest of his life reading, writing poems, and making pottery.

Reorganization of Omoto

On February 7, 1946, after the end of World War II, Onisaburo formally announced the revival of Omoto under the new name of Aizen-en, (the Garden of Divine Love). Thousands of his adherents joined him, and everybody was ready for the big start when on January 19, 1948, Onisaburo fell ill and died. The death of "the Master" was the end of one of the most fascinating religious careers in Japan and of the main attraction of Omoto. However, a religion that had been oppressed so ruthlessly by the government was bound to gain the interest and sympathy of many postwar Japanese, and in spite of the absence of Onisaburo, Aizen-en met with a fair amount of success under the leadership of Sumiko, Onisaburo's widow. Sumiko died in 1952, after which the youngest daughter, Deguchi Naohi, succeeded to the leadership of Aizen-en. At the same time the religion again became known as Omoto, which is still its official name. Since 1946 the reconstruction of most of the buildings in the two Kyoto Prefecture headquarters of Ayabe and Kameoka has taken place, particularly the huge Miroku-den (Grand Sanctuary) at Ayabe.

Present leadership of Omoto is divided between Deguchi Eiji, the president, and Deguchi Isao, who is in charge of ULBA. Membership as of January, 1959, was a little over 200,000.

Headquarters

The two headquarters of Omoto are Kameoka and Ayabe, both located in the western part of Kyoto Prefecture about an hour's ride from Kyoto City. Ayabe is the old religious center of the religion, where the main sanctuary is located, and where the great festivals and other ceremonies take place. People come here to worship and to be reminded of the life and death of the founders. Kameoka is the organizational center, where all the offices are located and where conferences and study courses are held.

Doctrines and Writings

The doctrines of Omotokyo are based on the revelations of Deguchi Nao and teachings of Master Onisaburo. This is expressed by the two "doctrinal" stone monuments erected on the summit of the headquarters area at Ayabe.

On the right stone is written the first utterance of Deguchi Nao after her revelation: "The Greater World shall burst into full bloom like plum flowers in early spring. The world shall be reconstructed and transformed into the former Heavenly Kingdom under the protection of the One Ruling God."

On the left stone is written the Fundamental Doctrine of Omoto, found in Onisaburo's *Reikai Monogatari:* "God is the all-pervading Spirit in the Universe. Man is the minister governing all Heaven and Earth. When man's unity with God is attained, he commands unlimited power and authority."

The Three Great Rules of Learning as expounded by Onisaburo of Omoto are:

1). Observe the true phenomena of nature, and you will think of the body of the true God.

2). Observe the unerring function of the Universe, and you will think of the energy of the true God.

3). Penetrate the mentality of the living creature, and you will conceive of the soul of the true God.

It is easy to find again the Fundamental Doctrine and the Three Great Rules of Omoto in the religions, which originated out of Omoto. Most founders of the Omoto group of new religions have taught the doctrines of Omoto, but only emphasized one particular side of the teachings of Onisaburo—for example, Nakano Yonosuke, who built the religion of Ananaikyo almost entirely on the second of the Three Great Rules.

The canon of Omoto consists of Nao's *Ofudesaki* and of the *Reikai Monogatari* by Onisaburo, which tells of his journey to the spiritual world.

The *Ofudesaki* was written during the last twenty-seven years of Nao's life from 1892 to 1918. It is claimed to be direct dictation by the spirit of God. Her writings consist of no less than 200,000 pages, from which just one typical quotation follows:

"All religions in the world are the forerunners of Omoto, Omoto being the one that came to give the last finish to the reconstruction of the world. All the pillars of the Spirit in the past were aware of the reconstruction of the world, but they did not know how to carry it out. Those who want to know something of the Divine Plan come to Omoto at Ayabe, and they shall be given Divine Virtue with which to see the whole world at a glance, and to see everything which shall happen in the world hereafter."4

The teaching of Onisaburo is said to have spouted forth from his mouth, and judging from the amount of his work it is a very apt statement. He has written more than 600,000 thirty-one syllable Japanese poems and numerous books, among which is the eighty-one-volume *Reiyukai Monogatari,* each volume of four hundred octavo pages. Here is one quotation from this main work of Onisaburo in which he relates of his journey to the spiritual world: "The God, who created all the universe, is but one. He is called Ame-no-minakanushi. It is because God is almighty that He created all things in the universe. God begot the Angels of Heaven and Earth for the administration of all the things that He created, and the Angels are engaged in the development of the whole universe."5

From these two scriptures all the doctrinal system of Omoto has been drawn. In the following pages the main points of this system will be explained.

God

Nao claimed that her revelation was from the God of Konko-kyo, and was for a short while a teacher of that religion. Other names were given to the deity later on, but usually he is called Creator of the Universe or Great God of the Universe.

Omoto teaches that God is invisible, and that *kami,* the Japanese word for god, is a contracted form of *kakuremi,* or the being in hiding. Everything on earth is said to be manifestations of this invisible God:

"Behind the phenomena of the universe is God, or One Reality, or whatever He may be called. All that exists is an expression of Him. Everything consists of these three elements of God: body, soul, and energy. These three elements are together called the Causative Factor. This can also be expressed as follows: 1. The Prime source of the universe is vitality, which is Divinity. 2. The universe is the manifestation of vitality, or the fragments of the Divinity."6

Onisaburo expresses it in the following way: "We find that our surroundings are full of God, Buddha, or Maitreya [the Buddhist saviour]. The grace of Heaven, and the grace of Earth, is it not all the substance of God, Buddha, and Maitreya? One drop of water, one gleam of light, a single act of kindness, the earth, sun, moon, and stars all give us happiness."7

The Two Worlds

According to Omoto, the world consists of two worlds, the spiritual one and the natural one. It is claimed that universe and man were created in the order of spirit first, and then the natural world. The law of the mastery of spirit over body says that. The people who live in accordance with its rule will be happy, but those who pervert the order and place nature or body before spirit are bound to become unhappy and miserable.

Man

Onisaburo writes about man as follows:

"What is a man? A noble creature is he born with God's life and love, God's son and citadel he ever is.

"Small as a man may be, weakling as he may be, endowed is he with a spirit just as great as the Universe.

"Spirit is man's essence, and a man is a spirit, his body being the garment, guarding his spirit always."[8]

Omoto explains the word for "man," *hito,* in the following way: *"Hi* means a spirit or soul, and *to* means "to stop," or "a receptacle." From this it is clear that man is a receptacle of the Divine Spirit, and hence, in Omotokyo, we have it that man is a Temple of God. Man is the lord of all creation, and the minister of Heaven and Earth, Heaven being the spiritual world and Earth the natural world."[9]

Man's purpose is to take the leading role in establishing the "Heavenly Kingdom" on earth. God and man are interdependent in this task. To carry out this task, man and God must be one, and this oneness is best realized by using the method of *chinkon kishin,* a direct method of communication with God (this is covered in detail under Ananaikyo). Man should be like a child, and live in the now—the present moment, which is a borderline between good and evil, God and Satan. His life should be guided by the Four Guiding Principles of Life: 1. Purfication, spiritually as well as physically, which is necessary in the life of the individual, family, community, nation, and world. 2. Optimism, meaning enjoyment of life with reliance upon God. 3. Progressiveness in active life, which is never confined to a narrow corner of life,

but ever expanding, always exploring new possibilities. 4. Unifica-
tion of microcosmos (man) with macrocosmos (God).

Art and Beauty

One of the most important tasks of man is the continuous
quest for art and beauty. Onisaburo based the art of man upon
the art of God and referred to God as the First Artist. He taught
that art is not for the gifted few but can be an integral part of
everyday life for all people—a means of expressing their special
abilities by injecting their own personalities into their job. Onisaburo himself tried out his genius in such divers fields as literature, poetry, painting, calligraphy, and architecture. He was
especially well known for his tea bowls and turned out more
than three thousand in gorgeous unorthodox colors.

Tokuchika Miki, when he founded PL Kyodan, emphasized
the concept of God as First Artist, building his religion on the
idea of using art in daily life.

Sin and Repentance

Omoto's concept of sin is a familiar one because it shares the
general new religion idea that sin is not irrevocably part of man's
nature—after all, man is the "minister of Heaven and Earth."
Man only becomes a sinner if he does not put the spiritual world
before the material and physical world.

At times Onisaburo speaks of a mediator who has borne the
sins of mankind in terms that are difficult to describe as anything
but Christian:

"In ancient times the Angel Susa-no-o came to this earth as
the Saviour. He redeemed mankind by shouldering all the celestial and terrestial sins upon Himself. Therefore it is a great
shame for man to be ungrateful to this Merciful Saviour."[10]

To overcome the ill effects of sin man must repent, but not
in front of man: "Confession in the presence of others is simply
a sinful act, because man, being a part and portion of God,
disgraces Him if he discloses his own humiliating secrets in public. It will not please the True God. It is all right to confess to
God, though it would be most indiscreet to reveal your own

misdeeds before ministers or priests of any others."[11] Further
true confession and repentance is regarded as something internal:
"...to make a turn-about from materialistic views of the world
to spiritual ones is the real meaning of man's repentance."[12]

Life After Death

Life does not end with daeth, according to Onisaburo: "We
are not felons, nor sentenced to death, but still we have to 'die.' Is
not this a tragic outlook on life? Oh, no! We are eternal, immortal, young life itself, one with God. Even though there is a
barrier which separates soul and body, our very substance will
never sink into perdition; it is resurrected in the world of spirit
permanently."[13]

Omoto teaches that "after death the body grows cold and
decays, but death means a new birth of the spirit into another
place of life in the spiritual world, where he will live on the
same patterns of thinking and in the same modes of living, as
he did in the natural world."[14] "He can meet and recognize his
beloved ones in the realm after death, if they lived with the
same love."[15] Reincarnation is not the rule after death, but can
take place under certain circumstances: "Man is destined to become an angel and live in eternal bliss in Heaven, but reincarnation is possible 1) when the disembodied has left something un-
done in the way of unfolding his inner being to be received in
Heaven, and 2) when an angel was ordained for the salvation of
mankind."[16] The ancestors, even though they died unsaved, can
be saved, and ancestor worship is as important as your faith and
dedication."[17]

Omoto often mentions the angels when life after death is explained. The angels apparently have been assigned roles and
tasks of all kinds: "Many people fancy angels to be winged beings
who dance and sing all the time. This is far from the truth. They
have their occupations—missionary, agricultural, industrial, com-
mercial, and others—not for the pursuit of their self-interest, but
as something to be used in the fulfilment of the Divine Plan.
Such a thing as labor trouble between employer and employee
is unthinkable. There are also governmental organizations in

Heaven, but they are governed as One World by One Ruling God, and perfect order is maintained."[18]

Other Religions

Omoto is conceived of as a religion without prejudice and discrimination. They maintain that Shintoism, Buddhism, Christianity, Islam, and all other religions are like so many branches on one tree that all come from one root—the One Truth, God. However, other religions have not yet perceived all the mysteries of the universe: "The founders of other religions and the saints of the past had but a peep into heaven, but no extensive exploration or wide experience of the spiritual world enabled them to expound with authority on the actual state of Heaven and Earth and Hell, as they really exist."[19] However, "this does not deny the fact that there exists a society of Christians, a society of Islamites, a society of Buddhists, and many other religious societies in Heaven."[20]

Omoto, therefore, believes in the unity of all religions, respects other religions, and does not attempt to make converts of people already belonging to another faith. At the same time they believe that Omoto is the fullest and most perfect religion on earth, the one which represents most truthfully the Spiritual World, which should be the model for all religion.

Activities

Training

A lecture course on Omoto teachings is functioning on a year-round permanent basis at the organizational headquarters of Omoto at Kameoka. It is a five-day program, rotating all the time so that anybody can join the training course at a convenient time.

A three-month seminar is held every summer. This is for special training of young people who, after finishing the seminar, can go home and become leaders of their local groups. The seminar will develop into part of the planned Omoto University.

Social Work

Since the establishment of Omoto, one of its chief concerns has been to do social work. This undoubtedly has its root in the poverty and misery-ridden life of Deguchi Nao. A recent poem by the present leader bears this out:

How fervently my heart seeks a world where
the distinction between the rich and the poor
can disappear, and all may live in peace.

Accordingly all kinds of social welfare work for orphans, the poor, the sick, and the old are carried out.

Especially well known is the activity to help farmers to get better crops, which has led to the establishment of the Bumper Crops Association with about four thousand branches and close to 100,000 members throughout the country. The main idea is that production can be increased with the aid of deeper spiritual insight. In the beginning, shamanistic mystical ceremonies were emphasized, and the farmers were told that fertilizer was unnecessary and could be replaced by spiritual insight. But for the last decade it has tended towards becoming an ordinary farmers' association with scientific experiments, publishing information to the farmers, giving special courses, and holding round table discussions with the addition of an emphasis on the dependence of man upon God, and on efforts to obtain deeper spiritual insight. Phenomenal results from Omoto-style agriculture are claimed—several hundred percent above the average crops in Japan. Below are the official Omoto 1954 statistics on the results in some areas. These figures are from a year where Omoto's record compares very favorably. The national average has risen since 1954.

ITEM	JAPAN'S AVERAGE CROP PER ACRE	OMOTO AVERAGE PER ACRE
Rice	1,260 kg.	3,660 kg.
Barley	900 kg.	4,140 kg.
Sweet potatoes	5,772 kg.	90,000 kg.
Potatoes	6,130 kg.	37,500 kg.
Soy Beans	448 kg.	2,826 kg.

Omoto is one of the religions which most strongly emphasize the international character of religion and make efforts to apply this to various problems, mainly of world peace.

Since the early days of the religion, Onisaburo endeavored to make contact with religious societies abroad, and the ULBA movement met with a large amount of success. It has for the last thirty-five years taught that a world language must be created for the sake of religion, and has ever since advocated the use of Esperanto for this purpose.

Omoto has done most active work in the peace movement, stressing world government and opposing nuclear tests. When the World Federation for the Advancement of One World Government held its world convention in Geneva in 1951, Deguchi Isao, then president of Omoto, was a delegate. Omoto participated actively in the Asiatic Congresses of the World Federation in Hiroshima (1952) and in Tokyo (1954), where on both occasions the delegates from various Asiatic countries were invited to Kameoka and Ayabe, which Omoto calls "our two World Federation cities."

The Omoto organizations launched a nation-wide campaign to arouse public opinion against the tests in 1954 and succeeded in collecting almost two million signatures for this purpose.

Practically all the new religions stress world peace, but there are probaby none which put words into action more than Omoto, and in this undoubtedly lies a good deal of the attraction of Omoto today, particularly among young people.

Summary and Future

Omotokyo's spectacular successes before the 1935 government suppression were in good part due to the fascinating personality of Onisaburo and to the religious emphasis on brotherhood and peace. There is good reason to believe that the religion would have risen to the size and influence of Tenrikyo or Soka Gakkai if the government had not stepped in and crushed it.

In 1946 Omoto got off to a new start, but this movement

lost much of its impetus when Onisaburo died in early 1948. Though leadership has remained in the Deguchi family, no one of Onisaburo's stature has come forth. This is probably the reason for the present rather small membership of a quarter of a million.

However, with its colorful and inspiring history—second to none among the new religions—and its reputation for martyrdom for the sake of world peace on the one hand and its core of young, dedicated, and unusually high-caliber leaders on the other, Omoto might well become much more important than it is at present.

2

三五教 / Ananaikyo

     Ananaikyo is a syncretic postwar new religion whose founder, Nakano Yonosuke, was originally a member of Omoto-kyo. In 1949, a year after the death of Omoto's founder, Nakano founded his religion. Though its teachings are almost identical with Omoto's, and relations between the two religions are cordial, Ananaikyo does not consider itself a branch-off from Omoto.

There are two large centers, one in Kurume in Kyushu, and the other, which is also the headquarters, in Shimizu, Shizuoka Prefecture. Ananaikyo is quite famous for the international religious conferences it organized and for the observatories which it has built all over Japan in recent years.

The name of the religion is coined from the word *ananai,* an old Japanese word which means "to tie," and the usual suffix-like *kyo,* the idea being that this is a religion which ties man to God, or builds a bridge between earth and heaven. The characters used, however, are the ones for the numbers three and five. They are read "ananai" but visually they have a different symbolism: the three is heaven, earth, and man; the five represents the five great religions of the world.

Founding and History

Nakano Yonosuke, the founder and present leader of Ananaikyo, was born in 1887. He started his religious activity well before World War II, having studied under Master Honda's pupil Nagasawa Katsutate. He was a fellow student of Ueda Kisaburo **143** and Okada Mokichi (who later founded the new religion known as Sekai Kyusei Kyo). When Ueda took the name Deguchi and became the co-leader of Omotokyo with Deguchi Nao, Nakano and Okada followed him. Okada left Omoto in 1934, but Nakano remained with Omoto, even being imprisoned with Deguchi Onisaburo in 1935. Nakano did not break away from Omoto until 1949, a year after Onisaburo's death.

Practically all the doctrines of Ananaikyo can be traced back through Onisaburo to Nagasawa Katsutate. These are mainly the teaching that the world is approaching catastrophe; that man, to escape this catastrophe, must receive God's spirit through the means of a special type of mediation (*chinkon,* or often *kamigakari*); and that God will send a saviour to bring about the happiness of the world after the catastrophe has been overcome.

Nakano was born in Yaizu, a small town close to Shimizu. His father was a farmer, and the family had for generations been in charge of the Shinto shrine of the village. At the age of thirty, Nakano entered the construction business and had a considerable amount of success. However, in 1926, at the age of thirty-eight, he claimed to have a revelation. According to Ananaikyo this revelation was "...a remarkable event in his life. He was not sick, but his condition of body was extraordinary. God came into his sight. His soul and spirit entered God's world, where he was endowed with divine wisdom and sense. By virtue of this supernatural power he could see his mission given by God."[1]

After this experience Nakano devoted his life to the study of such things as spiritualism and astronomy, under the guidance of Nagasawa. Later on, he joined Omotokyo, which in the meanwhile had been organized by Deguchi, his fellow disciple. In 1935 he was thrown into prison together with most other leaders of Omotokyo. Finally in 1949, he established his own religion, Ananaikyo.

The leadership of Ananaikyo has been organized in a rather unusual way. Nakano has chosen a young woman as his successor and given her his own family name. Her name is now Nakano Yoshiko, and she holds the title of Superior of Ananaikyo. Besides her, Nakano has adopted about fifteen young women and men and has placed them in organizational positions in the religion. This canny plan of putting one's own "children" into such positions is rather unique in the new religions, and probably was an attempt at building a firm foundation for the religion, a foundation which would work against secessionist movements (Nakano, of course, was himself one who had broken away from Omotokyo). The idea is that one's children cannot rebel against the father. Interestingly enough, so far none of the adopted children have rebelled, but Nakano's eldest real son is said to be in the process of creating a new version of Ananaikyo—a *shin* (new) Ananai. This split between father and son and the creation of a Shin Ananaikyo might signal the dissolution of the present religion because rumors claim that the son has lined up many of the best minds of Ananaikyo on his side.

Worship and Practices

Worship may be performed in three ways: at the two daily services, one in the morning and one in the evening; by daily chinkon meditation; and at the Grand Festival, held four times a year.

The Morning and Evening Services

The morning service takes place at 5.30 A.M., and the evening service at 7:00 P.M. Each service lasts about an hour. The big drum is beaten, and the believers bow as the procession of priests in magnificently colored robes enters the slightly elevated place in front of the altar. Sometimes the procession is accompanied by ancient Japanese music, usually bamboo flutes and *koto*. After the procession comes the service, which is almost identical with the service in any Shinto shrine. It is the pronounced purpose of Ananaikyo to lead its believers back "through the centuries of the wrong teachings of Buddhism to the ancient pure Shinto, before Buddhism ever came to Japan." The main part of the service is the reading of a *norito,* a typical Shinto prayer, in which blessings and protection are sought from various deities in heaven and on earth. There is no sermon nor speech. A part of the service that seems difficult to combine with "pure pre-Buddhism Shinto" is the hymn of Ananaikyo, which is chanted at morning and evening services, and is called "May the Holy Spirit be Glorified." As it throws an interesting light on the main doctrine of Ananaikyo, it is given here:

"Whether King of Day shines or not in the morn,
Whether Queen of Night may wax or wane,
Even if the earth sinks down into the deep,
Even if evil spirits will rave about us,
The Power of Truth shall shine upon us and the world.

As plum blossoms open at once all over the world,
Clear be made the Law of God.
Thus blooming, falling, and bearing fruit,
Know the grace of moon, sun, and earth,
All living gods who save this world,
Are assembling in the Holy Heavens.

God will make His appearance
To judge right and wrong.
Oh, Holy God, who created this world,
Thou art so gracious unto us;
Whatever may be in this world,
We will consider it in Thy light.
Let our faults be corrected in prayers,
Oh, may God's will be done on earth!
May the Holy Spirit be Glorified!"

The front of the worship hall, slightly elevated, consists of three altars. Here the five world religions are worshipped.

The front of the worship hall is slightly elevated and there are three altars. These symbolize heaven, earth, and man. Here the five world religions (Buddhism, Christianity, Islam, Judaism, and Shinto) are worshipped. This is the symbolism visually expressed in the name of the religion as it is written in Japanese: three and five (pronounced together *ananai*) plus the word *kyo*, which means "teaching." In front of the altars the "gifts of the earth" are placed preceding each service. These include water, rice, salt, fruit, and vegetables. The altar to the left is dedicated to the sixty-four saints of the world, including Moses, Christ, Buddha,

and Mohammed. The altar to the right is dedicated to the five
world religions and the center altar is dedicated to the God of the
Universe.

Chinkon

In all Shinto worship, as in all primitive worship, the idea
is to build a bridge between man and God, to establish the best
of relationships between man and god. In Ananaikyo chinkon
(divine meditation) is recommended as the best way toward the
realization of a union with God. On chinkon, Ananaikyo says:

"We purify ourselves in body and mind through chinkon. It
is a practical way of communing with God, a method of obtaining
capacity for spiritual enlightenment and susceptibility. It puts us
in the way of mending our present condition and growing in the
wisdom of God. In the practice of chinkon your mind will become
peaceful, quiet, and elated with your consciousness of communion
with God's spirit and of your purified divine self."[2]

The practice of chinkon is rather interesting. The participant
sits on the tatami floor with his arms stretched out in front of
him. Both hands meet, and the fingers are united in such a way
that a small opening is formed. Through this opening the participant fixes his eyes on a small black stone placed on a stand about
two meters away. With this, the meditation starts. The posture
is maintained throughout as the person enters a trancelike state,
concentrating on some thought—for example, "I am a God"—
that is repeated over and over.

Nakano claims this to be the quickest way to communicate
with the Great Spirit of the Universe. Although there is a formula
to repeat (see above), Nakano has this to say about the state of
mind during the practice of chinkon: "When one sits in chinkon
he must sit straight and try to have a zero state of mind, but
with the self-consciousness and firm conviction that he himself
is a god. He must not try to create a state of mind of nihility or
voidness, but he must let this nothingness grow up naturally in
him."[3]

Nakano also adds that this extinction of the self and the
merging of the microcosmos and the macrocosmos is not obtained
magically. Further, it presupposes a sense of gratitude. "One is

unable to recognize the significance of chinkon until one comes to have a gratefulness for the worth of the existence of everything created and of the Creator."[4]

The Grand Festivals

The Grand Festivals take place in February, April, July, and September. They are in form the same as Shinto festivals, and are some of the most magnificent such celebrations that can be seen in Japan. They consist of ancient Japanese music, colorful processions, purification rites, offerings, various prayers, and ancient dances.

The Saviour

According to Ananaikyo, the world would be facing a destruction that could erase all humans except for the gracious God who has sent a saviour to the world:

"We are waiting, day and night, for the coming of the king, who alone is qualified to claim his kingship on earth. He is our Saviour. Until he makes his appearance world peace will never come true, and human resurrection will be an impossibility. He is the center of mankind and is God incarnate, that is Living God. The power and virtue of the sun, the earth, and the moon are all being personified in Him."[5]

Sometimes it seems that the saviour is yet to come, but usually Nakano speaks as if the saviour had already arrived, though he is not yet ready to be announced: "God has already made preparations for the coming of the Saviour. The Saviour already exists on earth. I always meet with him in the Spirit and speak with him. But this is not the time for him to announce his appearance before the world."[6]

Nakano himself, interestingly enough, does not claim to be the saviour, but he is convinced that he is a forerunner or guide who is paving the way for the advent of the saviour.

Activities

Ananaikyo's activities have fallen in two stages, one an international stage, and the other, a program of construction of observatories all over Japan. The international stage refers to the arrangement of various international religious conferences held at Shimizu. Their object was to work for the creation of a world religion, and Ananaikyo's attitude at this time was that it is one religion among others. This is in contrast to the emphasis of Ananaikyo as a special religion which has taken place since a new revelation of Nakano's after which he started building the observatories. In this case Ananaikyo is seen as the religion invested with the power to interpret to man the laws of the Great Spirit of the Universe as they are written in the heavenly bodies.

International Religious Conferences

From the beginning of its existence Ananaikyo has stressed the importance of close relations with other religions. Numerous internal contacts have been made, among them with the World Red Swastika Society of China, and with Bahai. And in 1952 Nakano and Negami Shin, the president of Ananaikyo, went on a worldwide tour to Asia and Europe, during which they met with many religious and political leaders, among them Nehru of India and President Ben-zvi of Israel.

The attitude towards other religions is very tolerant. All religions are regarded as essentially the same. They are all manifestations of the Great Spirit of the Universe, and they will all accept the Saviour when He comes. Ananaikyo has emphasized this tolerant attitude by enshrining the founders of all religions in their main shrine.

This international outlook combined with extreme religious tolerance, another inheritance from Omotokyo, led Ananaikyo to arrange no less than eight International World Religion Congresses within the short span of three years, from early in 1954 to late in 1956. At the first congress about forty persons from eight different countries were present, and at the last congress more than two hundred persons representing sixteen different countries attended. Although no world-famous scholars attended, it was a remarkable achievement for this small religion, which had started only five years before the first congress. It gave Ananaikyo the status it had lacked before and put it on the "religious map" of Japan. The main result of the World Religion Congress was the creation of the so-called International Religious Federation, a loose organization of individuals in various countries that had some contact with Ananaikyo.

However, in the midst of this international activity Nakano claimed to have received a new revelation, which told him to change the activities of Ananaikyo from religious conferences to the construction of "Religious Observatories." After the Eighth Congress late in 1956 no more congresses were held, and the International Religious Federation, never much more than a "paper tiger" organization, seemed headed for oblivion.

Religious Observatories

The "national" phase of the activities of Ananaikyo began with the same energy that had characterized the "international" phase. Nakano began building *tenmondai* (observatories) in various parts of Japan. These were to be ordinary observatories, only with the exception that they should be used by Ananaikyo to "read the will of the Great Spirit of the Universe in the heavenly bodies." A steady stream of mayors and city councillors from all over the country came to Shimizu to ask Nakano to consider their town for the next tenmondai. Nakano and his staff went on "inspection tours" all over Japan to consider where the future observatories might be constructed. The eager officials of the respective municipalities paid all the expenses for these tours. Eight observatories have been built and a few others may follow. Nakano said that he hoped to build a hundred observatories in his lifetime. The ones he did build were equipped with such modern paraphernalia as 150mm refracting equatorial telescopes, reflex equatorial telescopes, 200mm Schmidt cameras, and revolving roofs.

The tenmondai idea was quite a success in the beginning, and Ananaikyo became known all over the country as the "observatory religion." However, recently there has been criticism of these "free trips" where there may never have been much chance of building an observatory. This unfavorable view of the financial matters has probably had its effect on the initial enthusiasm. One whimsical journalist expressed it in the following wordplay: *Tenmondai wa chotto mondai ni narimashita!* This might be rendered into English as: "Observation of the observatories has tended to become more critical."

Behind the tenmondai idea is the basic doctrine of Ananaikyo that religion and astronomy are one, and that the study of the universe (macrocosmos) is necessary to understand man (micro-cosmos). Without giving much in the way of the logic of it, Ananaikyo says, "If a religion has not instruction based upon the universe, it cannot be recognized as a real and true religion. The universe is the activities of the sun, moon, and the earth [which equals] God, the Great Spirit of the Universe."[7] According to Nakano, the will of God and the future of man is written in the stars, and by studying the universe man can learn to live in harmony and happiness. Through this we clearly see the combination of spiritualism with pseudo-science as taught by Nagasawa, Nakano's former teacher.

Nakano claims that "religion and astronomy are inseparable. It can be compared to a sheet of paper, religion being one side of it, astronomy the other. They cannot be parted..."[8]

However simply this basic doctrine is stated, the application of it in practice is extremely vague—in fact it is doubtful whether it is applied at all except in various superstitious practices involving the zodiacal signs and the like.

It is interesting to see how the "national" phase of the development of Ananaikyo has narrowed the tolerant attitude toward other religions so conspicuous during the "international" phase. For this reason it is all the more interesting that a second international phase has been in the making since the observatory movement lost much of its force. It seems that Nakano, remembering his earlier successes, began pointing for a conference of "religious, educational, and cultural" leaders to be held in 1961. The following is taken from a letter Nakano sent out to a large number of religious and cultural organizations as well as to various individuals in August, 1960:

Dear Friend in Faith:

I should like to have the pleasure of sending you this letter regarding the opening of "The International Foundation for Cultural Harmony." I have held world religious conferences eight times since April, 1954, and it was a great pleasure to have many people from various overseas countries in attendance....I have made up my mind to open a new conference on a large scale. It is sponsored not by Ananaikyo but "the International Foundation for Cultural Harmony" with the consent of spiritual leaders not only in Japan but all over the world. For this significant meeting I earnestly hope for your extensive co-operation by your presence and that of other representatives of religious, educational, and cultural organizations with which you are concerned.

Sincerely,

Yonosuke Nakano

Although Nakano takes pains to explain that the new congress is sponsored not by Ananaikyo but by the International Foundation, this latter organization is in reality almost identical with Ananaikyo, and, of course, the chief director of the group is Nakano himself.

The first congress was held in 1961 and was more or less a repetition of the eight previous ones. A second followed, and in spring of 1962 the third congress was held. About two hundred foreign participants, mostly from India, attended the 1962 affair.

Summary and Future

This new phase does not conceal the fact that Ananaikyo is in a critical situation that could affect its existence. Nakano, now seventy-four, has been ailing for some time. This, plus internal strife and recent unfavorable commentary in the papers, as well as certain financial difficulties could point toward an imminent collapse of the thirteen-year-old religion. Yet, observatories are still being planned beyond the eight now in existence.

3

生長の家 / Seicho no Ie

Seicho no Ie, the House of Growth, started in 1930 under the leadership of Taniguchi Masaharu, a former active member of Omotokyo. It started as a book publishing company and gradually developed into a religion. Just after the war its membership decreased sharply, partly because Taniguchi was purged for a while (due to his nationalistic writings during the war), but it has become popular again, and at present its members are between one and a half and two million. An impressive 300,000,000-yen headquarters has been built in Tokyo. The Holy Scripture of Seicho no Ie has been sold in more than eight million copies, and it is estimated that one out of every ten Japanese has heard Taniguchi Masaharu speak.

Founding and History

"It was born at six o'clock in the morning of November 22, 1894. According to the lunar calendar this was October 15, and the moon was full. It was sinking behind the mountains to the west but was still shining brightly. As the sun rose in the east I came into the world, illuminated, and protected by both the sun and the moon. Thus was the story transmitted to me by my father, who was a witness to this." In this dramatic account the founder of Seicho no Ie, Taniguchi Masaharu records his own birth.

As a boy Taniguchi was extremely reserved and sensitive, and events left a deep impression on him. Once he went to the school doctor with an eye ailment which the doctor diagnosed as tra- **153** choma and offered to cure by medicine. But Taniguchi did not believe him and would not accept any treatment. The next term his eye had completely recovered, and from this time he was extremely critical of medical diagnoses and treatment, an attitude he has applied to other areas of life.

After college, when he came to believe that "art is supreme" and "beauty superior to morality," he worked for a while in Osaka. He read avidly whenever he had time, mostly publications on psychotherapy, Buddhist sutras, and Christian books. Especially he seems to have valued the writings of Shinran (one of the patriarchs of Pure Land Buddhism in Japan) and St. Paul.

For a while he joined Omotokyo and became the editor of two of their publications at the headquarters at Ayabe. He also became one of their chief theologians. After the police clamped down on Omotokyo, Taniguchi left it. He was interested in Ittoen for a while, although he did not join as he found its adherents too "proud of their humility." Finally he started his own religion.

His religious breakthrough came about on December 3, 1928:

"One day, when I was in meditation, suddenly I heard an unseen voice saying 'On earth there exist no sins, no sickness, no death, no poverty. Nothing in the world restrains human beings. Thou art the son of God by nature. Thou art Buddha thyself. Thou shalt not become the slave of others.' Realizing that the voice had come from Heaven, I immediately took up a pen and wrote down all it said. What I have written and am going to write in magazines contains all that was revealed to me by God. These are not my own thoughts, but those from God in Heaven."[1] Later on he describes it in the following way:

"A light of truth flashed through my heart and dissolved my mental affliction. This manifest world, visible to the naked eye and felt with the five senses, is not God's creation. I was greatly mistaken in accusing and judging God. This world, as perceived with the five senses, is merely a production of our minds. God is love and mercy. The Real World, created by God's infinite wisdom, love, and life, is filled with eternal harmony. This Real World, this perfect and eternal world *always is*. This was the truth I discovered at that time. At the same time I realized the Real Self. The Real Self is the eternally enlightened Sonship."[2]

After this initial revelation of authority, so typical of most new religions, Taniguchi started his religion. First it was as a publishing company. This still continues and prospers, mainly due to the success of Taniguchi, who, besides his big 40-volume *Seimei no Jisso,* has written numerous books and pamphlets and must be regarded as one of Japan's most prolific authors. Later on, in 1930, the movement developed into a religion called Seicho no Ie (the House of Growth). Seicho no Ie changed its name four times after that, but returned in 1957 to the original name.

During the first period Taniguchi tried to demonstrate that Seicho no Ie was above religious boundaries, that is, it was the essence of all religions. He did not particularly want to found a new religion because of his fundamental idea that all religions are the same, and because he believed that his interpretations would be accepted by people of other religions. He therefore quoted from the important scriptures of all religions, trying to point out where these religions had made wrong interpretations. He stated during this initial period that his real task was to make the Christian a *real* Christian and the Buddhist a *real* Buddhist, and his followers were allowed to continue worshipping with the religion they already professed. However, this gradually changed, and a special Seicho no Ie worship was introduced. Now Seicho no Ie has all the marks and characteristics of a religion, although Taniguchi still prefers to call Seicho no Ie a "non-denominational enlightening truth movement through literary endeavor."[3]

During the war Taniguchi came out strong in favor of the Emperor, and throughout the war he was one of the most nationalistic religious leaders in Japan. He stressed in books published during this period that world order can only be attained by eliminating the self and devoting oneself to the "Ultimate Being," "the Only Existence," and this "Ultimate Being" is identified with the Emperor, "the only thing that really exists, and accordingly the center of our loyalty and devotion."[4]

After the war Taniguchi was a purgee for a while and could not participate in any public activity. However, he claimed that his fundamentally peace-loving doctrines had been distorted and made use of by the militarists.

Since 1954, however, Taniguchi is again a devout patriot.

There is no mistaking the nationalistic tone of *Warera Nihonjin To Shite* (We Japanese) and *Jinrui no Kiki ni Nozonde* (Facing the Crisis of Mankind), both published in 1958. Now the emphasis is not on the Emperor, but upon the "fatherland" and the national flag. And Seicho no Ie is one of the Japanese religions which most ardently advocate a "religious political movement."

Worship and Practices

Seicho no Ie has thirty-three churches and 1,173 meeting places, mostly in private homes. The believers are mostly from the middle or upper classes, and not a few intellectuals are among them. The great majority are middle-aged women.

The service, or meeting, begins with a unison recital of part of the scripture. Next there is the speech centering on the teaching of Taniguchi as it appears in his *Seimei no Jisso* (The Reality of Life)—often a speech of two or three hours. After that, or in between, come the testimonies, miraculous stories of healing from diseases, narrow escapes from death, and improved family relationships. These are told with an emotion and frankness which staggers the foreign observer who probably will find this entirely un-Japanese. And finally comes the *zadankai*, the important informal gathering with refreshments, where everybody chats and enjoys himself.

The devotional life of Seicho no Ie has been influenced by shamanism to some extent, at least up to and during the war, when mystical communications between the dead and members of their families were held by means of a shaman. Also, though charms do not officially exist in Seicho no Ie, the shorter scripture called *Kanro no Hou* is regarded as possessing the efficacy of a charm, and several stories are told of the miraculous saving of soldiers on the battlefield by this scripture.

Another interesting phenomenon in the devotional life of Seicho no Ie which at least borders on shamanism is the *nempa*, a peculiar term used only by this religion. It refers to a kind of spiritual waves which are said to have the power to influence other people at a distance. Taniguchi says that when a family holds a memorial service for a deceased member the nempa of the family is sent to the soul in the spirit world with the power to save him. An interesting instance of the power of nempa appears in the periodical *Seicho no Ie* of August, 1953 (pp. 35–36):

It says: "The thought waves are far more delicate than those of the radio, and distance will not be a hindrance to receiving them. We have an example of a patient in Manchuria who could neither walk nor sit with his legs folded. He was healed instantly by practicing meditation at the same time that we were praying for the benediction of all the members of Seicho no Ie. You require a delicate radio set to receive radio waves. Likewise, you must keep your mind peaceful by meditating on the perfectness of the Reality of Life in order to receive the benedictory waves broadcast from the headquarters of Seicho no Ie. We are praying for your health, prosperity, and world peace from 5:10 to 5:40 A.M. daily."

The center of the devotional practice of Seicho no Ie believers is the *shinsokan,* defined by Taniguchi as a "prayerful meditation in concentrating the mind."[5] This form of meditation is one of the elements of Omotokyo which Taniguchi took with him and adapted for Seicho no Ie.[6] Immense power is said to lie in this meditation, because "by meditating and praying to Avalokitesvara (the Bodhisattva Kannon) means not only to ask for the help of Avalokitesvara; it means to realize that one's true self and the life of perfect freedom of Avalokitesvara are one. Realize that the self is Avalokitesvara, the self *is* Buddha, the self is one entity with God."[7] By meditating in this way, man attains to unlimited power—evil, hate, and suffering disappear, and only love and happiness remain: "Meditate solely: 'The World of Reality is filled with goodness.' An evil such as resentment may appear to exist, however, it is non-existent. Love is the only real existence. Therefore that person loves me, and I love that person. This is the only true existence. This is the only true Reality."[8]

Writings and Doctrines

The canon of Seicho no Ie is the book written by Taniguchi called *Seimei no Jisso* (The Truth or Reality of Life). It is a huge work of forty volumes, but a few adapted excerpts are given to enable the student of Japanese religions to get a glimpse of the innermost thoughts of Seicho no Ie:

"One day an angel came to the Seicho no Ie and sang: 'God, who is the creator of the whole universe, is beyond the five corporeal senses, even beyond the sixth spiritual sense of human beings. He is the holy, consummate, infinite Spirit that permeates the universe, the life that pervades the universe, the law that regulates the universe throughout, Truth, Light, Wisdom, Absolute Love .... Nothing exists without God; God is holding all being in His hand; nothing indeed exists that does not come of Him .... When the Divine Mind unfolds itself into "the creative world," then develops the whole universe, and all the creatures come into existence .... All the beings are the creative Words of God; they are all Spirits, all of them are Mind, nothing is made of matter, matter is nothing but the reflection of the mortal mind.... God never created sin, God is the only being that creates, so there is no sin in the world that has been really committed, hence there is no sin that has to be revenged...., The angel continued, 'Reality itself is everlasting. Reality shall not fall ill, nor shall it get old, nor pass away. To realize this is nothing but to know the Way. Reality we call the Way, or Truth, as it permeates through the universe. The Way or Truth is always with God, and God is the Way and the Truth Itself.

(Man)

" 'A man is the Son of Light, and in pure Light of Reality does he live. He could meet with no darkness, neither could he see any failure, nor find any hindrance whatsoever. Just as celestials stroll about in Heaven in perfect freedom, and just as the fishes in the sea can swim to and fro quite freely, so man full of light and spiritual rejoicing strolls about in a world full of bright light.'

(Sin)

"The has recited our angel, when a cherub appeared and said: 'For the sake of humanity, in order to help them in attaining to enlightenment, pray give me a full account of the real nature of errors.' To this responded the angel, saying,

' "Error" is so called, as we dream false things that have no existence in reality. To be ignorant of the real aspect of beings is called "delusion" '. . . . 'Is our sin of real existence?' asked again our cherub, to which the angel replied, saying 'There is nothing real in the true sense of the word but God, and those that have come of Him. Sins are not perfect, so they are not of reality. Diseases are imperfect, so they are not real. Death is imperfect, so it could never be of reality. Do not take the things to be real, that have not been created by God. Never dream of things in your bad dreams which have no existence in reality, nor be afraid of things unreal. Sins, diseases, and death are not what God has created; they are therefore unreal, they are merely delusions, though they have ever assumed the garb of reality. I have come to unmask them to show that sins, diseases, and death have no existence in reality. Gautama [the Buddha] himself once came into the world for this purpose. Christ also once revealed himself for the same purpose. If sins were of real existence, even the truth that various Buddhas preached in all ages could not have demolished them, and Jesus Christ's crucifixion might have been, after all, ineffective for destroying them. How blessed are you to know that sins are all unreal. . . . Jesus Christ, too, could exterminate our sins by mere dint of the words: "Thy sins are forgiven." I, too, have expressed it in words, the Holy Sutras and Holy books of Seicho no Ie, and merely by dint of the words I unmask the so-called sin. He who happens to read my words may know the true aspects of Reality, and therefore all of his sins shall come to naught and shall recover without fail from all diseases and realize the Life Eternal, forever transcendent above death. . . . God is Spirit, therefore Man is also Spirit. God is Love, therefore Man is Love. God is Wisdom, therefore Man is Wisdom. Man in reality is Spirit, he is Love, he is Wisdom, he is Eternal Life. Therefore he could never commit a crime, he could neither suffer from any disease, nor could he pass away. Who would dare to call men sinners? God has never created sinners, so there could not be a single man on this earth, who is a real sinner. The idea of sin is contrary to the Sonship of

Deity. God is the source of Light, and Man is the Light that has come of God.

(The Kingdom of God)

" 'Christ has taught us "Behold, the Kingdom of God is within you." Verily, verily I tell you, here "within you" means nothing but man's real nature or the real-man, as the inner man of man's real nature is nothing but God-Man.

" 'Again, Christ has taught us "My Kingdom is not of this world." The Kingdom of this world is nothing but shadow of reflection, the land of eternal blessing is only to be found within.'

(End)

"When thus had spoken our angel, the celestial chorus of Heaven sounded in the sky, and down came numberless petals of holy flowers from Heaven, showering from where we knew not, as if to pay homage to the Truth that had been preached by the angel."[9]

Finally, before we take up the doctrines, I want to list the Seven Declarations of Light of Seicho no Ie.

1. We should not be prejudiced in favor of any sect or any religion, but believe in the spiritual nature of man, and live in accordance with the spiritual truth of Life.

2. We believe that to bring the great Life Principle into full manifestation is the way to infinite power and abundance, and that the personality of every individual is immortal.

3. We study and make known to all the Law of the Creative Spirit, so that humanity may follow the right path to infinite growth.

4. We believe that love is the best nourishment for life and that prayer and words of love and praise are the creative Way of the Word necessary in bringing love into manifestation.

5. We believe that we, Sons of God, have infinite power and abundance within us and can reach absolute freedom by following the creative Way of the Word.

6. We publish the monthly *Seicho no Ie* and other books and booklets filled with good messages so that man may follow the creative way of constructive words and live a happy life.

7. We organize actual movement in order to conquer all the

pains and troubles of humanity, including diseases, by means of the right view of life, constructive living, and true education, to finally bring the Kingdom of Heaven to the earth.

God and Man

As can be seen from the above excerpts from *Seimei no Jisso,* Seicho no Ie in a sense identifies man with God. This is illustrated by Taniguchi in the following way: "Gautama is not the only incarnation of the Eternal Buddha in flesh. We are all the Eternal Buddha that is embodied in the flesh. Jesus alone is not the only son of God. We are all sons of God. Jesus taught us to pray saying '*our* Father, which art in Heaven.'" This means they say that all humanity are sons of God, and he is everyone's father, everyone has infinite power as they are God's children.[10]

However, at other times Seicho no Ie seems to forget the identity of God with man and treat the two separately. The following illustration will serve to bring this out:

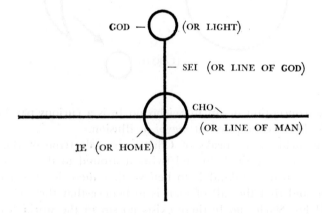

Seicho no Ie preachers often use this diagram to explain how God relates to man. The vertical line, the line of God, and the horizontal line, that of man, meet at one point only. This is called "the true home of man, the center of the world. God's line is called *sei* (life), and man's is called *cho* (growth). The meeting point is *ie* (home), thus they form the name Seicho no Ie (House of Growth). To illustrate the connection between God and man—

and this concept is still somewhat blurred—the lines are compared with a water pipe through which water (life) comes to man. The pipe can freeze at times, at which time only the "Light and Love of God" can thaw it. Two different worlds are spoken of: the world of God, with life and love; and the world of man, which depends on God for life by means of the life line that might be cut off under certain conditions.

Sometimes there seems to be a different sort of link between God and man. This one says that sometimes the light from God comes indirectly to man through the scriptures, the nempa, and shinsokan (see above). This is shown in another illustration often used by Seicho no Ie.

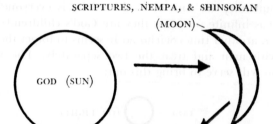

SCRIPTURES, NEMPA, & SHINSOKAN
(MOON)

GOD (SUN)

MAN
(EARTH)

Sin

The conception of sin in Seicho no Ie is a curious parallel to the Buddhist conception of *mayoi* or illusion.

Taniguchi often speaks of Christianity's doctrine of the Fall or of Adam's original sin and twists it around to the effect that the real sin of mankind is to believe that there is such a thing as sin, and that the fall of man is to believe that there ever was a fall! For Seicho no Ie there exists no sin in the world because they believe that God, being goodness and love, could only create things that are part of the same goodness and love. Taniguchi says: "The idea that 'I am a sinner' is the mother of all kinds of sin in this physical world. On the other hand, the idea that 'I am a son of God' is the mother of all the good things in this physical world."[11]

The application of the nonexistence of everything evil or bad is interesting. Here is an example of how it is applied to the Christian idea of loving one's enemy: "The Bible says we should love our enemy. Seicho no Ie says that originally there is no enemy. You can truly reconcile only when you realize that you have no enemy. If you first recognize the existence of an enemy and then try to love your enemy, you will find it almost impossible because the idea of 'enemy' contradicts 'love.' Only when you realize that you have no enemy will you be able to love anyone without trying to do so purposely."[12]

Another interesting application of the theory of "no sin" is the interpretation of the crucifixion of Christ as an act by God to clear away the sin-consciousness of man: "Christ had himself crucified as atonement for humanity's sin in order to exterminate humanity's sin-consciousness. The crucifixion of Christ meant that he was the humanity of his age, self-bound and self-restricted by the idea of sin, suffering because they believed in Adam's original sin and believed themselves to be children of sin. And although he preached that man is not a child of sin but a son of God, they could not believe it in any way, and therefore he suffered before the multitude, declaring: 'I will be crucified as an atonement for your sins; therefore original sin has disappeared, and there are no longer any sins. I will suffer this much in place of your sins.' What Christ wanted to pacify was not God's anger but humanity's sin-consciousness."[13]

Salvation

According to Seicho no Ie, salvation consists of the realization of the "Sonship"—that man is Son of God, that man is Buddha, and thus born to live in freedom and abundance with limitless possibilities. "To be saved by religion means restoration of the original freedom of life, and does not mean man's deliverance from sin into an exceedingly pleasant world called Paradise, as if man were a mud-smelling carp to be scooped up from the mud and put it into pure water."[14]

"Man's salvation by religious truth means the realization of the truth of Sonship, that man's essence of life is originally a perfect Buddhahood, and the originally perfect real aspect of the self should be made manifest and recover the original freedom, original liberation, and original free divinity. Such a truth that delivers and liberates man is true religion; therefore Christ taught in the Book of John: 'Ye shall know the truth, and the truth shall make you free.' "[15]

Usually Seicho no Ie speaks of salvation as something that occurs suddenly, in a moment. Two steps and a testimony, however, seem to be necessary. These are:

1) The reading of *Seimei no Jisso* and other related literature, hearing the speeches of Taniguchi, and attending the services of Seicho no Ie.

2) The practice of shinsokan (meditation), and through this realizing that the individual and God are one, that all people are brothers, and that there is nothing real in the world except love. This experience should generate gratitude, and is an important prerequisite to salvation in Seicho no Ie.

3) The testimony to others to the effect that one has recognized the Sonship and has been saved.

Disease and Faith-healing

To salvation belongs cure from any disease. The problem of disease is solved in the same way as that of sin: as God is Goodness and Love, He cannot create evil things, they reason. Therefore, since disease is an evil thing, it cannot have been created by God, and since all there is in the world has been created by God, disease simply cannot exist. It is just in man's imagination and unenlightened mind that disease and all kinds of suffering exist.

Taniguchi attacks the idea that disease is catharsis. Thus he says of a former Christian who entered Seicho no Ie:

"She had been a very earnest Christian and held the false faith of welcoming sufferings, as is too often the case with Christians. Sublimation of sufferings is a false faith. It cannot be that God is pleased to see man suffer. Yet many Christians think that diseases and misfortunes are given as a cathartic method for sin by God, and that therefore one should be pleased to accept them in order to destroy one's sin. Mrs. Miya was so pious that she thanked God when her eldest son died, but since she began to come to Seicho no Ie, she has begun to understand what the true God is."[16]

Diseases are explained in the following way: "You think that something can hurt you. This false idea arouses anger and fear which creates a negative mental wave (see *nempa* above). And according to the Law of Affinity your negative mental wave will call forth evil mental waves broadcast from the miserable and unhappy people prevailing in the universe. The objectification of these evil mental waves is so-called disease and misfortune."[17] Or: "There is a passage in the Vimalakirti Sutra of Buddhism, where Vimalakirti says 'I am sick because the multitude are sick.' "[18]

Seicho no Ie claims to be able to cure all diseases, to avert all calamities from bed-wetting to atomic burns. The following headlines from the May 1958 issue of *Seicho no Ie* made these claims: "Uterine cancer completely cured in a week; Cancer of the pancreas disappeared in a moment; Stomach cancer cured through reconciliation with mother-in-law."

Many religions lay claim to such cures, but the variety of those with which Seicho no Ie associates itself is such that several follow for illustration. In Taniguchi's words:

"Mr. Matsumoto Jukyo of Ochiai, Tokyo, was in the audience at my lecture given at Hochi Hall on December 19, 1934. His child had the bad habit of bed-wetting, and various treatments were of no avail. To tell the truth, the parents are usually responsible for the child's affliction—the bed-wetting is often the reflection of the parents' mind. When Matsumoto listened to my lecture his mind underwent a sudden change and his child stopped wetting the bed that very night."[19] (That such "miracles" are highly estimated by Japanese mothers appears from the detailed recounting of five such cures in the first four pages of Taniguchi's book.)

"Since she [a little girl] visited Seicho no Ie, she has acquired the firm belief that man is originally perfect, and that therefore her nearsightedness must be imaginary. Telling her doctor so, she persisted in her refusal to wear glasses. Her eyes got well before long, and when she took the entrance examination for school there was nothing wrong with her eyes."[20]

"A young lady came to me and asked for consultation. Her story was that she had been subject to chronic menorrhagia for eight years since the age of fourteen and thus unable to marry and conceive children. Her mental affliction was complicated, so it was necessary to visit me four times before she was cured."[21]

"Mr. Tanaka Ginnosuke, a principal of a primary school in Tatsuno, was in the audience at the Kokumin Kaikan [hall] in Osaka. He was a man of character, but had a big wart in the middle of his forehead which formed a distinctive feature in his physiognomy. As soon as my lecture came to a close, the wart suddenly dropped off. This is a true story and by no means strange because the flesh changes according to the mind."[22]

And this amazing claim: "Lately. . .I revealed true stories of how man has learned to live in harmony with such previous nuisances as mice, ants, ticks, and the like—all these once harmful animals and insects have become unharmful because of the conditions of our minds."[23]

There is no disease or abnormal situation that Seicho no Ie does not claim to have healed. The healing comes about, as claimed above, through the change of people's minds—bitterness turned into gratitude, hate into love, as they listen to Taniguchi, or practice the shinsokan. About the power of the shinsokan Taniguchi says: "It is not always necessary to practice shinsokan in order to meditate on the perfect nature of the person seeking help. If you can concentrate your mind on the perfect nature of the other person while you are carrying on a conversation with him, the illness will disappear."[24] The doctrine of shinsokan may be compared with similar doctrines in other new religions.

Because of the supposed unlimited power of the shinsokan, doctors, diagnoses, and medicine are held in contempt: "I sometimes see a patient suffering from lung disease taking his temperature all the time. Every time he checks his temperature he says to himself, 'I am feverish. I am really ill,' thus making the disease-idea stronger and stronger. This is not the way to be cured. Throw away your thermometer, realize your original true self, which is free from disease. Drive the disease-idea out of your mind and you are sure to recover health at once."[25]

The reader should not believe that Westerners are the only ones who might raise their eyebrows on hearing these accounts—there are countless Japanese as well who do so.

Life after Death

Seicho no Ie does not deny that there is a life after death, but it is not clearly defined. The emphasis on this life is carried to such an extent that Taniguchi claims that paradise and heaven are here: "The pilgrimage of faith does not mean in the literal sense a long journey to the Pure Land of Heaven. We are *already* in the Pure Land of Heaven, without making any laborious trip. We are in reality in Heaven and one with God, though we lead a life in this world. However, we must not be satisfied with mere intellectual understanding of it. We must go ahead and make it our own life and blood, nay, we must endeavour to live daily with this consciousness."[26]

Man of Infinite Potentiality

Perhaps the doctrine that has given Seicho no Ie most of its appeal to people is the idea which can be traced like a thread through all the other doctrines. This is the idea that man, once conscious of his "Sonship," has unlimited resources at his disposal and can live a life of infinite possibilities: "The fundamental principle expounded by Seicho no Ie is that our fate lies in our own hands, that we shape our fate freely ourselves, that we in other words are the masters of our own destiny. The law of destiny is provided by the fundamental truth that man is son of God. Since man is son of God, there is no impossibility, and he creates freely according to his heart's desire the phenomenal world, which is a reflection of the mind."[27]

"There is no impossibility for a person who is united with the life of God and burns with the will to make manifest the wisdom, love, and life of God on earth. Impossibility makes its seeming appearance, because we do not realize God within us. When we make the will of God our will, and cast ourselves into His work, forgetting ourselves in absolute reliance on God, negative words such as impossible vanish from our thinking."[28]

For the sons of God there is no such thing as fear: "Fear is indeed an enemy of life. The negative thought of 'impossibility' and 'all is up' will deprive you of the power of 'possibility' and drive you into an abyss of misfortune which is unnecessary and can be definitely avoided. Then what can we do to break away from fear and arrive at the thought that 'it can be done'? Here is the answer: Pray constantly in your mind saying 'I am a son of God. I will never fail because God is always leading and directing me with His infinite wisdom. God is my wisdom, power, and wealth—He is infinite supply.' "[29]

This theory of man as a being of infinite potentiality is used dexterously in the propaganda of Seicho no Ie. Lavish promises are made for all kinds of occupations: "Medical men will through this be enabled to make accurate diagnoses and prescriptions. Artists will be enabled to transfer to the phenomenal world the truth, goodness, and beauty of God's Kingdom. Scientists will be guided by the wisdom of God and be enabled to make great inventions and discoveries to benefit human life, or again, to discover complex and mysterious laws of the Universe and improve the destiny of man. Again, a technician will be able to make his skill a tool of God, to unite with the great and divine wisdom of God, and proceed one step further than he would be able to do if he relied merely on material knowledge."[30]

Seicho no Ie tells the parents that all problems will disappear. The children's studies will improve if just they close their eyes before each lesson and meditate on being a son of God and on the idea, "I know my lessons well." And a boy who is told often enough that he is a good boy will automatically become a good boy, just as a boy who is always scolded for being a bad boy will become a bad boy. Also, tension in the family, such as between husband and wife, between parents and in-laws, will become a thing of the past, or rather, a thing that never existed, if they apply the shinsokan meditation to their problems and use the unlimited resources waiting for those who realize the Sonship of man.

Similar miraculous stories are told about people who suddenly became able to pay their taxes when before it had seemed impossible;[31] people who through enlightenment were able to find things long lost;[32] people who had narrow escapes from death;[33] and on and on, all due to salvation through using shinsokan, once man has realized his potential as a son of God.

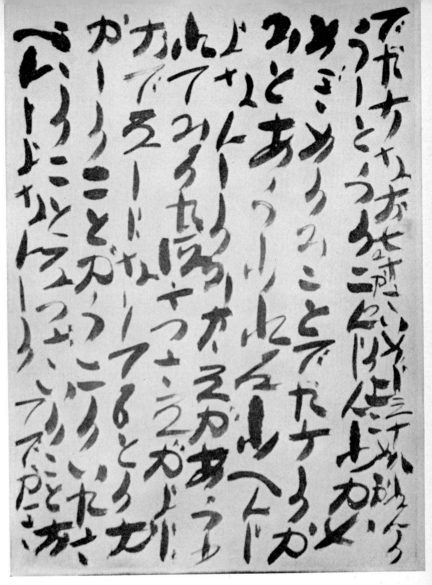

OMOTOKYO

17 ■ PART OF OMOTOKYO'S SCRIPTURE, THE "OFUDESAKI." IT
WAS WRITTEN BY THE BRUSH OF DEGUCHI NAO, FOUNDRESS OF
THE RELIGION. JAPANESE "KANA" IS USED ALMOST EXCLUSIVE-
LY RATHER THAN CHINESE "KANJI" CHARACTERS.

OMOTOKYO

19 ■ DEGUCHI NAO, ORIGINAL FOUNDRESS OF OMOTOKYO (1836–1918).

18 ■ DEGUCHI ONISABURO, COLORFUL CO-FOUNDER OF OMOTOKYO (1871–1948).

ANANAIKYO

20 ■ IN CONNECTION WITH THE WORLD RELIGIOUS MOVEMENTS, PRIME MINISTER NEHRU AND AN INDIAN RELIGIOUS LEADER POSE WITH ANANAIKYO'S NEGAMI SHIN.

21 ■ ONE OF ANANAIKYO'S MANY OBSERV-
ATORIES. THIS ONE IS ON KYUSHU NEAR
KURUME.

22 ■ THE PRESENT LEADER,
NAKANO YONOSUKE.

SEICHO NO IE

23 ■ THE LARGE TOKYO HEADQUARTERS OF SEICHO NO IE.

24 ■ A RELIGIOUS GATHERING AT THE HEAD-
QUARTERS IN TOKYO.

Seicho no Ie and Other Religions

Taniguchi and most other religious leaders of Seicho no Ie study other religions intensely but still claim their own superiority. Many are the stories of people who, by coming to Seicho no Ie, suddenly came to "truly understand" the sutras and doctrines of their *own* religions.[34]

Still, Taniguchi pays the highest tribute to Jesus and Buddha, if not to Christianity and Buddhism: "I have a profound respect for Buddha and Christ. This is because among the other numerous religious founders, these two persons preached the truth; but the followers of their various sects generally misunderstood the truth and could not genuinely transmit what Buddha and Christ taught, and they have consequently preached truth as well as untruth."[35]

It is the religions, Buddhism and Christianity, as they have developed, that are scorned by Taniguchi and regarded as inferior to Seicho no Ie: "There are many religious books, some of which were written by men of high virtue and profound learning. What they say is mostly correct. However, they are merely book-and-church religions, and cannot be applied to practical life because they do not have the realization that now is the time to act, and have not awakened to the truth that 'the Eternal Buddhahood is in me now; the eternal God is in me now.' This realization that now is the time to act turns a religion into practical life. This is Seicho no Ie. The difference between accomplished religion and the new revelation of Seicho no Ie is very slight, but this slight difference is extremely important. When this barrier is broken, religion becomes actual life, but till then it remains a religion of only church and book."[36] This stress on the connection of teaching with life is typical of a large number of the new religions and must be seen as part of the background for their success.

According to Seicho no Ie the present strifes and conflicts between religions will not disappear until all religions have found their way back, away from their founders, to the Eternal God: "When the Christians discover Christ, not in the material form of Jesus in the flesh, but in the eternal Divinity who said 'Before

Abraham was, I was'; when the Buddhists discover Buddha, not in Gautama in the flesh, but in the eternal Gautama, who told Ananda 'All Buddhas in the past are my disciples'; when the Seicho no Ie discovers Seicho no Ie not in the house, where Taniguchi in the flesh lives, but in the Seicho no Ie of eternal Reality, who said 'All religions will be rejuvenated by Me'—*then* first will religions no longer have to quarrel over their spheres of influence."[37]

Although Taniguchi has borrowed heavily from Buddhism, it is especially the Christian terms and doctrines he has colored for his own use, and at the same time has misquoted and mixed up some accounts (the above "Before Abraham was, I *was*," for example).

One of the stories in the Bible that Taniguchi most frequently uses is the story of Nicodemus. The following is his interpretation of it:

"If I paraphrase the words of Jesus to Nicodemus, it will be something like this: 'Even if the picture is distorted, do not think that the Real-Man is distorted. Even if the physical man is ill, the Real-Man is not ill. The physical eye cannot see the Real-Man. Can you see, from where the wind blows and where it goes? You can see the Real-Man no more than you can see the wind. To be born of the Spirit means to turn the eye from the physical man to the Real-Man—to come to the realization that you and God are one.' "[38]

Also the crucifixion of Christ, one of the few things concerning Christ that hardly ever is mentioned by Japanese religions, finds a place and an interpretation in the system of Seicho no Ie:

"True freedom lies behind the seeming freedom of being able to do as one pleases, and another name for it is meekness. What are we to be meek toward? It is to the mind of God that we must be meek. Christ prostrated himself in the Garden of Eden [this mix-up of Eden for Gethsemane is another example of superficial Bible study] and repeated twice these words in prayer: 'Oh, my Father, if it be possible, let this cup pass from me; nevertheless not as I will, but as thou wilt.' The bitter wine refers to the fate of Jesus, who was to be placed on the cross to die. Such is a bitter experience, and the mortal mind does not wish for it to happen. But finally Jesus surrendered everything to God's will. Jesus was crucified. Because of the cross the body was killed, but in spirit he was resurrected. He was released from phenomenal bounds and was given true freedom of the spirit. The act of ascending the cross does not symbolize any injunction to be crucified or to imitate any such barbaric practice as burning or torturing the body. It symbolizes the message which Seicho no Ie proclaims: *that his body does not exist, that matter is nothingness.*"[39]

Another phrase of Jesus that Taniguchi often (mis)quotes and gives his own interpretation to is 'Before Abraham was, I was.' This is how Taniguchi renders it: "Man is an eternal being. As God is immortal, man—a Son of God—is immortal. It is not when he was born from his mother's body that he came into this world as a man. Jesus says: 'Before Abraham was, I was.'"[40]

The words of Jesus and the teachings of Christianity that Seicho no Ie uses—with its own interpretation—are so numerous that they give a distinct Christian coloring to it. One of the most interesting questions in connection with the development of Seicho no Ie, and other new religions, is to what extent and in what way this wholesale adoption of Christian form and content will affect the attitude of these religions towards Christianity in the future.

Summary and Future

Seicho no Ie belongs to the medium-sized new religions. It has been adopted mostly by the middle classes and directs itself toward the intellectual in contrast to most other new religions which have had their great successes among farming classes. His formulation of a teaching that is a mixture of both Buddhism and Christianity has probably been greatly responsible for Seicho no Ie's appeal to the higher classes, but there is no doubt that Taniguchi's personality, his speeches, and the popularity of *Seimei no Jisso* have been mainly responsible for the success of his doctrines.

Seicho no Ie has a large number of devoted leaders throughout the country, and there is reason to believe that it will continue

172 as a fairly prosperous medium-sized middle-class new religion, although its durability and strength will not be truly tested—as is the case with so many other new religions—until it meets the challenge of surviving the death of its creator and present leader.

4

世界救世教 / Sekai Kyusei Kyo

Sekai Kyusei Kyo, founded under a different name in 1934 by Okada Mokichi, is another of the new religions which originated from Omotokyo. It is a typical syncretistic religion which in content and form is a mixture of Buddhism, Shinto, and Christianity but with strong overtones of Omotokyo. Naturally, much of the former three religions was filtered through the latter, but much has also been brought in since Sekai Kyusei Kyo became separate and independent.

The name of the religion has changed several times since its beginning. It started out as Kannonkyo in 1934, changed into Nippon Kannon Kyodan in 1947, then, in 1950, developed into Sekai Meshiya Kyo (World Messianity), under which name it is best known. It finally adopted its present name shortly after.

Sekai Kyusei Kyo is classified as a new religion by the government, but its believers prefer to call it a "truth movement, of which religion is only a part." They claim that Sekai Kyusei Kyo is a combination of science and religion, and consequently should be called a super-religion and super-science.

Sekai Kyusei Kyo reminds one strongly of Omotokyo. Its main teachings are that the earth is approaching the last judgment, that the judgment will be followed by a paradise on earth, that man in the meantime must build model paradises on earth, and that Okada, founder of the religion, was a prophet sent by God to this age to bring about heavenly paradise on earth.

Sekai Kyusei Kyo has established two "miniature paradises." The "paradise" in the Hakone mountains is known as Shinsen- **173** kyo and was built in 1952 at Gora. It consists of several buildings and a garden, the latter considered by many to be one of the most beautiful in Japan. One interesting feature is the Hakone Art Museum, which has a collection of unique objects of ancient art from China and Japan. Just above the museum is the Founder's Mausoleum, a structure done in a highly unorthodox architectural style, and which was constructed with the aid of four thousand members who donated their labor. A third "paradise" is under construction in Kyoto.

The more famous of the existing "paradises" is the one in Atami, the Zuiun-kyo, built on a hill about one hundred meters above the town of Atami. It was completed in 1955, and the Art Museum on the second floor was added in 1957. It is really the spiritual headquarters of Sekai Kyusei Kyo and the museum is just part of the center, but interestingly enough there are no signboards from below leading up to "Sekai Kyusei Kyo," whereas one will find a number of signs with the words "Atami Art Museum." In the main building is the impressive Messianic Hall with red-cushioned plush seats for three thousand and standing room for an extra two thousand. It contains a revolving stage and an acoustically well-designed hall. In this hall the two monthly services, on the 10th and the 23rd, are carried out. An underground ferro-concrete corridor, which was reserved for the use of the founder, connects the main building with the Crystal (or Sun) Palace (Zuishoden), which commands a magnificent view of the Atami bay. Surrounding the buildings, down along the sloping hillside, is a beautiful park with hundreds of plum trees given by believers from all over the country. The whole project is said to have cost more than 210,000,000 yen, an economic task easily performed by Sekai Kyusei Kyo, which is reported to have holdings and property to an amount of 2,500 million yen at present.

The purpose of the two museums is to introduce fine arts to the world and elevate human souls through contact with beauty— in other words, to experience religion through the medium of beauty. The collection of art objects in Sekai Kyusei Kyo is highly appreciated by the public, as they stress that most objects of art in Japan otherwise are the property of individuals.

Founding and History

The founder of Sekai Kyusei Kyo, Okada Mokichi, was known as "Jikan" (Manifestation of Kannon) in an earlier stage of his religion, now, among other titles, is known as Ohikarisama (literally, Hon. Mr. Light). He was born in the Asakusa district of Tokyo in 1882, the son of a poor shopkeeper.

He attempted the way to success through business and was successful. In a few years he had collected a fortune in wholesale business in accessories, only to lose every yen in the stock-market panic of 1920. This caused him to turn to religion, and for a few years he belonged to Omotokyo. He soon became the teacher of one of the largest churches in Tokyo. He became well known as a master of spiritualism, meditation, and shamanism, and soon he decided to part from Omotokyo and begin his own religion. The first step toward this was the adoption of his own method in faith-healing and the refusal to use the wooden spoons, which were distributed by Onisaburo Deguchi to all teachers of Omotokyo and used by them to heal diseases. Okada constructed instead a special fan and began to use it in the practice of faith-healing. This was in open opposition to the rules of Omotokyo, and Okada had to leave this religion in 1934 (fortunately for him, as Omotokyo was prohibited and its leaders jailed by the police the next year) and established his own religion, Kannon Kai, the same year. He claimed to be an incarnation of Kannon, the Buddhist Goddess of Mercy, and found friends and sponsors among many prominent men of his day (among them Admiral Suetsugu Nobumasa and novelist Satomi Ton).

Before this time, in 1926, Okada claimed to have a revelation from God, who asked him to be his messiah and prophet to mankind and gave him the "divine light" (*jorei*) to heal diseases and perform all kinds of miracles. From that day Okada was convinced that he was above all other men since he had been selected by God. He developed a strong feeling of superiority, claimed to be the greatest doctor in the world, and even sent in an application for the Nobel Prize—an honor he failed to receive!

Okada said that the jorei went out from him. He claimed that this was a power which could cure any disease just by applying a piece of paper on which he had written the character for the word light (*hikari*) to the sick part of the body. Many believed him to be divine; some paid as much as twenty thousand yen (much more to a Japanese than the $55.00 this is equal to) just to talk with him, and the hikari characters were sold at a price of two thousand yen apiece. No wonder that he in a few years had gathered an enormous fortune, part of which he used to build the two "paradises."

In 1947, after the World War, Okada changed the name of his religion into Nippon Kannon Kyo, and in 1950 he changed the name once more, this time into Sekai Meshiya Kyo (World Messianic Church). The changes of the name of his religion were probably carried out partly because Okada thought something *new* and something *international* would have stronger appeal to people, partly because Christianity came to interest him, more and more at the expense of Buddhism. He simply discarded Kannon from the name of his religion, and replaced her with Yahweh and messiah in his subsequent writings.

In 1950 Okada was put into jail on an 80,000,000-yen tax-evasion charge, and from this time on his health gradually weakened. Although he became worse and worse he refused to see doctors, and on the 1st of March, 1955, he died. He was given one of the most splendid funerals seen in Japan; all the 180 taxis of Atami were reserved for the funeral on that day, and twenty thousand attended the funeral service, which cost Meshiya Kyo more than eight million yen.

Just as Miki's death at the age of ninety had been a problem to Tenrikyo because she had taught that man's natural age was 115 years, the death of Okada, who claimed that his Divine Power could cure anybody or anything, posed a problem to his believers. Therefore they maintain that the word "death" cannot be applied to Okada, that he is not really dead but is in constant communion with his successor, and that he only "departed" to "finish his purification in the name of us all." Okada Yoshiko, the wife of the founder, succeeded to the leadership of the religion and held it until her death in January, 1962. Okada's married daughter,

Fujieda Itsuki, is the present leader. Since Okada's successors have been followers in the same family, their titles Nidai-sama (second generation leader) and Sandai-sama (third generation leader) reflect this.

Doctrines

The Two Worlds

Okada taught that "this world consists not only of the visible world, but that there is also an invisible, spiritual world. These two worlds are closely connected, indeed they are like two sides of a sheet of paper, the one not existing without the other. It is the spiritual world which is the main component of this universe because it is eternal and is the source of all life energy governing the universe. Everything occurs first in the spiritual world, and is then reflected in the visible world."[1]

Accordingly, all diseases as well as any other kind of misfortune have their inception in the spiritual world, and cannot be removed unless contact is established with the spiritual world.

Destruction of the World

According to Okada, man should live in accord with the spiritual world of God in order that the new world can come true, but man has chosen to turn his back to God and embrace the material world. To correct this, he said: "The old house must be destroyed before the new one can be built." The "present calamities" of the world are all part of this purification by God. And the closer we come to the "day of the construction of paradise on earth," the more numerous the calamities will become: "Not only the purification of human bodies, but the world-wide purification, a general house cleaning in every field is impending. This means the obliteration of the clouds of sin and vice which have accumulated in the past thousands of years. The purification may come not only in the form of disease, but in famines, wars, and also in natural calamities. This is what Christ Jesus prophesied as the Last Judgment. The Last Judgment does not mean punishment but a purification which must come in order that this world of discord may be changed into a world of harmony and peace."[2]

A Paradise of Art and Beauty on Earth

After the transitional period of destruction, humanity will enter the great period of construction, during which "the Kingdom of Heaven" will be built on this earth. Further, this great event must first have taken place in the invisible spiritual world, and Okada claims that it already has. "This turning from night to day first began in the innermost part of the spiritual world, in the very heights of heaven, and then gradually it has been reflected on the ethereal realm until now at last it is permeating this physical world."[3]

Okada stresses that this paradise will be a world of truth, virtue and beauty, especially the latter because "beauty can be expressed by form." As the time draws near, the "fine arts will accordingly have a marvellous development." And, as a contribution to this development, Okada built the two "miniature paradises" at Atami and Hakone because, as he says, "If a pattern is worked out somewhere in the world, it will in time be imitated on a world-wide scale."[4]

Their beauty, and that of every object of art, is not merely beauty but "an activity of salvation." The purpose of beauty and art is to elevate human souls and bring them closer to the spiritual world. Okada believed that this was a task especially given to the Japanese people:

"Every race in the world has its own thought and culture. The national characteristic of the Japanese people is to give expression through the medium of beauty and thus to contribute to the development of culture. From this viewpoint the future course of Japan is self-evident. I believe that eternal peace and prosperity will be brought about if we adhere to the above ideal."[5]

After the sharp blow that defeat had dealt to Japanese national pride and confidence it was necessary for some to rediscover their cultural heritage. People's first reaction to Okada's paradises was an appreciation of their beauty, then, coming as a proud after-thought, the realization that these creations are peculiarly Japanese. This was one key to Okada's success. He correctly saw that beauty is potential spiritual nourishment, especially for the Japanese with their historic esthetic sensitivity.

The Problem of Misfortunes

According to Okada, all evils, diseases, poverty, disasters, and other. ills can be explained by the theory of "spiritual vibrations."

"A kind of radiant energy is emitted by all living creatures, by all minerals and by all vegetables. The human body emits auras or light waves all the time. There are degrees of high vibrations and degrees of low vibrations according to the understanding and spiritual advancement of the individual. Also the aura changes according to the way we think. If man thinks of or does something good, the light waves become intense and vibrate at a high note. Conversely, when a man thinks of or does something bad, his aura will become clouded and the vibrations low. Those, whose auras are wide are fortunate and healthy, and those whose auras are narrow are likely to encounter misfortunes and be subject to sickness.

"The spiritual body was originally transparent because God created man pure, but now everybody has more or less non-transparent parts in the spiritual body. These impurities are called 'clouds.' They have been created by man's wrong thoughts and deeds. This has become so serious that these clouds are also found in the blood of every man, and they are the real cause of all man's misfortunes, disasters, calamities, and diseases."[6]

The Divine Light

The central doctrine of Sekai Kyusei Kyo is the teaching that *jorei* (divine light) can dissipate the clouds in the spiritual body of man and cure man from any misfortune.

Jorei is explained in the following way:

"It was revealed to [Okada], that the invisible ether is an element governing this universe, and may be called Universal Energy. It is a tremendously strong energy which brings into being all things in this universe and makes them grow. This force is not only invisible but omnipotent, and the source of this energy is God. The method of utilizing this power to disperse the clouds in the spiritual body as well as in the human body, is called *jorei*. Through the administering of *jorei* we believe the recipient is purified spiritually and physically. It can heal any sick person, but it must not be forgotten that the object of *jorei* is not so much the healing of the physical body as the purification of the spiritual body of its clouds and the attainment of the spiritual awakening of our inner soul."[7]

The jorei was supposed to be concentrated in Okada. Some even go so far as to claim that the power was actually contained in a ball-sized pearl in Okada's abdomen, the light from which sometimes came in the form of a white flame emanating from his hand.

Okada claimed that he could transfer this power from himself to the character for the word *hikari* (light). This was written by Okada himself and was to be carried as a charm (*omamorisama*) worn around the neck of a believer who had taken the Sekai Kyusei Kyo course of study. The bearer of this written character was also then able to cure others "...by raising his arm, whereupon the light will reach his hand and be emitted from his palm to the person to whom he is administering."[8]

Sekai Kyusei Kyo also terms jorei "prayer in action," and has made all sorts of extravagant claims. Its periodical *Eiko*, also published in English under the name *The Glory*, carries stories giving jorei the credit for easy births, protection from floods, and cures from blindness. *Eiko's* readers are told that followers of Sekai Kyusei Kyo at Hiroshima and Nagasaki survived the atomic explosion and that communists gladly forsake their doctrines when they experience the power of jorei. This will make a person virtuous, loved, and respected by all.[9] With it man can save not only his ancestors but his descendants.[10] Such are the powers of jorei that even if the man who administers it denies God, its powers are not dimmed.[11]

An interesting application of jorei is the claim that it makes fertilizer unnecessary. "If jorei is administered to the soil, the power inside the earth, 'transcendental soil,' will spring to the surface of the earth from the center of the earth. This is called natural cultivation."[12] This of course lets us realize the preponderant majority of the members of Sekai Kyusei Kyo are farmers.

This doctrine made Okada and, soon after, his followers completely sceptical of medicine, doctors, and hospitals. He frequently refers to medicine as poison because "it reduces the pain which was intended as the purification by God." And he sent an open letter to the Japan Medical Association proposing an open debate before an audience—a proposal which was politely refused. Even today, believers follow in Okada's footsteps, refusing to be vaccinated, not believing in the existence of such things as bacteria, and refusing to use fertilizer on their fields.

Life after Death

Sekai Kyusei Kyo teaches "eternal salvation through reincarnation." When the physical body becomes useless and dies, the soul separates itself, returns to the spiritual world, and, after a period of schooling and improvement, returns in a new incarnation: with a new mission to perform.[13]

Other Religions

That Sekai Kyusei Kyo thinks in terms of saving not only the Japanese, but also the Western world, is evident, among other things, from the title of a book Okada wrote with the title *America o Sukuu* (Saving America). And Sekai Kyusei Kyo has succeeded in establishing several churches in Brazil, Hawaii, and the U.S., not least important the one in Los Angeles, where several non-Japanese are members.

The attitude of Sekai Kyusei Kyo towards other religions is very friendly and tolerant. It is stated that members of any other religious faith need not abandon their church to enter "the gateway of Sekai Kyusei Kyo."[14] This statement must be qualified by the fact that Sekai Kyusei Kyo, as mentioned above, regards itself as a "super-religion."

Sekai Kyusei Kyo takes a special interest in Christianity. Okada took many of his ideas from the Old and New Testaments, and personally believed that he was the Messiah mentioned there. He stated that the purpose of Sekai Kyusei Kyo was to work together with Christianity, and he suggested that the world be divided into two mission fields, one for the Western countries under the responsibility of Christianity, and one for the Eastern countries under the responsibility and leadership of Sekai Kyusei Kyo.

Summary and Future

Sekai Kyusei Kyo reached its zenith during the last years of Okada Mokichi's life due mostly to his fascinating but somewhat bizarre personality. Since his death membership has decreased sharply, at present numbering only about 120,000 paying members (although the religion claims to have about 400,000 believers).

Sekai Kyusei Kyo has been involved in a couple of scandals caused by the death of believers undergoing "treatment" to expel evil spirits. These events, which occurred in the period 1957–58, seem to have been the beginning of a decline in popularity. Sekai Kyusei Kyo is at present one of the smaller new religions, though one of the wealthiest of these. Okada's successor, his wife Yoshiko, died only recently. It is hard to say how things will fare under the thirty-four-year old daughter Itsuki, but it is doubtful if the future holds great promise of any large-scale growth.

5

PL 教団 / PL Kyodan

Perfect Liberty Kyodan, the "Religion of Art," is the only Japanese religion which has used foreign words in its official name. Miki Tokuchika, the leader of Perfect Liberty Kyodan—or PL, as it usually is called—explains the extraordinary name in the following way: "We want to contribute to the modernization of Japan, and therefore we chose a modern American name, "Perfect Liberty." Kyodan means church or religious group.

Refounded in 1956 as PL Kyodan, PL is also called the "Golf Religion" because of the famous huge golf course they have made at the headquarters at Tondabayashi, near Osaka. The name is not entirely off the mark as several local PL churches, among them the downtown church in Kyoto, have roof-top golf driving ranges, and on the whole PL takes an immense interest in sports.

The aim of PL Kyodan is expressed in the following way: "The PL Kyodan seeks to elucidate the Way to eternal peace and welfare of mankind by promoting the realization that all men are children of God and by making people attain a state of mind whereby both they and others become blessed and happy through freely and powerfully expressing their individuality in the interest of their fellow men and society under the motto of 'Life is Art.' "[1]

PL is one of the most modern and streamlined religions in Japan and is, with more than 600,000 believers, a religious force to reckon with. That PL believers also believe in the future of their religion is obvious from the following quotation: "PL has at last discovered the significance and purpose of life—something that has been sought for by mankind since the beginning of his- **183** tory. Regardless of the kinds of problems met in human life, it has become possible to give a clear-cut answer according to the individual character, circumstances, and environment of any person concerned. This is a great discovery in the history of human culture. With the appearance of the PL Order it has become possible for all mankind to attain eternal peace and welfare."[2]

The central theme of an interpretation of life as art is a generous elaboration and emphasis of one of Onisaburo's ideas in Omoto-kyo. It permeates all their writings and sermons—the words "art" and "artist" being used continually. There are several general points of similarity between PL and others of the Omoto group.

Founding and History

Miki Tokuchika is called Oshie-oya by his followers. The English title he uses, Holy Father, is a rough equivalent. He is one of the strongest personalities among founders of new religions in Japan, and he is the most eloquent spokesman of Japan's League of New Religions, of which he is chairman. In 1946 he founded the PL Kyodan. In many ways the religion he founded is the continuation of a religion his father had created in 1924.

The seed of PL Kyodan was actually planted in 1912 with the founding of the new religion Tokumitsu-kyo, whose leader was an itinerant priest and spiritualist by the name of Kanada Tokumitsu. One of Kanada's disciples was Miki Tokuharu, Tokuchika's father. Miki had been a Buddhist priest of the Obaku Zen sect. After the death of Kanada in 1919, Miki planted a shrub called *himorogi* at the place of Kanada's death. He worshiped it for five years in accordance with the instructions given him by his master. At the end of the five years he claimed to have received the revelation promised by Kanada before his death. Miki then established a religion known as Hito no Michi (the Way of Man) in 1924. Hito no Michi was quite successful and is estimated to have had about one million believers by 1934. However, in 1937 the religion was prohibited by the government, and Miki and many of his leaders were arrested on the charge of lèse majesté. Soon after, in 1938, Miki Tokuharu died.

His son Tokuchika, was born in 1900. In later life he became the leader of Hito no Michi. This was not long before the 1945 Supreme Court verdict which upheld the earlier decision of lèse majesté and caused the disbanding of Hito no Michi. After the war, in 1946, Tokuchika and some leaders and members of the old group started Perfect Liberty Kyodan and established its headquarters at Tosu.

Headquarters

PL's headquarters was first in Tosu on Kyushu, then it was moved to Shimizu in Shizuoka Prefecture, and finally, in 1955, it was established at its present location, an hour's drive from Osaka. It is a huge area of more than 2,000 hectares, one of the largest of the religious headquarters. All PL's ambitious building plans have not yet been realized, and it will be some time before this is possible, but still, impressive progress has been made. At present a town of almost three thousand inhabitants has been created. The religion's leaders hope to create an "earthly paradise," and have already made an artificial lake, leveled hills, and have removed thousands of pine trees which have been replaced with cherry trees. Tokuchika was undoubtedly influenced by the already existing "paradises" of Sekai Kyusei Kyo.

PL's ambitious plans provide for excellent sports and education facilities. There is a kindergarten, an elementary school, a middle school, and a high school. A huge PL Youth (PLY) center has been constructed, an enormous golf course has almost been finished, and three baseball diamonds are in use. There are also golf courses for beginners and midget courses for children.

Among other buildings are the Saidan, the main temple, which is a marble structure built on a hill overlooking the golf links; the Founders Mausoleum, two remarkable semi-spherical buildings; and the Gaisaiden, a kind of mausoleum for the ashes and artistic works of deceased members of PL. In front of the Gaisaiden there is a tall white tower with a ring of sun rays with the letters PL on the top.

Close to the PLY building is the Hoshokai Hospital, the entire staff of which belongs to PL. The function of the hospital is explained in the following way:

"The Hoshokai Hospital aims at a firm establishment of PL medicine, by proving one of our religious doctrines that says illness is the revelation of God, and a man becomes ill when he violates the divine law. Both the doctors and the patients pray to God for mercy prior to the medical treatment, and also in the waiting-room the patients pray and worship in front of an altar placed there. Due to mutual trust between doctors and patients, all of whom are believers of the same religion, the cures are most effective."[3] In connection with the hospital, an interesting system of five training groups has been set up, in which people are given physical and spiritual training as well as medicinal treatment.

Worship and Practices

The main features of PL worship are the daily morning service, the informal round-table conferences held from time to time, the thanksgiving service celebrated on the twenty-first of every month, and the four annual festivals. The festivals have become nationally known for their gorgeous display of magnificent fireworks, and the summer festival is usually attended by crowds of up to 250,000 people.

The daily morning service starts before 5:00 A.M. and lasts for about an hour. It is called *asamairi* and is conducted in such a way that the participants can exchange "artistic experiences." At the appointed time, which varies from place to place, the PL people "gather at the headquarters and branches to pledge themselves before God to lead an artistic life during the whole day in a pleasant mood and in accordance with divine laws. This function is a unique form of PL faith, practiced throughout the year without interruption."[4]

"The morning service takes place in the following order: believers gather before the appointed hour, sweep inside and outside the church, and make various preparations at the teacher's instructions. This is called *misasage* (divine service). At the appointed time all stand before the altar, which is always covered with a white veil in PL churches. They then proceed to sing the PL Hymn in chorus, and then sit down and intone worship (*shi-*

kiri, a word borrowed from *sumo* wrestling) to God. Subsequently, those believers who wish to do so speak to the audience about their personal experience of leading an artistic life. After this follows the sermon of the teacher. The actual meeting is closed after again singing the PL hymn. Afterwards talks are given for the people who have newly entered PL."[5]

PL believers attach the greatest importance to the morning service and particularly the sermon. "The pleasant and bright atmosphere of the morning service is something, no other religion can produce."[6] "If one attends the meeting and listens to the sermon, and afterwards asks questions, then all necessary expressions [teaching] will be given, until one fully understands."[7]

An interesting element of PL worship is the newly introduced PL Prayer accompanied by a series of peculiar hand postures—nine for sitting and seven for standing.

The PL Hymn, along with the sermon, is considered the center of the morning service. The hymn goes as follows:

"Born as children of God in the beautiful world,
Wishing to express the individuality,
Unique on this earth
People have gathered at PL Kyodan.
Earnestly wishing to be blessed

With a way of life completely new,
Upon giving up selfishness and depending solely on God,
People have gathered at PL Kyodan.
Realizing piously that it is the way of man
To devote himself, heart and soul, to the task blessed by God,

And to pray for the happiness of mankind,
People have gathered at PL Kyodan.
Wishing to follow to the last
The Way preached by the Master,
To save man, who has forgotten God,
People have gathered at PL Kyodan."[8]

Laws of Art

PL makes a distinction between the so-called Human Law and Divine Law given by God and revealed to Miki: "The law of the great nature is called Divine Law in our Order. Mundane laws or ethics are made by man, are products of man's art, and are therefore called Human Law. Man is always under the control of Divine Law. The expressions 'Life is Art' and 'Man's life is a continuous succession of self-expressions' mean to engage in creating art through expressions of the self in conformity with this divine law, giving due consideration also to human law. Problems of human life cannot be expected to be solved if one does not recognize God or forgets Divine Law because human law is always imperfect. The Divine Law, to be adhered to by all means in leading a human life, has been revealed by our Order in the Twenty-one Precepts for Conduct in Life. One can perfectly and beautifully express oneself as a manifestation of God, only when one follows these precepts."9

Creed of the Artist

The following is a translation of the Twenty-one Precepts for Conduct in Life, Shosei-kun, which PL says were revealed in part to Miki Tokuharu five years after the death of Kanada, and in full to Miki Tokuchika at Hiroshima in 1947:

1. Life is art.
2. The whole life of the individual is a continuous succession of self-expressions.
3. The individual is a manifestation of God.
4. We suffer if we do not manifest ourselves.
5. We lose our self if we are swayed by our feelings.
6. Our true self is revealed when our ego is effaced.
7. All things exist in mutual relation to one another.
8. Live radiantly as the Sun.
9. All men are equal.
10. Bring mutual happiness through our expressions.
11. Depend on God at all times.

12. There is always a way for each person.
13. There is one way for men, and there is another for women.
14. All things exist for world peace.
15. Our whole environment is the mirror of our mind.
16. All things make progress and develop.
17. Grasp the heart of everything.
18. At every moment man stands at the crossroad of good and evil.
19. Practice at once whatever your first inspiration dictates.
20. Attain the perfect harmonious state of mind and matter.
21. Live in Perfect Liberty.[10]

All PL doctrines have been extracted from these twenty-one precepts, and they are constantly referred to in the sermons and the daily worship.

The precepts do not form a clear-cut doctrinal system. Thus precept nine, "All men are equal," seems to conflict with thirteen, "There is one way for men, and there is another for women." It is also difficult to see how number five, "We lose our self if we are swayed by our feelings," can be harmoniously combined with nineteen, "Practice at once whatever your first inspiration dictates." These precepts are part of a conscious attempt to popularize and simplify PL's doctrines, but it has resulted in oversimplification and partial obscurity.

The influence from Shinto is evident. Thus, precept eight, "Live radiantly as the Sun," is a reference to the Sun Goddess of Shinto. On the whole, PL is more influenced by Shinto than any other traditional religion, especially in its external worship, rites, and ceremonies. When the heritage from Shinto and Omotokyo have been subtracted, not much is left of PL. Its main characteristic is the attempt to explain everything on the basis of "Life is Art." Their development of this theme—man is an artist, God is the "Artist of Artists," sin is an unartistic life—is of course unique, but it is an elaboration of an Omotokyo doctrine.

God, the Artist of Artists

PL claims to be a monotheistic religion, although it is a question as to whether this claim is quite justified. The "Parent God" of PL is called Mioya-okami, a name which is not found in the myths of Shinto, but is similar to the Tenrikyo Oyagami, which may be the original of the PL version.

The existence of God is argued in the following way: "There is nothing man can do by his own efforts. It is by the Power of Nature that man is born, is enabled to grow up, live, work, and make self-expressions during the whole span of his life. Besides mankind, the progress and development of the whole creation also depends solely upon the Power of Nature, if we examine all phenomena closely, one by one. There exists a great power in this universe. We are manifestations of that great Power of Nature and are allowed to live our daily life in accordance with the breathings of that great nature. This power of great nature, the spiritual power constituting the fountainhead of life and activity not only of man but also of everything else, is called God. In our Order we call Him Mioya-okami."[11]

Mioya-okami is not a transcendent deity but is regarded as one with man: "God is not something that exists outside of man, and favors or punishes him. In fact, God manifests Himself in man, and therefore God and man are one. Consequently, man cannot lead a perfect artistic life unless he makes self-expressions with the knowledge that God is his substance."[12]

Mioya-okami is in fact so immanent that not only man but everything in this world is in him: "God embraces everything. Good and evil, beauty and ugliness, truth and falsehood, happiness and misfortune, in short, all things are nestled in his bosom. God is power and love which, while embracing everything, creates everything, nurtures everything, and makes everything progress and develop. Everything, originating thus in God, always makes development by trying to transform evil into good, ugliness into beauty, falsity into truth, and misfortune into happiness."[13]

Man, An Artist

Although man occasionally is regarded as being one with God, he is also said to be outside of God and different from Him. This apparent contradiction PL explains in the following way: "Man is God manifested as a human being. Man is not God Himself and remains man to the last, but man possesses the essential qualities of God."[14] Man's connection with God from the cradle to the grave is described thus: "At the moment man gives his first cry on leaving his mother's womb he is given a divine spirit of his parent deity Mioya-okami; and later his spirit consecutively communes with this parent deity from moment to moment, whereby his life is sustained; and when he dies, his spirit returns to that of his parent deity, leaving only his body on this earth."[15]

This close relationship with God gives man a singular position in this world, far above that of the animal kingdom: "Everything appearing in this world is a manifestation of God, but man in particular possesses the body, intellect, individuality, and desire for expression, which surpass all other beings, and is moreover endowed with liberty. Man is the lord of creation; indeed, there is nothing nobler than man."[16]

This singular position of man, however, is not unconditional: "Man can live a worthy life only when he consciously communes with God. None can live apart from God. As we return to God after death, man lives a human life only for so long as he is allowed to do so by the grace of God."[17]

Salvation, Becoming an Artist

Salvation, as conceived by PL, is obtained through spiritual as well as material endeavors: "It is needless to say that you have to listen to the teachings and believe in God, but you also have to make efforts. To strengthen your faith, you should attend morning services at a branch of our Order. To live righteously is in short to get rid of your ego and serve the world and others. To embody this faith you have to go at least once to the Holy Land, where the headquarters of the Order is being built for the purpose of establishing eternal peace in the world."[18]

The course a would-be believer must follow is clearly marked. As the first step, the person "...who has some knowledge of PL but wishes to study further and thus appreciate it better by experiencing the charm of a pleasant life, should officially join. This requires an introduction by a believer. Once a member, the aspirant should attend morning services for some time without fail. After study of about a month, including listening to the sermons, talks, and testimonies by believers; and after receiving the Twenty-one Precepts for Conduct in Life and asking for explanation [*kaiketsu*] of them, the accumulation of these experiences will cause the realization that without a doubt PL is the true teaching that the aspirant sought for these many years."[19]

An important prerequisite to salvation is the financial contribution. PL requires regular contributions from its followers and has acquired the fame, or reputation, of being one of the strictest religions in Japan on this point. Upon joining PL the newcomer is requested to pay for his copy of the *Shin no Iiyu* (Believers' Handbook), for his badge, and for half a year's contribution to *Geijutsu Seikatsu* (Artistic Life), the PL monthly. Later on he receives a "treasure bag" (*hoshobukuro*), in which he is supposed to put daily offerings. "In this way he expresses his gratitude to God for the happiness brought to him by his faith in PL," the handbook explains. The treasure bags are collected and brought before the altar at headquarters on Kansha-matsuri, (Thanksgiving Service), the twenty-first of every month. The treasure bags pay for all the propaganda expenses and finance the expansion program at headquarters.

The external conditions for salvation mentioned above are not sufficient. Salvation is only brought about through a combination of the efforts of the believer, the grace of God, and the "divine function" or intervention of the founder himself (*tensho*), who in this case acts as mediator and brings about the salvation of others. The latter function is a recent doctrine which is not yet clearly developed.

The Artist Expresses Himself

One of the most important words in PL terminology is "self-expression," a term which is used to explain that every person should live in close connection with God and let his own abilities come to full expression in life. Just as the artist expresses himself through the objects of art he creates, in the same way man should express his abilities in whatever he does and make his work a continuous series of expressions of himself or of his own personality: "From day to day man lives his life by expressing his self from the cradle to the grave. Man's life is a continuous succession of self-expressions, and man dies when his self-expression comes to an end. Self-expression is an instinct man is endowed with from the moment he appears on this earth."[20] "Life is pleasant and interesting because man has this desire for expression, and because man is made to feel joy and satisfaction by endeavoring to manifest this desire. The progress and development of human society can be said to be based on this boundless desire for expression."[21] "Man is noble because he has an individuality. Human society is multifarious, multicolored, and full of indescribable charm because a multitude of such unique individualities are expressed in a complex way and woven together like the most exquisite figured brocade."[22]

The Art of Life

The self-expression of man must result in the "creation of art," whatever his work is. It is the main thesis of the founder that art has been much too narrow a concept in human history, and that the conception of art must be widened to include all human occupations:

"A conscientious artist, when engaging in artistic creation, completely devotes himself to his work, does not think of position, honor or money, and makes extraordinary efforts even at the risk of his life. After having taken such great pains he succeeds in creating an object of art. In this process of creation he feels spiritual pleasure akin to religious exaltation. This is because he takes delight in expressing his own individuality through creating an object of art.

"But is such pleasure a privilege of professional artists alone? No, it is not! Art consists in expressing one's own individuality through an object. Man can express his individuality in every act he does: in cooking food, in sweeping a room, in making tea, in nurturing a child, in stocking merchandise, in displaying merchandise in his store, in selling to customers, in negotiating a loan, in digging coal, in raising crops, in engaging in education, social welfare works, or politics—all people engaged in all kinds of professions in this world can express their respective individuality every day in all matters."[23]

With this conception of art in mind it is possible to see the background for the following kind of PL propaganda, which otherwise puzzles the reader: "In order to cultivate the finer senses and as an encouragement for better art, PL advocates the composition of thirty-one syllable poems as well as modern poems, dancing, baseball, and golfing."

Happiness, Joy of the Artist

Happiness consists in living an 'artistic life'; that is, to regard one's work as art and put into it all one's individuality. This will bring the zest of life that all men need: The Master says: 'To be happy is the same as to create art,' and that means that everybody can create art. If the purpose in life is to create art—that is, to express oneself—then in life there can be nothing but happiness, and unhappiness cannot exist."[24]

A variation of the same thought will be seen in the following paragraph: "When inspired expressions are made, man always feels good, regardless of how difficult their processes may be. Toil itself becomes a great pleasure and joy. The frame of mind after the goal has been achieved is of course pleasant, but compared with the pleasure and fun experienced in the midst of its processes, it resembles the taste of the rest of what one has thoroughly relished and enjoyed, like chewing gum after it has been chewed thoroughly."[25]

Unhappiness, Non-Art

If man forgets that he is a manifestation of God or even forgets God, then his life is no longer artistic, and he will meet various difficulties. Diseases, problems, and all kinds of misfortunes will come: "If man lives a kind of life based on his egocentric feelings and interests, all things in his environment develop unfavorably for him. Nothing goes as he wishes it to, he meets with disappointments, makes errors, fails in his business, loses his friends, his home life becomes unhappy, calamities arise one after the other, and he may at last suffer from illness."[26]

These sufferings and misfortunes in PL terminology are called *gasho,* and this signifies warnings from God, or manifestations of selfishness. If they are recognized by man as warnings from God, they may be blessings in disguise: "Since everything is material for man's art, we must also gladly make use of *gasho* as material for our art. When we approach *gasho* with the purpose of creating art, we will find that here is a splendid way of achieving this purpose. There is always a way to make every *gasho* without exception take a favorable turn."[27]

In order to know the nature of a gasho and what must be done to avert it or to turn it into a blessing, the believer must turn to the "Master" (Miki), or to one of the few consultants appointed by him, and ask for a *kokoroe* (prescription or instruction) applicable to the situation. PL members believe that the Master, who is said to be in constant contact with God, is able to diagnose the nature and cause of every misfortune and to prescribe a treatment. In cases of emergency, where time is scarce, the Master is said to be able to save the believer from calamity by "vicarious suffering," a rather obscure and unfinished PL doctrine.

The World and the Artist

PL teaches that everything in the world is a manifestation of God, and that things only exist as material for the use of man's creation of art. All things are therefore "potential objects of art." "Everything constitutes some material for the building up of human culture. In fact, the whole of creation is there to be utilized by mankind as material for making respective self-expressions and for building up eternal peace and happiness of mankind by mutual assistance. Mankind has incessantly been busy, and will always be busy in expressing self and creating art. What we ought to be thankful for in this connection is that in keeping with the progress of man's art, its object, the whole creation, progresses too, and that materials needed for man's art are produced endlessly and inexhaustibly. The part of the whole creation man has managed thus far to utilize as materials for his art is infinitesimal. A boundless world has been left for the present and the future, waiting to be utilized for man's art."[28]

Man as an artist is not alone but is surrounded by other artists whose joys he must share, and to whose expression his art must not become a hindrance: "Although man is a being that can freely express his own individuality by working upon the whole of creation, he does not do so as an isolated individual, but he is a social being from birth. There can exist no individual or art apart from society. Self-expressions should not become a hindrance to others or bring misfortune on society but become blessings for oneself as well as for others. The joy of self-expression is a joy which can be felt only when there are other people who appreciate, utilize, and welcome one's art. A joy shared with others becomes a joy twice blessed."[29]

One of the greatest arts in society is the harmony in the homes of the artists: "The most essential point in home life lies in leading a truly amicable life with man and wife becoming one in mind and body. Every member of the whole family should always strive to fulfill his respective task in a peaceful, joyous, bright, and pleasant mood without any restraint or hindrance."[30]

PL Kyodan is a modern religion, and from the quotation above we see how man and woman should become one in mind and body. Nevertheless PL has its roots in Shinto, according to which women are inferior to men, and the words of precept thirteen referring to "one way" for man and another for women reflect this. PL tries to explain this seeming contradiction by saying ". . . the divine law concerning how a married couple's life should be lived, and what the relationship between a superior and a subordinate should be is this. The greater part of the reason why home-life art generally does not go smoothly is attributable to the fact that the divine law is being neglected. The masculine, husband, and superior cannot become happy unless he expresses himself in a masculine way. Likewise, the feminine, wife, and subordinate has to express herself in a feminine way if she is to become happy."[31]

World Peace: Towards an Artistic World

Like all other new religions, PL also stresses that its ultimate goal is world peace: "We firmly believe that the larger the number of people who embrace PL faith and live an artistic life, the sweeter and lovelier this earth will become. Various evils such as grudging, hatred, and strife will disappear, and the world of perfect liberty and absolute peace that has been earnestly desired by mankind for a long time will become a reality, and it then will become possible for all of us to live our life artistically with a radiant heart and a peaceful mind."[32]

Propagation

They feel that to attain this goal of peace and harmony, mission is necessary to make all people in the world realize that PL is the answer.

PL carries out vigorous propaganda, even outside of Japan. There are already believers in Brazil, the United States, Australia, Argentina, Paraguay, Thailand, and Vietnam, but these are almost exclusively people of Japanese descent.

All believers are supposed to be missionaries, and all PL groups in Japan are divided up into smaller groups called *kumi*. Each kumi must bring in twenty new people every three months, whereupon the names of the people converted, as well as of those who converted them, are written on paper strips on the walls inside the church. To stimulate the missionary activity of the members, ranks are conferred upon the churches as well as upon the individuals, and the promotion in rank is according to the number of "new artists" brought into PL by the church or group in question.

The teachers and missionaries of PL are given a course which is quite unique as preparation for a missionary life in Japan or anywhere. The prospective missionaries are given instruction in all kinds of art: music, old and modern poetry, sculpture, painting, advanced calligraphy. Most popular is the composition of the thirty-one syllable Japanese poem, the tanka. This instruction is supposed to enable the missionary to become a real artist in more than one sense of the word. It should also be mentioned that PL capitalizes on the present renaissance of the tea ceremony, invites famous tea masters to PL, and carefully instructs its missionaries (not least those going abroad) in this and other old Japanese arts.

Summary and Future

During the past fifteen years PL Kyodan has acquired a membership of about 700,000, and it is now putting the finishing touches on what will become one of the most impressive religious

198

centers in Japan. PL's financial strength is considerable and it has able leadership under Tokuchika Miki (who is president of the League of New Religions).

Because of its able leadership and its having gone one step further in the typical Japanese association of daily life and religion by synonymizing the two, PL has been successful.

PL Kyodan could face future difficulties because of its "perfect liberty" in moral and doctrinal issues, but its present strength is so considerable that it must be counted among the new religions that will stay and survive, though it is doubtful that much expansion will occur.

IV

Miscellaneous New Religions

Among those new religions that cannot be classified and grouped so easily as those in the previous three sections are both large and influential groups and smaller religions whose futures could go either way. Also included are some groups which do not claim to be religions as such, but which exhibit enough of the characteristics of the new religions that they play an important part in the overall social and religious spectrum under consideration in this book.

The first two organizations covered, Odoru Shukyo (the Dancing Religion) and Ittoen, should be considered as equal in importance to any of the previous religions covered in the first three sections. Those remaining, at least for the present, are minor groups here covered under the heading "Other New Religions."

1

天照皇大神宮教 / Tensho Kotai Jingu Kyo

The
Dancing
Religion
has no
mark

Though the official name of this new religion is Tensho Kotai Jingu Kyo it would mean little to the average person. Throughout Japan it is known as Odoru Shukyo, the Dancing Religion. The outstanding feature of the religion is the person-

ality and history of the woman who founded Odoru Shukyo, Kitamura Sayo. She is regarded as a living god (*ikigami*) by her followers and, indeed, every aspect of the religion is permeated by
this remarkable woman.

Kitamura Sayo started preaching in 1945 shortly after she
claimed that the Shinto deity Tensho Kotai Jingu "took possession
of her." The name of this god is used in the official title of the
religion, combined with the usual word *kyo* (teaching), attached
in the manner of a suffix.

The headquarters of Odoru Shukyo has always been Kitamura
Sayo's farmhouse in the little village of Tabuse in Yamaguchi
Prefecture, two hours by train from Hiroshima. Now a very large
headquarters building is being constructed.

A passage from *The Paradise of Tabuse* gives considerable insight into the attitudes and beliefs of this striking religion:

"In a corner of Japan, in Yamaguchi Prefecture, there is a village called Tabuse, where one can actually find a separate world
that is beyond imagination—the world that all human beings have
eagerly sought. This heavenly world is the Kingdom of God founded by Kitamura Sayo, our Saviour. There, at the Preaching Hall
of our headquarters, she delivers her sermons day and night.
Great numbers of people from all parts of Japan visit our headquarters in order to polish their souls and to participate in our
Saviour's sacred task of creating God's Kingdom here on earth
and establishing world peace. Our God delivers her sermons in
both the form of psalms and in ordinary conversation, but she
never has to prepare them beforehand. When she opens her mouth
sermons issue forth like spring water gushing from the earth. She
says, 'The moment I open my mouth the divine radio commences
and you can listen to revelations directly from God.'... The community of followers believing in her is nothing less than God's
Kingdom itself, the Kingdom of Sincerity where there is no need
for police to enforce the law, where ranks, titles, and wealth are
unnecessary and unwanted. In this sense the headquarters at
Tabuse can be called a Spiritual Homeland for all followers, and
our followers all know that some day it will become the same for
all the people of the world."[1]

Kitamura's approach is direct: "Awake you maggot beggars.

Awake you traitor beggars! The door of Heaven has now opened for pious souls to enter."[2] "Maggot beggars" and such expressions mean unbelievers in Kitamura's language.

Founding and History

Born in 1900, married in 1920, Kitamura lived most of her life as an ordinary farmer's wife, having no religious pretensions until shortly after her house burned down in 1943. The coincidence of this dramatic event and her spiritual awakening has given rise to various ideas concerning the reason for her subsequent conduct—these include "insanity caused by shock." Followers, however, stoutly believe that she had a divine revelation.

According to Odoru Shukyo, on November 27, 1944, and again on August 12, 1945, Kitamura was possessed by a female-male Shinto god called Tensho Kotai Jingu. (These are "main" revelations; there were others in between). Once again a person destined to be the founder of a new religion was told to establish the "Kingdom of God" on earth. The religion's account of this event also shows that Odoru Shukyo is aware of outside opinion:

"From 1944 a most mysterious phenomenon occurred in her body. A spirit entered it and began to communicate with her. Perhaps materialists and intellectuals would call this hallucination, and psychiatrists would call it a sign of psychosis, nevertheless it truly did happen. The spirit told her of future things unseen to man and ordered her to do various things. She found it a nuisance to be ordered about—on occasions the ringing voice made her feel as if she were wearing a jar over her head. The One in her body gave invariable accurate weather forecasts and even went so far as to teach her modern techniques of such things as cooking and laundering. He told her about balanced diets that included the correct amounts of vitamins [i.e., so she could be a model farm woman in the postwar economic chaos of Japan]. When she refused to do as the One directed, he would say: 'If you disobey me I will kick your stomach to give you internal hemorrhage, or I shall beat your head and give you cerebral hemorrhage. Which do you prefer?' After this she had to give in. The One would tell her: 'Join your hands together when you pray, as that symbolizes com-

plete coordination of God and man. And shout, shout at the top
of your voice, until your throat bleeds. The more you shout, the
more people will understand your teaching. Travel at your own
expense, carrying a sack on your shoulder. You have been selected
to perform a Salvation Dance, when the present world is on the
verge of collapse. Therefore, since your birth I have trained you
in various lines of farm work, and with these experiences as a
background you are now to perform the salvation of the world.' "3

After the "authorization" by revelation Kitamura started her
evangelistic work by delivering her first public sermon on July
22, 1945, when she invited friends and neighbors to her home.
The religion spread rapidly, and in March, 1947, it was registered
formally with the government as a religious body, and was given
the name Tensho Kotai Jingu Kyo.

Kitamura Sayo is undoubtedly one of the most extraordinary
persons to be found anywhere in the world. Her appearance, her
voice, her speeches and sermons, everything about her is unusual
and remarkable. The author agrees wholeheartedly with a Catholic
scholar of Japanese religions who said: "Kitamura Sayo is a
woman so remarkable that she could easily win an international
ladies' contest for breath, brawn, and bravura."4 She was one of
the first women in Yamaguchi Prefecture to ride a bicycle. She is
at home with a sewing machine or a dairy cow, and she often sets
out to preach on horseback. She always wears men's clothes, but
somehow people do not notice this at first. What strikes one is the
magnetism of her face and stentorian voice she uses as an effective
vehicle for humor as well as for invective.

The story of her arrest and trial in 1945 (from *The Prophet
of Tabuse*), just after the war, is a striking illustration of her
eccentric character:

When the 1945 autumn harvest of rice was reaped, Kitamura
refused to give the obligatory quota to the government, saying:
"This rice is for God's servants. We have nothing to waste on
maggot beggars." The matter was reported to the police, and on
April 22, 1946, an officer of the district court came to Kitamura's
home, produced a court order telling her to acknowledge the
receipt of the order and submit her quota of rice without further
delay. Kitamura's answer was: "Is this toilet paper? I have enough

of that and need no more. Anyway I won't waste time arguing with a messenger like you. Go and tell the district governor to come and see me." A few days after the police came and took the rice, and Kitamura was taken to the police station, where she began to sing in the faces of the outraged policemen: "Beggars and traitor maggots in neat uniforms are taking on high airs, while the True Redeemer is placed under arrest." Crowds of her followers gathered outside the jail and shouted the Odoru Shukyo Prayer. Kitamura answered them by singing out a sermon from the jail window.

The matter was finally brought to court and the prosecution accused her of refusing to pay her rice quota and inducing others to do likewise. She was asked point-blank whether or not she had on several occasions tried to induce more than ten different people not to submit their quota. "That last is not true—I have told not ten but ten thousand not to do so. Further, I have told them not several times but thousands of times. I am not asking you to give me a light sentence—don't hesitate to give me the maximum penalty."

The nonplussed prosecutor was doubtless relieved when the day's unorthodox proceedings came to an end.

Moved to a different cell, Kitamura continued her eccentric ways. She enquired of the jailor as to just who was the prisoner, the one who had a nice room, bed, toilet, and someone to bring her three meals everyday, or the one who had to see to all her various needs. Next, she piled cushions under the window so she could stand on them and watch the prisoners working in the fields. She commenced to sing a sermon to them, whereupon the chief warden, summoned by the jailor, warned her to keep silent. She called him a fool and explained that she was "establishing God's Kingdom on this earth." No one could silence her "rightful prayer for the salvation of all the evil spirits."

When a wealthy friend came to see her and offered to arrange for bail, she refused the offer and said she was determined to stay there until she had converted the young district attorney who was prosecuting her.

At the final court session, Kitamura stood up and sang a sermon at the top of her voice, danced around the court room, and banging her fist on the newspaper reporter's desk she said: "Print a picture of my enraged face in your papers and tell the world exactly what you have seen and heard here. Then I'll give all my rice to all the maggot beggars."

The case finally came to a conclusion, and the district attorney—now the leader of the Tokyo branch of Odoru Shukyo—came and told her that she would be released the following morning. She refused this offer, saying, "Let me stay here until the end of the month. Jail is not a place that one can come into and go out of easily." Finally about a month later Kitamura was released. She immediately gathered her followers about her and sang a sermon on her experiences in jail.

As the religion grew, believers traveled to all parts of Japan on evangelical missions. After only five short years of proselytizing and propagandizing Odoru Shukyo had gathered over a hundred thousand members. At about this time Kitamura went to Hawaii, where she spent some time campaigning, ending up with eight branches in the islands. In 1955 and again in 1961, she went to Hawaii and mainland United States and spent some time there preaching. In 1955 she succeeded in establishing eight more branches there. These successes were mainly among people of Japanese ancestry.

At present Odoru Shukyo seems to have lost some of its initial appeal, but its membership remains at about 110,000.

Doctrines and Writings

God is Among Us

Kitamura claims to be, and her followers believe, that she is divine. Accordingly she is addressed as "Goddess" (*Ogamisama*); her son is "Young God" (*Wakagamisama*); and Kitamura's ten-year-old granddaughter, who is the appointed successor to the leadership of Odoru Shukyo, is called "Princess-goddess" (*Ohime-gamisama*).

It is interesting to see, how Odoru Shukyo attempts to widen the heretofore narrow conception of the Shinto deity Tensho Kotai Jingu.

"Tensho Kotai Jingu is the name of the Absolute God of the Universe, and is the same as the Heavenly Father in Christianity and the Eternal Buddha of Buddhism. Tensho Kotai Jingu is not a guardian deity of the small islands of Japan. Ogamisama explains that the Almighty God is a couple formed by a male and female God, and that they came into her body and made it a temple for themselves, thus forming a trinity. Therefore the meaning of Tensho Kotai Jingu Kyo is 'the Teaching of the Absolute God.' "[5]

Sometimes Kitamura speaks of herself as "Christ" or as the "mediator" of God: "Be grateful that you were born in this century. Three thousand years ago it was Buddha who preached this Gospel, two thousand years ago it was Christ, today I am the Christ." And: "God used my body as His temple and descended from Heaven. He dwells in Me and chooses pious people. God convokes them with His holy power. He purifies their spirits so that they may become His innumerable angels and may guide and reform, one by one, all the other spirits astray. This is God's way. Since I serve as God's Mediator no fear have I. Because God has vested His authority in Me I shall redeem the sincere and the pious."[6]

As a deity Kitamura is supposed to have prophetic insight and power to heal disease:

"Ogamisama possesses these superhuman powers: She has Divine and spiritual eyes to penetrate the present, past and future of the whole universe—there is nothing of which she is ignorant. She has Divine power and insight to penetrate into the bottom of all people's hearts, to lead them according to the circumstances and needs the case may warrant and to free them from their past destinies, and thus She foresees their future lives and leads them accordingly; She has the power to heal all incurable diseases. Although She possesses miraculous power, She always states: 'I am but a farmer's wife with six years of elementary education. I am a fool, a fool of non-ego, but not that much of a fool. The One who is great is the God within me. My body is the temple of God, and the Divine Radio is switched on at all times.' "[7]

Kitamura's supposed prophetic power has given occasion to numerous miracle stories. Here is one of the most widely circulated accounts, taken from one of Kitamura's trips aboard a train:

"She continued her preaching from car to car on the train. As she delivered her sermon in one car, a man suddenly took off his overcoat and said: 'Shut up, you hag, or I'll beat you.' The sinister-looking man advanced a few steps, got hold of Ogamisama's blouse and slapped her cheek twice. She immediately held up her right hand, formed it into the shape of a pistol, and, pointing it at the man's heart, yelled twice. Suddenly the color drained out of the man's face, and he dropped down into a vacant seat, his legs losing their strength. 'You shall die three days from now. Drink water to your heart's content, for it shall be your last drink in this world!' Asked by bystanders what she did, her answer was: 'This is God's pistol. In the maggot world no pistol can shoot freely. The pistol I used does not kill on the spot. By my yell I simply impressed a death mark on him. He has now been ruled out of Heaven.' "[8] This latter ruling him out of heaven is as far as his "death" apparently went.

Coupled with Kitamura's conviction of being divine is a rather incongruous air of superiority and pride. Thus she says: "The God in my body is always proud of having made me the most impolite and sharp-tongued person under Heaven. I would like to know if there is any similar leader in this world!"[9] Or this double-edged remark: "I did not go to America for enjoyment, but to save America. I gave talks at Harvard, at Columbia, and elsewhere. You should have seen those learned doctors listening in awe to what I told them. One of them said after my sermon: 'Madam, if you are right, we are all mad here!' They could answer nothing to what I had to say."[10]

The self-assertion of Kitamura has also led her to establish a new calendar. The "modern age" look began on May 4, 1944, when Kitamua received her first inspiration, and is called "the Year of Ogamisama." At present (1962) we are consequently living in "the twenty-fourth year after Ogamisama." However, this is not taken too seriously; thus the author has received several letters from Kitamura and other Odoru Shukyo leaders marked appropriately for the twentieth century. It also brings up a technical difficulty concerning Kitamura's birthday, which according to the new calendar would be the Forty-fourth Year Before Ogamisama!

Sermon and Prayers

Kitamura's "singing" sermons are extraordinary in that they often are given in the form of poems delivered without preparation. They are always delivered in a state of ecstasy, but usually in everyday language. Kitamura says about her sermons: "I just open my mouth and out come the words of God—you are immediately tuned in on the Divine Radio and are in contact with God." Here is part of one of her sermons:

"The war, fought for eight long years, was designed by His wish to reveal the true human road and to convert all people to His Kingdom.

"They have spoiled His land with egoism, with selfishness and with the delusion that honesty is disadvantageous. But at last this age of corruption has ended.

"God descends, subjugates, and controls the degraded human world with His hand. He changes it into His most wonderful and amazing Celestical Kingdom.

"Cultivate patriotic spirit and pray for victory. But if you prayers are selfish, God will take no notice of them.

"Do not expect selfish prayers to be answered, but endeavour instead to be reborn as His child. Only His children will survive and enjoy Celestial Bliss forever."[11]

There are two types of prayer. One is personal prayer, different as the individual sees fit but based on the principle that one does not pray for himself. He must pray for world peace and the salvation of others. The second type of prayer is *the* Prayer of Odoru Shukyo. In form this was apparently inspired by the Lord's Prayer, but reveals Buddist influence in its reference to the Six Evils and the use of Nichiren's *Daimoku* at the end.

"Almighty God of the Universe, source of deities,
Peace of the whole world, peace of the whole world,
When all the people comply with the will of God.
Give us a Heavenly Kingdom, which is pleasant to live in.
Six Roots of Evil, Six Roots of Evil,
Six roots of evil of my spirit are now entirely purged.
Since the six roots of sin have been purged

It cannot be that this prayer will not be fulfilled.
Adoration be to the Lotus Sutra [repeated]!"[12]

The Prayer of Odoru Shukyo is said in a remarkable way—in fact it is "spoken" with the whole body. The believers work themselves into complete religious ecstasy, tears run down their cheeks, and their limbs vibrate. They shake their hands and lift them above their heads again and again with vehement movements. In the *Prophet of Tabuse* it is explained as follows:

"In the beginning Ogamisama prayed *Namu myoho renge kyo* to expel evil spirits, but later on, all the comrades joined her in prayer. During the course of one such earnest prayer a most wonderful phenomenon occurred among the comrades. Their clasped hands quivered up and down involuntarily as they prayed. At first they were surprised at these unaccountable movements, but Ogamisama explained that 'It is a psychic activity. When your hands are shaking high at your breast it means that your living spirit is activated. When the unconverted or stray spirits of the dead influence you, your hands will shift downward and will make downward movements. But as soon as these spirits are converted or leave you for the moment, your hands will rise above your head.' "[13] Some Christian observers of this dance may recall the Biblical account of Aaron keeping the arms of Moses raised so the Israelites might be successful in battle, but others are probably reminded of Holy Rollers or of some evangelical meetings where the participants "speak in tongues."

Besides the Prayer of Odoru Shukyo there is only one other sacred writing. This is the Miuta (Divine Song), written and composed by Kitamura herself. All the followers sing it at every gathering, just as the Prayer is chanted at every meeting.

How beautiful is the dawning of God's Kingdom!
Almighty God has descended when the world degraded so low
In order to establish His Kingdom on this earth
By bringing the human world back to His hand again.

At the juncture of great catastrophes
God chose you to serve Him for His sacred mission.

Be ever thankful for your good fortune to receive His call
And exert yourself to advance on the Road to His Kingdom.

The dawn of His Kingdom is now with you
Hasten in waking your spiritual eyes.
If you become aware that human beings are Sons of God,
Begin to tread the righteous road, being worthy of His name.

The path of human life should be a routine,
To guide yourselves towards His Kingdom.
Through diligent practice of polishing your soul
You may enjoy a Heavenly Life on this earth.

As long as you have built your courage to follow me
Anyone can be serviceable for this sacred task.
Do your utmost for the sake of His Kingdom
Until the day when people can enjoy world peace.

Simplicity, in Teaching as in Organization

Of all religions in Japan there is none that practices simplicity to the degree that Odoru Shukyo does. Kitamura consciously keeps her teaching at a level where even the most unlearned can understand her, and her sermons are always built on the principles of simplicity, straightforwardness, and the use of illustrations. The following quotation from one of Kitamura's sermons will illustrate this: "God's world and that of maggots are as different as two trains passing each other going in opposite directions. The celestial ship is about to depart for Heaven from a maggot harbor while the maggot ship of mud is foundering. If you realize that you are on board the ship of mud, then the only thing for you to do is to transfer to God's ship."[14]

This same simplicity is seen in the organization, or rather the lack of it. Kitamura's approach emphasizes the lack of impediments on the road to salvation:

"I have destroyed the prayer paper that fettered you to the maggot world. I have freed you from such impediments to enable you to be reborn in Heaven. Hear, all of you that hereafter no prayer, no idol, no church, nothing will be needed as Osayo's [i.e.,

Kitamura's mouth alone will teach the way to the Heavenly Kingdom."[15]

The simplicity goes so far that Kitamura and her followers claim to avoid anything to do with money. Money is said "to belong to the maggot world and commercialized religion." When Kitamura travels, she always takes with her all her food and other necessities, in order not to trouble others. She also pays her own traveling expenses (a concession to society, it seems). She says: "If I were to demand even a penny from you, there would be no need for you to hear my sermons. There is no God who needs money or donations. You have been redeemed by God freely; therefore you must have part in God's missionary work."[16]

There is no clergy in Odoru Shukyo. All are "missionaries," and no one pays or is paid by another. Under "Qualifications for Missionaries" in the document of registration as a religious body is written: "All who can serve God, and who can be utilized by Him, are qualified to convey teachings to others." There is no difference of rank or degree, and no clerical clothes of any kind are worn: "In this religion there is no place for. . .discrimination or seniority among comrades. You must discipline yourselves. Therefore hold meetings among yourselves. The leader of each meeting is God Himself."[17]

There are to be no churches. "Ogamisama prohibits the building of special halls or churches for meetings—a follower's home is designated as a meeting place."[18]

One of the most remarkable points in the program of simplicity is that special cemeteries and tombstones are said to be unnecessary. This is so much more remarkable as the burial system and the ancestor worship connected with it are considered the backbone of Japanese Buddhism and strong tenets of Japanese religion in general. It is significant that so many believers are flocking around Kitamura in spite of her criticism of the burial system, and the religious observer must ask: are we witnessing the beginning break-up of the ancestor cult, at least in its present form?[19] Kitamura says: "The time will come when no graves will be needed. There were no tombs in the ancient Divine Age. People began to build tombs after they became so degenerate that they turned into ghosts after their death. The world is again in God's era, and all the ancestors will be saved, and since you are reformed, there will be no need for graves. A corpse is merely a body from which the soul has departed and it is only a substance. Therefore it does not matter how you dispose of it. Either bury in under the ground, or in the sea, or cremate it, or dispose of it otherwise. God in my body said in 1944 that if this earth is left in the hands of foolish humans, the earth will soon be covered with cathedrals and graves. I am now creating a world in which churches, temples, idols, and graves will have no place. On the contrary, I will deprive physicians and clerics of their means of livelihood."[20]

The "no nothingism" goes on. Concerning marriages: "For marriage in the world of God there are no go-betweens, no clerics to officiate at perfunctory marriage services, no wedding feasts, no honeymoons, and no expenses. God Himself is the go-between."[21] Concerning funerals: "The Heavenly Father will take charge of your children and bring them up as His children hereafter, since you have parted from your body and have been reborn in Heaven."[22]

This World of Sin

This world, says Kitamura, lies in the throes of sin. She identifies sin with a Buddhist concept: "The first step in religious practice is to purge oneself of the Six Roots of Evil, which are regret, desire, hatred, fondness, love, and being loved. They are the cause of all the evil you commit in your human life. Regret means feeling sorry for what has been done, and desire means a longing for something which cannot be had. To have hatred in your heart, and to have extreme fondness are both very sinful. Being loved excessively and loving excessively are no less sinful."[25] Here it is easy to see the profound influence from Buddhism, which teaches man to beware of his emotions, and not to become excessively attached to things—whether they are good *or* bad—thus binding himself to the wheel of karma and endless rebirths.

The Buddhist concept of transmigration of souls—that man is bound to the wheel of cause and effect and must reappear again and again in endless existences until he finds salvation in Nirvana—is often mentioned in Odoru Shukyo to illustrate the sinful nature of man, who has sinned in previous existences and in this present one: "From God's view all of us are sinful in the long run. We must all have committed countless sins during the long pilgrimage our souls have made in the endless chain of transmigration."[26] This inescapable sinful nature of man reminds the Christian observer of the doctrine of original sin.

Further, Kitamura says that sin is not merely a personal matter that can be limited to each individual. According to her, the law of karma binds family members, ancestors, and all living beings together: "All people are invariably under the control of the law of causation—the cause and the effects of past, present, and future existences. Children of the same parentage will have different fates because the circumstances of their individual past lives are different. A human being is not only responsible for the causes of his own past in this present life, but he is also affected by the karma of all his ancestors. Therefore, many ordeals may come upon you, one after another, while you are practicing this true heavenly doctrine."[27]

The "sinful nature of man" is also reflected in the world of politics, which finds no favor with Kitamura and her followers. (In this connection it is interesting to note that one of the most important leaders of Odoru Shukyo is a former young politician who renounced politics and became a follower of Odoru Shukyo.) Right and left, Emperor and democracy, all are scourged by Kitamura: "The Emperor is good for nothing, and he is not a living god. If he were, why could he not detect the many traitors who surrounded him? Look, even I, a farmer's wife, can see them!"[28] "Democracy is easily misinterpreted as egoism or individualism. Real Democracy is performing one's duty before claiming a right"[29]

Science also belongs to the "world of maggots": "Science is only imitation of nature. When the time for natural life comes, science will fade away just like the snow that fell in spring."[30] "People once thought that they could realize Utopia by their own knowledge, but at present this seems impossible. On the contrary modern civilization has thrown mankind into confusion, crime, and disillusionment. Rationalism has come to a deadlock with itself, and is unable to solve anything. Material civilization and science have made our living easy and convenient to a certain extent, but they have given us the Atomic and Hydrogen bombs, which threaten our very existence."[31]

Why is the world in the throes of sin and evil? Kitamura advances two reasons that, however, seem to be contradictory. These are karma and evil spirits. It appears that Kitamura has tried to answer the question from the point of Buddhism as well as of Christianity at the same time. The two have not been convincingly combined: "All agonies and troubles in this world are caused by evil spirits. Living hell is a shadow of hell in the spiritual world. Karma is the historical prospect of the relation between the phenomenal world and the spiritual world. Just like a chain used to tie animals, karma is the chain which ties men and prevents them from going to heaven. By redeeming our ancestors' spirits we can be redeemed. By redeeming and purging the spiritual world and cutting off all karma, modern history would be suspended and God's New Era begun."[32]

These evil spirits play an important role in the teachings of the Dancing Religion. They are blamed for all man's calamities: "The phenomenal world has come to an end and has become a living hell due to the fact that the spiritual world has been flooded with evil and straying spirits—accordingly the world in which we live now is only a shadow of the spiritual world."[33]

"The Way to the Kingdom of God"

In order to obtain salvation of every man and peace on earth it is, according to Kitamura, necessary first of all to redeem the evil spirits. The means of effectuating this redemption is the chanting of the Prayer of Odoru Shukyo. Whenever this Prayer is said, many evil spirits are said to appear asking for redemption and salvation. They are said to speak in all tongues, English, French, German, Indian, etc. as well as Japanese, and according to Kitamura, "more foreign spirits will come for the purpose of salvation in the future, and as a consequence we may be able to learn foreign languages by them."[34] The latter by-product of the redemptive activity has become a popular doctrine.

The "march to Heaven" cannot begin before the ancestors have been redeemed: "It will be a futile effort to redeem others unless you are converted yourself. But, to be converted yourself you must first redeem your ancestors, who are suffering in Hell. Trying to reach Heaven by yourself, forgetting your ancestors, will avail you nothing."[35]

But it is not enough to redeem the ancestors. Man must always strive for his own salvation, before, during, and after redeeming his ancestors. To bring about final victory man must "polish his soul," practice *magokoro* (sincerity), and combine religion with his daily life: "First of all the words, the thoughts, and the deeds must become one, and the soul must be polished every day with one's conscience."[36] "God praises all acts of sincerity, and those merits will be credited and accumulated in our account with the Heavenly Post Office Savings Bank, and its pass-book will be conveyed to our posterity as an unlimited fortune. Therefore, sincerity is the treasure of human beings."[37] "Religion is not merely to worship and believe in God, but also to advance along the Road to God by practicing God's teaching. Human life is holy, and therefore one's home and community are the places where the soul must be polished. No religion can exist which is not intimately related to one's daily life."[38]

However, the road to Heaven is difficult, and many setbacks and dangers will be met. Thus, to enable man to continually progress on the Road the believers must excercise *mutual discipline* and *confess their sins*: "Instead of listening to a sermon made by an unqualified professional religionist, you can train your soul according to God's teaching not only during mutual disciplinary meetings but whenever you have a chance to be with the followers. You can polish your souls mutually. However, it is of the utmost importance that the mutual discipline should never be a process of accusing others of their faults without first reflecting upon yourself. You will find that it is very difficult to find your own fault and very easy to find that of others. [cf. Matt. 7:3] When you notice the offence of another person, first ask yourself if you have committed the same sin. [cf. John 8:7] Then you can advise the offender with sincerity. This is true mutual discipline. When others point out your faults, you should accept what they say with gratitude."[39]

Confession must be made not only to man but to God: "When your earnest confessions are accepted by God, your tarnished records kept in Heaven will be erased and become white as snow . . ."[40]

The various practices mentioned above will take man to the gate of the Kingdom of God, and the *Muga no Odori* (the Dance of Non-ego) will take him inside the gate. This dance has made Odoru Shukyo famous all over Japan and given to it the name of "The Dancing Religion."

The Dance of Non-ego is an ecstatic dance which is aimed at the redemption of the performers of the dance as well as of all evil spirits in the world. "You will get rid of your ego in the ecstasy dance. When you pray in such a state all evil spirits, including malignant spirits of living persons, are redeemed instantly. People in such a state of ecstasy are *tenshi* (angels), whom God utilizes to establish His Kingdom on Earth."[41]

It is a strange experience to see the Dance of Non-ego of Odoru Shukyo whether performed under the cherry trees on a farm, or on the platform of a railway station as a farewell dance to the Founder, who is about to leave by train. It has been one of the strangest experiences of the author to see the latter event happen: about two-hundred followers gathered on the platform to say good-bye to Kitamura. First they prayed *Namu myoho renge kyo,* and then they started the Dance of Non-ego. All singly they danced around and around on the platform to the accompaniment of the deafening voice of Kitamura Sayo, which outshouted all other sounds at the station. All, including Kitamura, with eyes closed and tears streaming down their cheeks, seemingly in complete ecstasy and self-forgetting trance, although it must be said that the Founder did not miss the train.

Whatever may be said about the Dance of Non-ego, there can be no doubt about its propaganda value. It is one of the most effective of the numerous attractions and drawing-cards of postwar New Religions. And it is followed up by the zealous missionaries of the Dancing Religion, who "shout, shout, and shout their teaching, until their throats bleed."

"The Kingdom of Heaven on Earth"

The Kingdom of God is something that can be obtained here and now. It is not "on the other side of the river," but right in

our midst: "If you come to God's world you will find all the necessary supplies you need piled up in quantities ready to be allocated. Come and see the Kingdom of God! There is no worry,
agony, sickness or suffering in God's Land. There you can enjoy a
heavenly life with the body you now possess. God's Kingdom
is nowhere remote. It sprouts in your heart and grows within
yourselves."[42] Sometimes the Kingdom is identified with the headquarters of Odoru Shukyo: "The community consisting of Ogamisama's followers is God's Kingdom, the Kingdom of Sincerity,
where there is no need for laws or police."[43] Accordingly the headquarters is called "the Paradise of Tabuse."

In the Kingdom of God there will be no diseases nor wars:
"With her (Kitamura's) divine power she has performed such
miracles as Christ performed. The dead have been revived, the
crippled walk, the blind see, the dumb speak, and manifold
diseases have been cured by her prayers."[44] And again: "The
absolute peace of the whole world can only be attained by establishing the actual Kingdom of God on this earth. In order to
achieve this it is essential that everyone should first secure peace in
their own heart, and extend it to all the members of the entire
family, neighbors, countries, and then lastly to the whole world."[45]

Odoru Shukyo and Other Religions

Odoru Shukyo is the only new religion besides Soka Gakkai
that is completely intolerant of all other religions. As we have
seen, other new religions operate with varying degrees of tolerance.
Kitamura claims that she is the only one who can save the people
of Japan and all the rest of the world. The picture she paints of
other religions is not flattering, and smacks of Nichiren, who,
however, has little new to teach Kitamura Sayo. Here are some
examples of her more mild views: "Saint Shinran [the Founder
of the main Pure Land sect in Japan], is not yet saved, but is still
suffering in Hell."[46] "Look at the past. All professional religionists
have become more and more corrupt. They have built idols, temples, and beautiful cathedrals, collected money and property from
people, and studied religious books without spiritual awakening
themselves. They preach that people must go to Heaven, but how

PL KYODAN

25 ■ PL'S SYMBOL APPEARS ON A COLUMN BEFORE THE HEADQUARTERS NEAR OSAKA.

26 ■ THE PL YOUTH HALL WHERE SPORTING EVENTS AND MEETINGS CAN BE HELD.

SEKAI KYUSEI KYO

27 ■ SEKAI KYUSEI KYO'S "PARADISE" IN HAKONE.

28 ■ OKADA MOKICHI, THE FOUNDER OF SEKAI KYUSEI KYO.

29 ■ OKADA YOSHIKO, THE PRESENT MATRIARCH.

30 ■ THE MESSIANIC HALL AT THE SECOND "PARADISE" IN ATAMI.

ODORU SHUKYO

31 ■ KITAMURA SAYO, LEADER OF TENSHO KOTAI JINGU KYO, OTHERWISE KNOWN AS THE DANCING RELIGION (ODORU SHU-KYO), IS SHOWN PERFORMING THE "DANCE OF NON-EGO" WITH CHILDREN.

32 ■ HERE KITAMURA SAYO POSES WITH HER ELEVEN-YEAR-OLD GRANDDAUGHTER AND ANNOUNCED SUCCESSOR, THE "PRIN-CESS-GODDESS."

33 ■ THE NINETY-YEAR-OLD LEADER OF ITTOEN, TENKO-SAN, THE "ST. FRANCIS OF ASSISI OF JAPAN."

ITTOEN

34 ■ ITTOEN FOLLOWERS GO OUT TO PERFORM THEIR "PRAYER IN ACTION." THIS INCLUDES ALL SORTS OF MENIAL AND DISTASTEFUL TASKS SUCH AS EMPTYING AND CARRYING OFF REFUSE FROM TOILETS.

could people follow religionists who have nothing to offer but idealism and imagination."[47] "The religions divided into numerous sects, and their teachings became abstract and more impractical. They are dead religions, which have no power to redeem the souls of the living or the dead."[48] The new religions receive no better treatment:

"When the world is about to end, a great number of heresies and false prophets appear. With fine speeches these heretical religions proclaim the advantages of believing in them, but they are in reality trying to deceive honest men. They may flourish for a brief period but will soon vanish like bubbles. In contrast to them, true religion will spread its roots deeply, grow trunks, stretch branches with thick leaves, and bear flowers and fruit."[49]

Odoru Shukyo and Christianity

It may be open to debate whether Kitamura was subject to much Christian influence before 1944, but there can be no doubt of it afterward. Odoru Shukyo has borrowed terminology and doctrines and used them to suit its own ends. Not forgetting its Buddhist doctrines, it is possible to say that Odoru Shukyo has more resemblance to Christianity than any other new religion.

Many incidents from Kitamura Sayo's life seem to be a conscious adaption of New Testament events. Thus, Kitamura is told by the spirit inside her that "you are now to work for the salvation of the world for three and a half years."[50] It is not said why this time span was chosen, but there is mention of three and a half years in connection with Christ's preaching in the April 1958 issue of the Odoru Shukyo publication *Tensei*. But on page ten of the same article Kitamura adds "but I have been preaching continuously for more than twelve years" to show Odoru Shukyo's superiority. This is the posture most of her adaption of Christian terms and ideas takes; in other words, "anything you can do I can do too, and better!" There are the words of Kitamura to her younger brother: "I am not your sister, nor are you my brother. I am being utilized by the Absolute God of the Universe and am serving Him as he pleases,"[51] which can be compared easily with Matt. 12: 47–49. Further, Kitamura is just as sure as Christ in

Matthew 19: 23–24 that a person of the higher classes will have a hard time entering the gates of heaven.[52] Kitamura "experienced," as did Christ, temptation at the hands of spirits who, in her case, offered to make her "queen of the angels."[53] In the *Mioshie* it is stated that "Christ wandered for more than forty days and fought the battle with the evil spirits. Ogamisama too fought a similar battle."[54] The word for the holy book telling Kitamura's life story is called *Seisho*. The pronunciation of this word is the same as that of the word for the Christian Bible; however, the characters are different. "Holy" book is replaced by "living" book. The same is true of the word for faith, *shinko*. The characters, rather than being merely the ones used heretofore, have the meaning of holy action. This latter probably indicates Odoru Shukyo's feeling that life and religion are one in their philosophy but not in others. Often she merely adapts events from the life of Christ without bothering to change the scene and the characters. There are numerous examples which could be added to the above.

The introduction of Christian thoughts and expressions seems to have increased gradually, and probably has some connection with the fact that the wife of Kitamura's son as well as the young former politician mentioned above were earnest Christians before they became disciples of Kitamura.

Summary and Future

As we have seen, Odoru Shukyo, even more than other new religions, is centered around its leader. She is completely responsible for the success and the attraction of the religion. This true *femme formidable* has created a religion that rebels against all the rules and regulations of established religions as well as giving an emotional outlet to its believers in much the same way as have the emotional religious sects that have developed in Europe and America since the days of World War II. But for all of this, Tensho Kotai Jingu Kyo would not be much without Kitamura Sayo.

Kitamura is sixty-two and is still going strong. The big question is what will happen after her death. Anticipating this, she officially named her successor on May 27, 1951: the baby girl which had just been born to her son and his wife. The child, known as Kiyokazu-chan, was given the title *Ohimegamisama* (Princess-goddess). It is remarkable that Kitamura did not choose her son, who is only in his forties. Her preference for her granddaughter may have something to do with the fascination for the life and sayings of Christ that Kitamura has consistently shown. She has said: "I love children. They are much closer to God than adults. They could be perfect citizens of His Kingdom if they were brought up from birth as children of God."[55]

At present Odoru Shukyo is working on a large headquarters at Tabuse, which is being built mostly by the voluntary labor of its members. It will be one of the largest such headquarters in Japan— quite an achievement for a comparably small religion. This is one of the things that seem to indicate a change in the status of Odoru Shukyo toward a second stage—a possible change away from un-restricted free-form emotionalism toward a more established re-ligion with cemeteries, churches, and preachers.

2

一燈園 / Ittoen

Depending upon the definition of Ittoen (Garden of Light), it can be said to signify a village, a religious movement, or a person. Ittoen allows members to maintain their own former religion if they desire, making it difficult to classify this group as a new religion. Further, its leader and members claim that Ittoen is a "way of life" and not a new religion. Since, however, it illustrates one of the most important sides of the new religions it has been included here.

As a village, Ittoen consists of the settlement known as Kosenrin. It is situated in Yamashina on the outskirts of Kyoto, where the rather modest number of three hundred people are "living" Ittoen and demonstrating its ideas. As a religious movement it is anything but modest. It is no exaggeration to say that its impact is felt throughout the country, making the study of this organization a necessity for the serious student of the religious situation in Japan. Finally, as a person, Ittoen can be identified as its founder and present leader, ninety-year-old Nishida Tenko, regarded by many as the greatest religious personality in Japan today. Tenko-san, as he is called, has often been compared to Tolstoy, Gandhi, and, especially, St. Francis. The study of Ittoen must start with a study of this personality.

Founding and History

About sixty years ago Tenko-san led a group of one hundred families to Hokkaido as a part of a large-scale agricultural project. He was successful in this venture and could have lived a life of wealth and leisure, but mainly because he saw the struggle for existence in everybody around him, he found no satisfaction there. Finally, after deciding to see whether a life without struggle, lived in absolute dependence on God or Buddha, could be practiced, he left Hokkaido and for several years wandered around seeking for this new way of life. The turning point came in 1905, when he was fasting in a small temple at Nagahama. After three days of this he gained a sort of insight that came about after he heard the voice of an infant crying out for its mother's milk subside immediately after receiving it. The crying out for its mother's milk became to Tenko-san an image of man's situation—that is, the infant receives and is happy; the mother gives and is happy. In this way men should cease struggle and strife and be happy in giving as well as receiving. This is how he analyzes his experience: "If man is born of God, God is responsible for his existence in this world. God should feed, clothe, and house his creature. Man should be glad to live and do whatever is good, even if on a modest scale, and simply wait for God to direct him to what he should do every day."[1]

Tenko-san gave away all that he owned and decided to live a life of altruism, putting all his trust in "the Light." He started working for others, often doing the dirtiest kind of work—cleaning up refuse, sweeping streets,—and he never asked for money as it was his conviction that "the Light" would take care of him if he put complete trust in it. He was always given the necessities of life by various people who witnessed his labors.

His penniless life of service attracted much attention from spiritually minded people, and gradually, as followers gathered around him, his movement took form. In 1928, a rich man donated twenty-five acres of land in Yamashina, and Tenko-san and his followers settled there. This was the beginning of the movement, which now reaches out far beyond the little village of Kosenrin to an estimated one or two million people all over Japan. The popularity of Tenko-san and his movement grew so that just after the war he was elected to serve in the Upper House, where he served for six years and, among other things, introduced a bill on "repentance of the nation." This bill, however, was not passed by the house.

The Ittoen Brotherhood at Kosenrin

Ittoen is the "spiritual conception" or "ideal" of the movement. Senkosha (the Evangelical Society of the Light) is an association of people trying to live up to the ideal of Ittoen. And Kosenrin, a name which is composed of the three Chinese characters for "light," "spring," and "wood," is a branch of the Senkosha, the village where Tenkosan and about seventy-five families are "living" Ittoen.

The Kosenrin is a quiet little village beyond a small stream, two minutes walk from Yamashina. It consists of a cluster of about one hundred buildings situated in beautiful peaceful surroundings: bamboo and pine groves, a small rivulet with waterfalls, ponds with goldfish, and a garden with beautiful cherry trees.

The religious life of the community is based on the *Komyo Kikan,* the Prayer of Light:

1. Have us born anew and let us have our being by the Providence of Light.
2. Teach us to respect the essence of all religions, and lead us to learn the One Ultimate Truth.
3. Have us render our services out of penitence, and perform our tasks out of gratitude.
4. Help us to perfect the way of our living by complete submission to the Laws of Nature.
5. In a word, grant that we may return to the land of "perfumed nook of heavenly flowers" (Nirvana), and that we may tread in the Paradise of Light.

The contents of this prayer are expressed in the following three main principles, which form the essence of the teaching and life of Ittoen: 1) simplicity and non-possession, 2) worship of God through all religious truths, and 3) a life in service and action.

Doctrines and Writings

Simplicity and Non-Possession

The members of Kosenrin have no private property, and no one works for profit or exploitation. Everything belongs to the brotherhood, which distributes all that is necessary: house, furniture, clothes, etc., to each individual according to his need.

Food is prepared in the village kitchen, which can take care of about five hundred. The food, simple but nourishing, is a vegetarian diet including, of course, rice.

There is no abundance of floor space at Kosenrin, but neither is there less than the *johan-ro* (one and a half *tatami* mats, or about three square meters) that is assigned as living space to each person. A bachelor at Kosenrin gets his *johan-ro,* and a family of four has six *tatami* in a strict multiplication of the basic unit. This sets a keynote for the simplicity that characterizes Ittoen.

As another living symbol of this simplicity, the building that was given to Tenko-san and his wife when they were in Kyoto and which was used as a lodging for about twenty people in the early days of the movement, was moved to Kosenrin when it was established. This reminds members of how the twenty went out to perform free labor during the day and then returned in the evening to share their simple experiences, a simple meal, and an essentially Zen worship.

The life of simplicity and non-possession is not thought of in financial terms, but is regarded as a way of self-denial and character training. Tenko-san says: "Let not the center be the self but the whole, not pleasure but self-renunciation, then there will be peace on earth." Or "In having nothing lies inexhaustible wealth."

The main principles of the way of life of Ittoen are expressed in "One Cup of Water,"[2] which is a dialogue between Nishida Tenko and a "visitor"; part of it is quoted in the following:

Visitor: "Will you be so kind to give me a brief explanation of the life of Ittoen?"

Nishida. "Suppose there was only one cup of water for two persons, and both urgently needed every drop of it to sustain their lives. Now, what would you do in that case?"

V: "Of course I would drink the water first myself."

N: "In Ittoen life in such a case we would let the other party drink it."

V: "Can such a thing be practicable?"

N: "Well, I am not sure whether we come to face such a situation, but our way of life impels every one of us do so, if the situation should arise."

V: "Is it not queer to make an ideal of what is impossible?"

N: "But it is not impossible. It may sound so to you because we have not confronted such a situation yet, but similar things are taking place every day among us here in Ittoen."

V: "What, for example?"

N: "For instance: would you consider working for others without expecting any remuneration?"

V: "I certainly would not."

N: "I don't blame you for that because your mode of living prevents you from doing so. Ours gives us the facilities to do so. In fact, every one of us is doing it at this very moment. Don't you think the mind which feels no uneasiness in living without any saving for himself, but dedicates all his time to the service of others and the mind which is willing to starve, if necessary for others, is the mind we talked about?"

V: "Well, maybe so."

N: "Therefore, when the last drop of water in the cup should come in question, it would be only natural for any of us who live in Ittoen to concede the water and die, if necessary, for the other."

V: "Then it is just contrary to the way of modern civilization."

N: "Yes, this life starts with the words 'Live only with the permission of providence, and never try to live at the expense of the well-being of others.'"

V: "If that be the case, it must be quite uncertain and precarious...why, it even seems like a revolt against the very instinct of man!"

N: "You may well feel that way. But the fact is just the reverse.

We feel no uncertainty, no danger, and not only do we indulge little in our natural instincts, but at times we are even annoyed with our over-abundance! Most of the people in the world, on the other hand, seem always to be complaining of insufficiency and longing after things they would like to possess; they are thirsty, dangerous, and apt to rebel against their own religious and moral instinct."

V: "I think that you are right, but what can be the cause of all these troubles?"

N: "That is quite simple: If we struggle for the possession of this cup full of water, do you think that the cup would remain full, or that it would be spilt during the struggle? Rather, let me ask this: Do you think that three quarters would be left?"

V: "I don't think so."

N: "Do you think that half the cup would be left?"

V: "I am not sure..."

N: "Or even a quarter?"

V: "It is hard to tell..."

N: "Or maybe nothing of it would be left, for they might go so far in their struggle that they would break the cup itself into pieces. The very fragments of the cup might even cause blood to flow. We might say that a struggle for possession results in double loss or even in double death."

V: (Silent)

N: "However, in our way of conceding to others, at least one of the two parties can be saved. Not to concede will invariably lead to struggle, to the destruction of the things we were to enjoy, and eventually to death."

V: "I see your point."

N: "If you act full of love and concede the water to the other, a miraculous thing might even happen—that the water is shared equally without wasting so much as a drop. The two might be both saved from need despite their earlier fear that they would surely die if each did not drink the entire cup. This is what happened in the story of Christ when he fed three thousand persons with only five loaves of bread. There are many such instances that occur within the life of Ittoen."

The resemblance to the Sermon on the Mount—which incidentally has its place in the canonical writings of Ittoen—and the reference to Jesus as one model of life shows that Ittoen is considerably indebted to Christianity.

Tenko-san, however, never talks in terms of Christianity, and rarely in terms of Buddhism. His term *Hikari* (the Light) or *Funi no Komyo* (The Light That is not Two) refers to an infinite omnipotent reality embodying ultimate truth. Ittoen puts it this way: "Tenko-san believes not only in God, Buddha, or Confucius for he believes that the essence of each and all is within the gate of the One and Only Light." This is quoted from *Ichijijitsu* (One Fact of Life), a short but important document read at the service every day. Since this is the central writing of Ittoen, it is given in its entirety here:

"Here is one fact of life: A man stands at the roadside. Though he appears no different from any ordinary man, he has his being through the providence of the Light.

"Sometimes he seems to worship by pressing his palms together and bowing [the *gassho,* a greeting to the gods used by several religious groups including Shinto]. Sometimes he enters the house of others and straightens up the footwear in the entrance, sweeps their garden, tidies up their store room, and cleans the toilet.

"When hungry, he stands by the side of the kitchen, palms pressed together, but whenever he feels that the giver's mind is not sincere, he declines the offered food. Other times, after accepting the offered food, he meditates in prayer and thus purifies the mind of the giver.

"Unless unavoidable he does not take a meal better than that of a servant, and rarely does he take a seat or accept any gratuity.

He lodges at homes where he is offered an invitation and renders whatever service he can. In these homes he makes no difference in degree of intimacy with the family members. He respects all, is grateful to all, and ever serves with gratitude of mind.

He is neither a priest nor a layman. Having a limitless sanctified treasure [*fukuden,* a Zen Buddhist expression] he is provided for by the Light. He is a laborer, but he does not work for livelihood, being taken care of by the Light, but rather renders his services in thanksgiving.

Rich men, having worries in spite of their wealth, come to

this 'poor' man asking him for relief. Without uttering many words he seems to show them the cause of their worries.

"Poor men, lamenting their poverty, come to him for their salvation. He seems to lead them to realize their 'richness,' to make them grateful, and to cause them to enjoy their life with thanksgiving.

"The authority of civilization has no value for this man. Civilization is built up and simultaneously destroyed by itself. And human beings, living by it, become like fools who worry over having nothing and suffer for having.

"The gospel of the heavenly kingdom or the joy of the world means nothing to this man. Asked of life and death, he smiles without answering. Asked who he is, he turns his head, presses his palms together and resumes his sweeping of the dust off the road. Asked of his way of conduct, he answers that he is made humble for the lack of virtue. If further persistently asked he, answers that he, led by Light, walks in formless form [*muso,* another Zen Buddhist term] and renders his service.

"He believes not only in God, or in Buddha, or in Confucius alone, for he believes that all of their essence is within the gate of *Funi no Komyo,* 'The Light That Is not Two.'

"The cause of human suffering, worry, want and conflict, even the rise and fall of nations or the ways of reconstructing this world, all are constantly clarified by him. When admired for wisdom, he always states that it is because so obvious are things when viewed in the light of the One and Only Light.

"He is meek, humble, and industrious without harboring any thought of conflict and struggle. Though he holds no idea of acquiring possession he enjoys producing things.

"He neither affirms nor negates the prevailing world ideologies. With his naïve simplicity of mind he seems to trust completely in the laws of nature [the Light].

"Is this an ordinary human being? Is he Light himself? Or is he mad? He does not know himself, and how much less do others.

"Nevertheless, such is his way of life, and this in One Fact of Life."[3]

The *One Fact of Life* has been quoted in full as it is one of the earliest writings of Tenko-san and the most treasured writing of his believers. *One Fact of Life* is of the greatest importance in the study of the present situation and the future development of Ittoen.

The essence of this document and Tenko-san's" life in service" is contained in the following poem often quoted by Nishida Tenko:

"With one rice-bowl, a thousand homes,
 Alone I roam for countless autumns,
Being neither empty nor phenomenal,
 Returning to life without pleasure or pain.
Warm days and green grass at river's bank,
 Cool breezes sweeping calmly beneath the bridge.
Should you, by chance, ask 'Who are you?'
 A bright moon floating over the water."[4]

Worship and Practices

Worship through all Religions

The worship of Ittoen takes place in the Hall of the Spirit (Reido), in which the only ornaments are a picture of Tenko-san on the back wall, and two oblong wooden signs with Zen Buddhist words on the front wall.[5] In the middle of the front wall is a large round window, through which a bamboo grove can be seen, an indication of the union of man and nature so typical of Japanese religion, particularly Shintoism. In the front are three altars. The one to the right represents the essence of Christianity, the one to the left represents the essence of Buddhism, and the one in the middle is dedicated to the Light (*Ohikari*). On the altar in the center is a lantern which is never extinguished. It has been made by combining more than one hundred fragments of ancient lanterns from the oldest temples and shrines all over the country.

The symbol of Ittoen is also displayed in the Reido. It consists of an old Buddhist symbol, the swastika, on a red or orange sunburst. The arms of the swastika bend so that it also forms a circle. That the cross-bars of the swastika form a cross is emphasized by a Greek-Maltese cross in green in the center. This means that the rays of the Light from Buddhism and Christianity merge and form a single circle of harmony. This same idea is reflected in the first two parts of the above-mentioned Ittoen prayer.

Accordingly there are people of various religions in Ittoen. Among the leaders are several Zen Buddhists, a former Baptist minister, as well as a former teacher at the Christian Doshisha University. All are free to maintain their beliefs if they wish. This lends a peculiar character to the life in Kosenrin, where a church bell is struck at six in the morning and a Buddhist temple bell sounds at six every evening. The service shows the same syncretic tendency. It is predominantly Zen Buddhist in form, but among the various Buddhist sutras included among the scriptures used at the service the Sermon on the Mount and the Lord's Prayer are also found. In this connection it should also be mentioned that a special service is held on Christmas and on the celebration of the Buddha's birthday.

Life in Active Service

Nothing is more emphasized in Ittoen than a life in "action and service." Tenko-san refuses to call Ittoen a religion and chooses to call it way of life (*seikatsu*), He always says: "It is useless to argue—go ahead and *do* it!" Or: "There are truer prayers in one's devoted work than in prostrating oneself before an altar. Things which you think you have earned are worthless and perishable. Only the toil, you have undertaken with the sweat of your brow is that which is imperishable and noble."

As a practical demonstration of this life in service, the members of Ittoen often go out and do all kinds of work free of charge. They are best known for their *rokuman gyogan*, euphemistically referred to as "life of creating peace" but actually involving the emptying and cleaning of Japanese toilets in homes without modern sewage. This may take place once a week. With a towel bearing Ittoen's emblem wrapped around their foreheads and buckets under their arms they gather in the schoolyard. After singing the Rokuman Gyogan Song they file through the village, across the bridge, and off to their assigned destination of that day. Those remaining bow in silent greeting as the workers pass by.

This form of service may seem a little strange, not only to Westerners, and the rokuman gyogan has been the target of many jokes (thus it has earned Ittoen the name of the W.C. religion). But there can be no mistake about the sincerity of the people who perform it. For them it is not a propaganda stunt or an amusing experience. They regard it as an important means towards establishing world peace and call it "prayer in action." Also they are conscious of the sense of humility, that this "low and contemptible work" gives them. Tenko-san thus said, when asked by a Christian missionary why such a rather unproductive and negative work had been chosen for the special service of Ittoen: "Jesus was a noble man—he washed the feet of his disciples!"

A special feature of the life in service is the two Swa Raj dramatic troupes of Ittoen, which perform every year throughout the country, especially in prisons and penitentiaries. The dramas are based upon the religious and moral principles of Ittoen and are seen by an enormous number of people. A "drama" in itself is the curtain used at the performances. It consists of more than a thousand different handkerchiefs of all shapes and colors that have all been picked up by the actors when they sweep and clean the auditorium after the performance.

The Swa Raj drama is one of the two activities that account for the far-reaching influence of Ittoen. The other one is the training meetings (*chitoku kenshukai*), which take place from the seventh to the tenth of every month at Kosenrin. On each occasion a large group of young people gather for a special training course in the rokuman gyogan and the life of Ittoen. From all over the country business managers and other people who are interested in the moral and religious training of their youth send their young employees to these training courses. The influence of Ittoen on such firms and companies is quite considerable. The training courses started thirty years ago, and until now about two hundred thousand people have attended them.

Other Activities at Kosenrin

The people at Kosenrin work in the ricefields, vegetable gardens, bamboo groves, and are able to support themselves financially through this work.

Another activity that goes on at Kosenrin is the publication of

Hikari and other pamphlets and books from the printing house of Ittoen, which has carried on for more than thirty years.

In the Kosenrin is also the the Hall of Light (*Ohikarido*), a beautiful two-storied building, which has been built for the use of people outside of Ittoen. In this house several international conferences, (including, for example, some Quaker groups), have taken place. In the main hall of this building the flags of all nations are displayed to symbolize the unity of all.

Outside the real compound of Kosenrin is a little camp that is called "The Rag Pickers Village." Any homeless wanderer or tramp who cannot find food or lodging is welcomed here. Lodging and two meals are provided, and in return the people who come are supposed to help with the raising of pigs in the pig-sty located here. The average number of people who come is about twenty-five every day.

The unique school system must also be mentioned. The tiny village of 350 inhabitants has within its compound a school system that takes the children from kindergarten through university. The teachers in the kindergarten and the elementary school are Ittoen members, but most of the teachers in the high school and the university are from outside Kosenrin, usually people from various schools and universities in Kyoto who take a special interest in Ittoen and therefore teach without remuneration. The educational system is extremely democratic and based on the Ittoen way of life—it is probably the only school in Japan where the teachers are called "uncle" and "aunt."

Ittoen and Other Religions

Tenko-san was probably influenced by Christianity in his youth. He states that some of the ideas which left the deepest impression on him during his youth were: "Give away all you have, and then take up my cross and follow me." "These words, which I at that time did not know were from the Bible, have ever since been the motto of my life," says Tenko-san.

Some of his Christian influence emerges in his often-quoted remarks, such as: "Genuine religious ecstasy will come only after you have borne your cross....Serve with no thought for rewards and things will be given you when you need....He who gives will live....Respect all men, give thanks for all things and be diligent in works of gratefulness."

The influence from Buddhism is just as evident. Tenko-san studied Zen Buddhism for ten years as a young man. Most of his terminology is from Zen, and many of his sayings are pure Zen. On self-negation he says: "True faith is self-negation. It is a state in which the self is merged with the cosmos....He who has negated himself is Buddha. The ultimate negative is the ultimate positive....matter and mind are one."

Apparently Buddhism has had the greater influence on Tenko-san. Whereas he seldom makes use of the word "God" he does mention Buddha, but it must be said that he usually combines the two into his term "Light."

Ittoen does not concern itself with questions of the superiority of, for example, Christianity over Buddhism or Christ over Buddha. The problem of life after death does not come up. Tenko-san maintains that there is only one Light, and that man and God, as well as man and life, cannot be thought of in segments but only as a whole. Usually he will not answer such questions as the above except by "speaking silence" (c.f. the "thundering silence" of Zen) or he will give an answer that reflects his sense of humor: "Death solves all problems. If you have any problems, assuredly it is because you have not yet died completely."

Summary and Future

The selflessness and winning personality of Tenko-san have appealed to the idealism and selflessness in others. Ittoen's thriving community is perhaps nearing the end of its spontaneous growing period—at least there is the possibility that this period of the organization could be near a point of stagnation. One of the customs of Ittoen may throw some light on this point.

Every year at midnight of the last night of December, when a new year is being born, Tenko-san leaves Kosenrin and returns to what is called his "home," that is, the streets and roadsides (his house at Kosenrin is called his "place of service"). The community at Kosenrin must then, if they want him back, go out on the following day, locate him, and bring him back again.

Inviting Tenko-san back has become more a ceremony than anything else, important for its symbolic value. Tenko-san usually goes to the same place in Kyoto every time, and the community send the same representatives every year to invite him back. In reflecting on the early days of the movement when Tenko-san's home was literally the roadside, one begins to wonder if the development of this custom is the signal that the vitality has begun to go out of Ittoen—that is, is it only possible that an idealistic movement like Ittoen can exist as an organic growing force for a limited period of time?

As with any of the movements we have discussed, the death of the leader is always a crisis that only the strongest religions can overcome. What will happen after the death of Tenko-san, who is now in his early nineties? Ittoen could continue to be a "way of life" or it could become a new religion with Tenko-san as its principal deity. Of course, it is impossible to predict this with any certainty but there are some hints of things to come. It can be seen that the *One Fact of Life* bears in it the seeds of a future deification of Tenko-san.

Various Other New Religions

Tenchi Kodo Zenrinkai

Tenchi Kodo Zenrinkai, which means Heaven-Earth-Public-Way-Good-Neighbor-Society, was started in 1947 right after the war by Rikishisa Tatsusai, who was born in 1908. It claims to have 35 meeting places, 272 teachers, and close to 400,000 members. The headquarters is in Kyushu.

Zenrinkai is registered as a religion but specializes in group therapy. A technique of psychotherapy has been worked out to the minutest detail, and Zenrinkai is one of the most interesting new religions in Japan that perform faith-healings.

The purely religious elements of worship, such as prayer, hymns, and sermon are only used so far as they can help towards curing diseases. Zenrinkai people say that a religion is not a true religion if it only takes care of the soul of man—the whole man, body and soul, should be taken care of by religion.

The Prayer of Zenrinkai runs: "Lord, lead us unfortunates to you. Show us, who are confused, the way to enlightenment. Give us, weak of heart, the food of health. Lead us on the way of mutual friendship to the paradise of love and peace. Let us follow always in the footsteps of God. Oh, Lord, oh, Lord, Great Ancestor of Heaven and Earth! *Yarimasu, yarimasu!*" The word *yarimasu,* "let us do it," is shouted at the top of the voice of the believers, and the last syllable *maaasu* is drawn out in a peculiar way.

The headquarters of Zenrinkai is in Saga, Kyushu, and until recently was the large estate formerly belonging to Baron Nabeshima, Lord of Saga. The main point of interest was the thirty-mat hall, where the service was held. There was a little Shinto altar with offerings of vegetables and fruits, and a picture of the fifty-year-old founder, Rikishisa. On the walls and everywhere strips of **235** paper had been plastered with the watchword of the religion: *yarimasu.* The loss of this establishment may remove one big popularity factor.

To become a member of Zenrinkai the only condition is to have an introduction by a member. By paying the entrance fee one becomes an ordinary member and holds membership as long as a low yearly fee is paid. To become a special member, which entails several advantages, the whole family must be converted to Zenrinkai, whereupon they exchange saké cups with the founder and are given an honorary diploma.

The alpha and omega of Zenrinkai is the faith-healing, which take place at the *gosenko,* the healing sessions held daily. As a bell rings, and a heavy gong sends its deafening sound through the room, the first teacher jumps up to the platform and begins a talk lasting about twenty minutes and accompanied with dramatic gesticulations and movements. As soon as he gets tired, another teacher makes a similar dramatic entrance and takes up the same subject: "You are sick, but you will be cured, if only you repent and confess your sins." The lectures continue and get more and more violent as people, especially middle-aged women, start weeping. At the climax the founder enters as the teachers set the cadence to the rhythmic cry of *yarimasu!* The founder's speech is similar to the ones by the teachers, and after ending his speech he pretends to leave the hall. However, now all the teachers rush up to him and surround him, clinging to his body. At their cry: "The Founder is leaving, get hold of him and be cured" the whole crowd, now worked up to a frenzy of delirium, get on their feet. They throw themselves upon the founder, who often is bruised by their violence, embracing him and pawing him wherever they can touch him. The founder finally escapes through the aid of the teachers, and a voice on the microphone says: *"Keikendan, keikendan"*—has anyone been cured? Come forward and tell us all about it!" Several people go to the platform and give their healing story, and the meeting ends with an earsplitting *yarimaaaasu.*

There can be no doubt that certain diseases, mainly psychosomatic ones, can be cured by a kind of therapeutic shock in the midst of the melee. However, there is no doubt either, that a large number of the healing stories are coached and fabricated.

Dotoku Kagaku

Dotoku Kagaku is an educational corporation or organization rather than a religion as such, and it is not registered among religions with the Ministry of Education. However, there are certain sides of Dotoku Kagaku, which must be called religious, and the trend seems to move towards the status of a religion.

The name Dotoku Kagaku means "moral science" or "moralogy." And Dotoku Kagaku is a way of life or a system of ethics based upon a syncretistic code of morals. "Our system contains the essence of the following great moral systems. Firstly, that of Amaterasu-o-mikami (the Sun Goddess of Shintoism), the Heavenly Ancestress of the Imperial House of Japan. Secondly, that of Confucius of China. Thirdly, that of Sakyamuni from India. Fourthly that of Jesus Christ of Judea. And, fifthly, that of Socrates of Greece."[1] It is claimed that the essential principles of thought and morality which constitute these five great moral systems are all displayed in Supreme Morality, or Dotoku Kagaku. It is also claimed that Dotoku Kagaku's system is higher than that of any one because of the further additions of the other four systems. Any statement to the effect that these principles may contradict each other is answered thus: "They might have been so, if it were not for the genius of our founder, who overcame the danger of contradiction by taking from each system only the doctrines and ideas that agreed with his principles."

Dotoku Kagaku was started by Hiroike Chikuro, the founder, in 1912, when Hiroike had a nervous breakdown during which he had an "illumination," that brought him deeper insight into the true purpose of life. He promised obedience to "the One True God in the Universe," studied Shinto and Tenrikyo to find the application for his ideas, but was dissatisfied with these religions, and finally founded his own system in 1928, when **237** he made a pilgrimage to Ise to select disciples. On the return trip he sat by the River Izu "imitating Jesus and giving his disciples an instruction like that of the Sermon on the Mount."[2]

After the death of Chikuro his son, Hiroike Chibusa, carried on the work. Study clubs were formed in most larger towns in Japan after the war, and instruction courses were held at the center established at Koganei in Chiba Prefecture, where Dotoku has an extremely large site with a variety of schools, dormitories, and a library and college. At present it is estimated that about 100,000 people have some contact or other with Dotoku Kagaku, with about half of the regular members paying dues and in return receiving various literature from headquarters.

Dotoku Kagaku teaches that God is two things: the fundamental spirit of the universe, and God Incarnate, such as the Emperor, the Imperial Ancestors, the sages, Christ, Socrates, and the rest. Jesus is respected very highly: "Jesus Christ suffered crucifixion with the spirit of loving-kindness in his heart, and at the bitter end he possessed no home, no property, no clothes, no family, and even no disciples. His great spirit of universal love, however, roused the faith of many followers and caused them to believe in his teaching and in his resurrection. Thus the spirit of Jesus did not pass away but spread to the remotest parts of the Roman Empire and later throughout the world. Though it is doubtlessly impossible to prove scientifically that Christ was the Son of God, we know that he was possessed by a divine nature. Indeed, it is his teachings that have made people believe in the existence of a universal God."[3]

Dotoku Kagaku teaches that man must follow and abide by the Five Rules of Conduct (*Kihon no Gogensoku*).
1. Forget yourself.
2. Duty first (towards your principals and towards your ancestors).
3. Always follow the true line of succession (of which there are three kinds: political, familial, and spiritual).
4. Attain to enlightenment through which God's love and kindness becomes part of man.
5. The law of causality.

Dotoku Kagaku is a pseudo-religious system of learning based upon the thoughts of Buddha, Confucius, Christ, Socrates and

Shinto: a system, in which the essence of the teachings of these five sages is composed into a system built upon modern scientific ideas. To close with the words of Hiroike: "Moralogy has been closely examined and has stood the test from the standpoint of the history of mankind, from the sociological point of view, from present-day scientific standards, and also from my own personal experience in life. Indeed, it is the most suitable and rational morality for the attainment of perfection in this existence and development, security, peace and final happiness of mankind now and in generations to come. This then is the all-important reason why I feel it to be my duty to urge upon all mankind the practice of Supreme Morality through the medium of this new science 'Moralogy.' "[4]

Ritsudo-kyo

Ritsudo-kyo, with headquarters in Osaka, is a religion with adherents mainly from the so-called intelligentsia. Its aim is to create a personal awakening coupled with a national and international awakening. Its teaching is seen from its ten "Tenets of Faith":

1. We believe in One Absolute God, because there is nothing in the universe but God.
2. We believe that God is absolutely perfect because God is the absolute Being.
3. We believe that God and man are one, and that all nations are basically one, having been created by the One God.
4. We believe that when we believe in God, sickness, poverty, and other misfortunes will disappear and supreme happiness will be given to our lives.
5. We do not believe that life has any other purpose than that of realizing God.
6. In order to realize and unite with God, we promise to live by the ideal of 'non-self.'
7. We believe that God through our prayer will give us an impetus towards right thinking and living.

8. We believe that our prayer will be realized because we believe that God, the root of the Universe, is the One who is urging us to pray.

9. We call the mind which God gives us in answer to our prayer Ritsudoho, and we strive to realize and be united with God by this Ritsudoho.

10. As we believe that God is love, we will also be given the power of love when we unite with God, and thus we shall be enabled to do great things.

Ritsudo-kyo claims that it is no new religion, but a movement that by grasping the real nature of God and the Universe is able to give life to the "dead" truths taught by Christianity, Buddhism, and other religions. Therefore Ritsudo-kyo not only teaches the "Ritsudo-ho" but also studies and teaches the doctrines of Christianity, Buddhism, and other religions.

Ishin-kai

Ishin-kai, with headquarters in Tokyo, owes its origin to the revelations received by Dr. Kishi Kazuta in 1927. Dr. Kishi was a well-known specialist of ear, nose, and throat diseases and continued his practice even after having started Ishinkai. He was followed by Kawamata Hitoshi, who is the present leader. Ishinkai had five shrines, fifty other meeting places, 451 teachers, and 48,330 believers as of January 1, 1958.

Of special interest in the teaching of Ishinkai is the conception of God. The principal object of worship is Yagokoro-omoikane-no-okami, the god who, according to Shinto tradition, acted as Master of Ceremonies when the Sun Goddess had hidden herself in a cave, and Ame-no-uzume-no-mikoto by her dance won the applause of the other gods with the effect that the Sun Goddess, overcome with curiosity, opened the door of the cave in order to see for herself. However, the believers of this religion in their homes worship the ancestor gods, *ujigami*, of the clans to which they belong. According to the *Engi-chiki*, the old Japanese book on ritual, there are 168 of these old clan gods who take care of their children, *ujiko*, the members of the clan. In Ishinkai the first thing for the believer to do is therefore to find out to which clan he belongs, since he otherwise will not know to which God he has to direct his prayers. This phenomenon, that the official worship at the headquarters of a religion and the private worship of the members of the same religion are directed towards completely different gods (and even vary in 168 names), is rather unique in Japanese religion.

Shinrikyo

Shinrikyo has its headquarters in Fukuoka Prefecture in Kyushu. It is a Shinto sect with a rather long history. At present it has 602 shrines and 117 other meeting places, 2,683 teachers and priests, and 557,911 believers (as of January 1, 1958).

Shinrikyo, "Divine Reason Religion," worships eighteen Shinto gods and regards its founder Kannagibe Tsunahiko (1834–1906) as a direct descendant of Nigihayashi-no-mikoto, who was a grandson of the Sun Goddess Amaterasu Omikami according to Shinto tradition. He is declared to have had a revelation in 1876, in which Nigihayashi-no-mikoto commanded him to start a new religion, and he is regarded by his followers as the mediator between man and the gods.

In addition to the practices and beliefs usually found among Shinto sects, Shinrikyo encourages sacred writing and drawing, sacred music, dancing, flower arrangement, and the tea ceremony in order to stimulate national customs and preserve the etiquette of ancient Japan. Modern Japanese are urged to return to their native culture.

Jikkokyo

Jikkokyo has its headquarters in Saitama Prefecture and is one of the so-called mountain sects of the New Religions. It has 333 **241** shrines, 1,878 priests and teachers, and 194,835 believers, as of January 1, 1958.

Jikkokyo emphasizes practical activities rather than ritual and dogmas. Believers are urged to show the inner spirit of the "Way of the Gods" in their everyday life, all philosophical arguments and discussions are discouraged, and all existing dogmas are made so simple that they can be understood by everybody. They especially emphasize universal brotherhood as the goal of man.

The most important part of the religious practices of Jikkokyo are the numerous pilgrimages to Mount Fuji, which is conceived of as the holy dwelling place for the three Shinto gods of creation, and consequently is the principal sacred mountain and object of worship to Jikkokyo adherents.

Shinshukyo

Shinshukyo is one of the purification sects of Shinto. Its headquarters is in Tokyo, and it has 534 shrines, 1,935 priests and teachers, and 580,795 believers as of January 1, 1958.

Shinshukyo worships the usual Shinto pantheon of gods, but gives a special place to Ame-no-minai-nushi-no-mikoto, one of the three gods of creation in Shinto teaching, whom they worship as the absolute spiritual being and the source of everything.

Shinshukyo practices numerous ceremonies as a means of washing away evil and pollutions of every kind, and does not pay much attention to doctrine or philosophy. Its principal rituals include a fire-subduing ceremony, a hot-water ceremony, a ceremony of twanging of bowstrings, and a rice-cooking ceremony. These four practices are performed together with the recitation of prayers for the purification of mind and body. Divination and exorcism are also practiced, and altogether Shinshukyo is one of the New Religions with most emphasis on shamanism and any kind of superstition. Probably the most interesting ceremony of the sect is a practice for producing an ecstatic state of mind in order to commune with the deities and become one with the gods.

Seishoin Kyodan

Seishoin Kyodan, with headquarters in Tokyo, is a postwar New Religion which had its start in 1946, when the foundress and present matriarch, Mrs. Yae Sata, had a revelation. It is also called *magokorokyo*. It practically exists only in Tokyo, and no statistics are available about its present strength.

Seishodo has four main teachings:

1. A true mind: the more who attain to a true mind through our way, the happier the nation and the world will become.
2. A patient mind: the way to happiness is to change unsatisfaction to joy and suffering into gratitude through patience in all happenings of life.
3. A mind of humility and love: with this mind obtained, one will gain a healthy body, prosper in one's business, and pay tax with joy.
4. A mind of helpfulness: always help your neighbor, and remember that as man is, so will the nation and the world be.

Entrance into Seishoin is easily obtained; there is no qualification except the payment of five yen per month. There is no special entrance fee, and withdrawal can take place any time without any obligations.

The words on the official pamphlet of Seishoin are typical of the atmosphere of most new religions, and indicative of the soil they grow in: "Come freely, those who have sufferings, all who have troubles in life. We give you consultations on family problems, marriage, child talents, business opportunities, sickness, agricultural matters, etc. You will be taught the way to be happy in this world of suffering, and you shall have sufferings no more."

General Information

Headquarters:	271 Mishima, Tenri City, Nara Prefecture.
	Tokyo office: 9, 1, Kanda Nishiki-cho, Chiyoda-ku.
Foundress:	Miki Nakayama (1798–1882). Founded in 1838.
Patriarch:	Nakayama Shozen. Official title: shimbashira.
Bulletin:	Michi no Tomo.
Statistics:	15,162 churches and 5,066 preaching places (225 abroad).
	102,000 priests and missionaries.
	2,350,595 believers.
Festivals:	January 1: New Year Festival.
	January 26: The Great Vernal Festival. x
	March 27: Vernal Commemoration of the Dead.
	April 18: Anniversary of the Foundress. x
	May 18: Holy Labor Day.
	August 4: Apostolate of the Press Day.
	August 18: Day of Wayside Preaching.
	September 21: Autumnal Commemoration of the Dead.
	October 26: Great Autumnal Festival. x
	x: Three Grand Festivals.

KUROZUMIKYO

Headquarters:	35 Kami Nakano, Okayama City, Okayama Prefecture.
	Tokyo office: 143 Ikejiri-cho, Setagaya-ku.
Founder:	Kurozumi Munetada (1780–1850). Founded in 1814.
Patriarch (kyoshu):	Kurozumi Munekazu.
Bulletin:	Nisshin.
	Michizure.
Statistics:	383 shrines and 15 meeting places.
	3,347 priests and evangelists.
	751,770 believers.
Festivals:	April 17—18: Founder's Festival.

245

Headquarters:	270 Otani Konko-cho, Asaguchi-gun, Okayama Pref. Tokyo office: 5, 4 Muro-machi, Nihonbashi, Chuo-ku.
Founder:	Kawata Bunjiro (Konko Daijin) (1814–1883). Founded in 1859.
Patriarch (kyoshu):	Konko Setsutane.
Bulletins:	Konko Kyoho (monthly) Konkokyoto (three times monthly) Konkokyo Seinen (monthly) Wakaba (monthly) Tsuchi (bi-weekly) Hotsume Shimbun (bi-weekly) Yatsunami (5 times a year) Toritsugi (semi-annually)
Statistics:	1,621 churches besides forty-eight meeting places 3,569 teachers and ministers 634,303 believers
Festivals:	January 1: New Year Festival Vernal Equinox: Spring Festival April 4, 7 and 10: Grand Festival June 10: Foundation of Church Festival Autumn Equinox: Autumn Festival September 29: Festival of Founder's Birthday November 15: Foundation Memorial Day December 10: Mission Day Also minor festivals on the 10th and 22nd of each month.

SOKA GAKKAI

Headquarters:	Administrative headquarters of Soka Gakkai: 6–32 Shinano-machi, Shinjuku-ku, Tokyo. Spiritual headquarters of Nichiren Shoshu: Taiseki-ji, Kamijo, Ueno-mura, Fuji-gun, Shizuoka Pref.
Founder:	Makiguchi Tsunesaburo. (1871–1944) Founded in 1930.
Refounder:	Toda Josei (1900–1958). Re-founded in 1946.
President (kaicho):	Ikeda Daisaku.
Official Bulletins:	Daibyaku Renge (monthly) Seikyo Shimbun (weekly) Seikyo Gurafu (weekly pictorial)
Statistics:	2.9 million households, or about 10 million believers.

Headquarters:	4–2 Iigura-cho, Minato-ku, Tokyo. A huge new headquarters is at present (1962) being built on the Izu Peninsula in Shizuoka Prefecture (near Ito City).
Founder:	Kubo Kakutaro (1890–1944). Founded in 1925.
President:	Kotani Kimi.
Bulletins:	Reiyukaiho (monthly) Myoho (monthly youth journal)
Statistics:	5 main temples and an unspecified number of meeting places. 593 teachers and missionaries. 3,465,688 believers
Services:	On the 8th, 18th, and 28th of each month.

RISSHO KOSEI KAI

Headquarters:	27 Wada Honmachi, Suginami-ku, Tokyo.
Co-founders:	Niwano Nikkyo (1906–) and Naganuma Myoko (1899–1957). Founded in 1938.
President (kaicho):	Niwano Nikkyo.
Bulletins:	Kosei (monthly) Kosei Shimbun (weekly)
Statistics:	84 training halls and 114 local branches. 4,650 teachers. 2 million believers.
Festivals:	March 5: Foundation Festival.
April 8:	Flower Festival.
October 12:	Grand Festival.

OMOTO

Headquarters:	Administrative Headquarters: Kameoka-cho, Kyoto Prefecture. Spiritual Headquarters: Ayabe-cho, Kyoto Prefecture. Tokyo Headquarters: Shichiken-cho, Ikeno-hata, Daito-ku.
Founder:	Deguchi Nao (1836–1918) and Deguchi Onisaburo (1871–1948). Founded in 1892.
Patriarch (kyoshu):	Deguchi Naohi.
Bulletins:	Omoto (in Japanese, English, and Esperanto).

Aizen-en (monthly)
Jinrui Aizen Shimbun (ULBA) (every ten days)
Statistics: 618 temples and 640 meeting places.
335 teachers.
203,888 believers.

ANANAIKYO

Headquarters: 481, Shimo Shimizu, Shimizu City, Shizuoka Pre-
fecture.
Founder: Nakano Yonosuke (1887–   ). Founded in 1949.
Bulletins: Ananai (monthly)
Ananai Kyoho.
The Ananai (irregular periodical in English).
Statistics: 65 shrines and 217 meeting places.
510 priests and teachers.
104,436 believers.
Festivals: Four Grand Festivals: February 2–3.
April 21–22.
July 22–23.
September 22–23.

SEICHO NO IE

Headquarters: 266–3, Harajuku, Shibuya-ku, Tokyo.
Founder
and Patriarch: Taniguchi Masaharu (1894–   ). Founded in 1930.
Bulletins: Shitohato (monthly)
Risosekai (monthly)
Seicho no Ie (monthly)
Seishin Kagaku (monthly)
Hikari no Izumi (monthly)
Seicho no Ie (English)
Statistics: 33 churches and 1,173 meeting places.
5,300 teachers
1,472,280 believers

SEKAI KYUSEI KYO

Headquarters: 996–2, Okubo, Izusan, Atami City, Shizuoka Pref.
Founder: Okada Mokuchi (1882–1955). Founded in 1934.
Matriarch: Fujieda Itsuki.
Bulletins: Eiko (newspaper).
Chijo Tengoku (monthly).

SEKAI KYUSEI KYO (CONTINUED)
                    The Glory (English).
Statistics: 95 Churches and 522 meeting places.
                    2,201 teachers.
                    393,534 believers
Festivals: Spring Equinox and Autumn Equinox.

PL KYODAN

Headquarters: Shindo, Tondabayashi City, Osaka Prefecture.
Founder: Miki Tokuharu (1871–1938). Founded in 1920 as
                    Hito no Michi.
Refounder: Miki Tokuchika (1900–   ). Re-founded in 1946
                    as PL Kyodan.
Patriarch: Miki Tokuchika.
Bulletins: PL News.
                    PL Seinen (monthly).
                    Geijutsu Seikatsu (monthly).
                    Tanka Geijutsu (monthly).
Statistics: 203 churches and 269 meeting places.
                    631 teachers.
                    605,213 believers.
Festivals: January 1.
                    April 8.
                    July 6.
                    September 29.
                    And a special service on the 21st of every month.

TENSHO KOTAI JINGU KYO (Odoru Shukyo)

Headquarters: 903–1, Namino, Tabuse-machi, Kumage-gun, Yama-
                    guchi Prefecture.
Foundress: Kitamura Sayo (1900–   ). Founded in 1945.
Matriarch: Kitamura Sayo.
Bulletin: Tensei (monthly)
Statistics: 136 Meeting places (among them 16 in the USA)
                    221 teachers
                    110,124 believers
Festivals: January 1: New Year Festival.
                    February 9: New Epoch Festival.
                    July 22: Anniversary of Kitamura's First Sermon.
                    August 12: Anniversary of the Advent of God.

ITTOEN

Headquarters: Ittoen, Yamashina, Kyoto.

Founder and present leader:	Nishida Tenko (1872–)
Bulletins:	Hikari (monthly)
	Koyu (monthly)
	Light (occasional bulletin in English)
Statistics:	Members of the village of Ittoen: about 350.
	People influenced by Ittoen: 1–2 million.
Training course (seikatsukai):	generally held the first weekend of each month.

Notes

THE NEW RELIGIONS

1. From a sermon by Kitamura Sayo, leader of the new religion Tensho Kotai Jingu Kyo (also called Odoru Shukyo), hereafter to be referred to as TKJK.
2. TKJK, *Guidance to God's Kingdom* (Tabuse, 1956), p.7.
3. TKJK, *The Paradise of Tabuse* (Tabuse, 1953), opposite picture nr. 17 (no page numbers).
4. Masaharu Taniguchi, *Divine Education and Spiritual Training of Mankind* (Tokyo 1956), p. 136.

I THE "OLD" NEW RELIGIONS
1. TENRIKYO

1. See title page of Henry van Straelen's *The Religion of Divine Wisdom*. This book and two books issued by Tenrikyo. (*The Doctrine of Tenrikyo,* and *A Short History of Tenrikyo*) are the main works in English on this religion.
2. Keiichi Nakayama, *Tenrikyo Kyoten Kowa* (Tenri, 1951, p. 3.
3. *Tadamasa Fukaya,* Mikagura Uta Kogi (Tenri, 1956), p.1.
4. For further explanation on this point read *Japanese Religion in the Meiji Era* by Hideo Kishimoto, pp. 330–333.
5. This first line is the important prayer in Tenrikyo mentioned above.
6. Heavenly nectar is another word for the *kanro* or sweet dew mentioned above.
7. Concerning the *jiba* see above. Yamato, the district around Nara, played an important role in the early history of Japan.
8. The special fertilizer: three measures of rice bran, three measures of ash, and three measures of soil—a mixture which, according to Miki, would be as effective as 150 kg. of artificial fertilizer, if used with faith and trust.
9. All the twelve hymns are divided into ten parts.
10. The construction of Tenrikyo.
11. Concerning *hinokishin* see below under "Propagation."
12. Usually interpreted as the Foundress or God, not Master Iburi, who, incidentally, was a carpenter and built Miki's first temple.
13. As the basis for this translation the author has used the original Japanese text as well as the *Choseki Mikagura Uta* by Kurakichi Nakagawa and

251

the *Mikagura Uta Kogi* by
Tadamasa Fukaya.

14. This has given to Tenrikyo
the nickname of "kana no
shukyo," i.e., the religion with
a canon written in the Japanese phonetic alphabet.

15. In this early stage of Tenrikyo
teaching, and to some extent
even today, there is no clear
distinction between the Foundress and God. For further
reading, *On the Idea of God
in the Tenrikyo Doctrine* by
Nakayama Shozen is recom-
mended.

16. Tenrikyo, *Ofudesaki* (Tenri
1952), XIV, 35.

17. Tenrikyo, *The Doctrine of
Tenrikyo* (Tenri, 1958), p. 14.

18. *Ibid.,* p. 42.

19. Until recent years Shintoism
had been exclusive among
Japanese religions in having
a creation story. According to
Buddhism the world moves
"from beginning-less beginning to endless end."

20. Takeshi Hashimoto, *Tenrikyo
to wa,* p. 15.

21. Tenrikyo, *Ofudesaki (op. cit.),*
III, 126.

22. Tenrikyo, *Osashizu,* February
14, 1889.

23. Tadamasa Fukaya, *Tenrikyo
Nyumon* (Tenri 1954), p. 12.

24. Yoshinari Ueda, *The Outline
of Tenrikyo Doctrine and Its
History* (Tenri), p. 195.

25. *Ofudesaki, op. cit.,* I, 52–53.

26. G.B. Sansom, Japan, *A Short
Cultural History* (London
1952), p. 51: "Throughout
their history the Japanese
seem to have retained in some

measure this incapacity to
discern, or this reluctance to
grapple with, the problem of
evil."

27. Ofudesaki, *op. cit.,* III, 52.

28. The Doctrine of Tenrikyo, *op.
cit.,* p. 71.

29. Ofudesaki, *op. cit.,* XII, 172.

30. Tenrikyo, *A Short History of
Tenrikyo* (Tenri 1958), pp.
68–69.

31. Ofudesaki, *op. cit.,* III, 99–100.

32. Osashizu, *op. cit.,* October 3,
1900.

33. Thus the title of the patriarch is shimbashira, or main
pillar.

34. The Doctrine of Tenrikyo,
op. cit., p. 93.

35. Osashizu, *op. cit.,* 1892.

36. *ibid.,* 1898.

2. KUROZUMIKYO

1. Goro Tanaka, *The Brief Outline of the Kurozumikyo*
(Omoto, Okayama 1956), pp.
2–3.

2. *ibid.,* p. 3.

3. *ibid.,* p. 9.

4. Kurozumikyo, *Kurozumikyo*
(Okayama 1957), p. 2.

5. Poem by Munetada.

6. Tanaka, *op. cit.,* p. 5.

7. *ibid.,* p. 5.

8. Kurozumikyo, *op. cit.,* p. 3.

9. *ibid.,* p. 5.

10. Tanaka, *op. cit.,* pp. 8–9.

3. KONKOKYO

1. Kazuo Sato, *Konkokyo, A New
Religion of Japan* (Konko
Headquarters Konko-cho, Oka-
yama Prefecture 1958), p. 4.

2. *ibid.,* p. 8.
3. William K. Bunce, *Religions in Japan* (Charles E. Tuttle, Tokyo 1955), p. 144.
4. All from Sato, *op. cit.,* pp. 6–7.
5. Konkokyo, *Konkokyo Kyogi* (Konkokyo Headquarters, Konko-cho, Okayama Prefecture, 1954), p. 1.
6. Sato, *op. cit.,* p. 2.
7. Sato, *op. cit.,* p. 2.
8. Sato, *op. cit.,* p. 3.
9. Sato, *op. cit.,* pp. 2–3.
10. Sato, *op. cit.,* p. 10.
11. Sato, *op. cit.,* p. 7.
12. Sato, *op. cit.,* p. 1.
13. Sato, *op. cit.,* p. 7.

II THE NICHIREN GROUP
1. SOKA GAKKAI

1. From an article in the English *Mainichi Daily News,* March 7, 1958.
2. Nichiren Shoshu, *Doctrines of Nichiren Shoshu* (Soka Gakkai Headquarters, Tokyo, 1957), pp. 2–3.
3. Anesaki Masaharu, *Nichiren, the Buddhist Prophet* (London 1949) p. 43.
4. Nichiren Shoshu, *op. cit.,* p. 4.
5. This is one of the essays of Nichiren most valued by Soka Gakkai and Nichiren Shoshu.
6. From "Hokke Shuyo-sho" (*Works of Nichiren,* p. 2051).
7. From "San Dai Hiho" (*Works of Nichiren,* p. 2051).
8. Excerpts from an article by Nichiren Shoshu in the English *Mainichi Daily News,* April 28, 1956.
9. From *Rissho Ankoko Ron,* an essay written by Nichiren.

10. *Chugai Nippo* (a religious daily newspaper in Japanese), May 31, 1957.
11. *Shukan Asahi* (a weekly magazine in Japanese), June 21, 1959.
12. *ibid.*
13. From a letter by Nichiren to his disciples (*Works of Nichiren,* p. 1875).
14. The famous words, in Japanese: *Nembutsu muken, Zen temma, Shingon bokoku, Ritsu kokuzoku.*
15. Yoshihei Kohira, *Shakufuku Kyoten* (Tokyo, first edition 1951– the following excerpts all from the 1954 edition), p. 339.
16. *ibid.,* pp. 340–343.
17. *ibid.,* pp. 345–346.
18. *ibid.,* p. 347.
19. *ibid.,* p. 344.
20. *ibid.,* p. 351.
21. *ibid.,* p. 336.
22. *ibid.,* p. 308.
23. *ibid.,* p. 310.
24. *ibid.,* pp. 322–323.
25. *ibid.* pp. 325–326. Considerable changes have been made in these chapters on other religions by Soka Gakkai in the latest, 1961, edition.
26. The English *Mainichi Daily News,* June 22, 1957.
27. *Shukan Asahi, op. cit.,* June 21, 1959.

2. REIYUKAI

1. Kimi Kotani, *A Guide to Reiyukai* (Tokyo 1958), pp. 19–20.
2. A reference to the propaganda tactics of Soka Gakkai and

others of the new religions.

3. RISSHO KOSEI KAI.

1. Rissho Kosei Kai Headquarters, *A Guide to Rissho Kosei Kai* (Tokyo 1959), p. 2.
2. Concerning the names mentioned in the mandala see above.
3. The growth of Rissho Kosei Kai has been phenomenal and shows at present no signs of stagnation. The rate of its growth will appear from the statistics below:
   1945:   1,000 members
   1947:   4.000 members
   1951:   300,000 members
   1955:   700,000 members
   1958: 1,008,000 members
   1959: 1,200,000 members
   1962: more than two milion members
   Incidentally, the statistics of Rissho Kosei Kai are more reliable than in most other new religions.

III THE OMOTO GROUP
1. OMOTO

1. Omoto, *The Basic Teachings of Omoto* (Omoto, Kameoka, Kyoto Prefecture 1955), p. 1.
2. Omoto, *Scripture of Omoto* (Omoto Headquarters, Kameoka, Kyoto Prefecture 1957), p. 4.
3. Akio Saki, *Kyoso* (Tokyo), p. 79.
4. *Scripture of Omoto, op. cit.,* pp. 4–5.
5. Omoto, *A Guide to God's way* (Omoto Headquarters, Kame

oka, Kyoto Prefecture), p. 4.
6. *The Basic Teachings of Omoto, op. cit.,* pp. 20–21.
7. Omoto, *Memoirs by Onisaburo Deguchi,* (Omoto Headquarters, Kameoka, Kyoto Prefecture), p. 18.
8. Omoto, *Didactic Poems by Onisaburo Deguchi* (Omoto Headquarters, Kameoka, Kyoto Prefecture), p. 9.
9. *The Basic Teaching of Omoto, op. cit.,* p. 37.
10. *A Guide to God's way, op. cit.,* p. 4.
11. *Memoirs –, op. cit.,* pp. 15–16.
12. *The Basic Teachings of Omoto, op. cit.,* pp. 34–35.
13. *Memoirs –, op. cit.,* p. 11.
14. *The Basic Teachings of Omoto, op. cit.,* p. 23.
15. *ibid.,* p. 30.
16. *ibid.,* p. 30.
17. *ibid.,* p. 31.
18. *ibid.,* pp. 33–34.
19. *ibid.,* p. 27.
20. *ibid.,* p. 26.

2. ANANAIKYO

1. Yonosuke Nakano, *A Guide to Ananaikyo* (Ananaikyo Headquarters, Shimizu City, Shizuoka Prefecture 1955), p. 8.
2. *ibid.,* p. 18.
3. Yonosuke Nakano, *The Universe Viewed from the World of Spirit* (Ananai Headquarters, Shimizu City, Shizuoka Prefecture 1957), p. 71.
4. *ibid.,* pp. 72–73.
5. *A Guide to Ananaikyo, op. cit.,* p. 23.
6. *ibid.,* p. 24.

7. *ibid.*, p. 16.
8. *The Universe Viewed from the World of Spirit, op. cit.,* p. 137.

3. SEICHO NO IE

1. Masaharu Taniguchi, *Seimei no Jisso* (Seicho no Ie Headquarters, Tokyo, first edition in 1937, reprinted numerous times), VI, p. 7.
2. Masaharu Taniguchi, *Divine Education and Spiritual Training of Mankind* (Seicho no Ie Headquarters, Tokyo, 1956), p. 129.
3. *ibid.*, p. 137.
4. Masaharu Taniguchi, *Shin no Chikara* (Seicho no Ie Headquarters, Tokyo, 1941), pp. 5–9.
5. *Divine Education-, op. cit.,* p. 152.
6. This meditation is called *chinkon kishin in* Omotokyo and is often followed by divination, which is not the case with the *shinsokan* of Seicho no Ie.
7. *Divine Education-, op. cit.,* p. 105.
8. Seicho no Ie, *Seicho no Ie* (Seicho no Ie Headquarters, Tokyo, a periodical magazine in English), February 1954, p. 21.
9. *Divine Education-, op. cit.,* pp. 231–249.
10. *ibid.*, p. 164.
11. *ibid.*, p. 118.
12. *ibid.*, p. 160.
13. *ibid.*, p. 205.
14. *ibid.*, p. 196.
15. *ibid.*, pp. 196–97.

16. *ibid.*, pp. **28–29.**
17. *Seicho no Ie, op. cit.,* August 1953, pp. 7–8.
18. *ibid.*, p. 20.
19. *Divine Education-, op. cit.,* p. 3.
20. *ibid.*, p. 28.
21. *ibid.*, p. 153.
22. *ibid.*, p. 154.
23. *ibid.*, p. 138.
24. *Seicho no Ie, op. cit.,* June 1958, p. 10.
25. *Divine Education-, op. cit.,* p. 13.
26. *Seicho no Ie, op. cit.,* February 1954, back cover.
27. *ibid.*, January 1958, p. 14.
28. *ibid.*, p. 21.
29. *ibid.*, July 1953, back cover.
30. *ibid.*, January 1958, p. 19.
31. *ibid.*, January 1958, pp. 22–23.
32. *ibid.*, February 1954, pp. 7 and 35.
33. *Divine Education, op. cit.,* pp. 101–102.
34. *ibid.*, p. 5.
35. *ibid.*, p. 194.
36. *ibid.*, p. 136.
37. *Seicho no Ie, op. cit.,* July 1953, p. 9.
38. *ibid.*, July 1953, pp. 12–13.
39. *ibid.*, June 1958, pp. 21–22.
40. *ibid.*, May 1958, back cover.

4. SEKAI KYUSEI KYO

1. Sekai Kyuseikyo, *World Messianity and What It Means* (Sekai Kyusei Kyo Headquarters, Atami City, Shizuoka Prefecture, 1957), pp. 7–8.
2. *ibid.*, pp. 22–23.
3. *ibid.*, p. 22.
4. *ibid.*, p. 30.

5. From *Handbook of the Hakone Art Museum and the Atami Art Museum* (both run by Sekai Kyusei Kyo), p. 3.
6. *World Messianity-, op. cit.*, pp. 9–11.
7. *ibid.*, pp. 11–14.
8. *ibid.*, pp. 25–26.
9. *ibid.*, p. 29.
10. From *The Glory* (a newspaper published by Sekai Kyusei Kyo), March 10, 1958, p. 1.
11. *ibid.*, January 10, 1958.
12. *World Messianity-, op. cit.*, pp. 32–34.
13. *ibid.*, 17–18.
14. From *Church of World Messianity* (pamphlet by Sekai Kyusei Kyo).

5. PL KYODAN

1. PL Kyodan, *Shin no Jiyu* (Believers' Handbook), cover.
2. PL Kyodan, *Perfect Liberty—How to Lead a Happy Life* (PL Kyodan Headquarters, Tondabayashi, Osaka Prefecture 1950), pp. 5–6.
3. PL Kyodan, *PL* (an illustrated pamphlet without page numbers, published by PL Kyodan, 1959).
4. *Perfect Liberty, op. cit.*, p. 74.
5. *ibid.*, p. 74.
6. *ibid.*, p. 75.
7. *ibid.*, p. 73.
8. *ibid.*, pp. 79–90.
9. *ibid.*, pp. 35–36.
10. The translation by PL Kyodan itself.
11. *Perfect Liberty, op. cit.*, pp. 32–33.
12. *ibid.*, p. 34.
13. *ibid.*, pp. 38–39.

14. *ibid.*, p. 37.
15. *ibid.*, pp. 37–38.
16. *ibid.*, p. 41.
17. *ibid.*, p. 38.
18. PL Kyodan, *A Guide to a Happy Life* (PL Kyodan Headquarters, Tondabayashi, Osaka Prefecture—a pamphlet without year of issue), p. 5.
19. *Perfect Liberty-, op. cit.*, pp. 75–77.
20. *ibid.*, p. 7.
21. *ibid.*, p. 8.
22. *ibid.*, p. 13.
23. *ibid.*, pp. 16–17.
24. PL Kyodan, *Essay on the Way of Life* (PL Kyodan Headquarters, Tondabayashi, Osaka Prefecture, 1950), p. 109.
25. *Perfect Liberty-, op. cit.*, p. 50.
26. *ibid.*, pp. 56–57.
27. *ibid.*, p. 58.
28. *ibid.*, pp. 42–44.
29. *ibid.*, pp. 44–46.
30. *ibid.*, p. 63.
31. *ibid.*, pp. 64–65.
32. *ibid.*, pp. 71–72.

IV MISCELLANEOUS

1. TENSHO KOTAI JINGU KYO (ODORU SHUKYO)

1. Tensho Kotai Jingu Kyo hereafter to be referred to as TKJK), *The Paradise of Tabuse* (TKJK's Headquarters, Tabuse, Yamaguchi Prefecture, 1953), first page.
2. TKJK Headquarters, Tabuse Yamaguchi Prefecture, 1956), p. 4.
3. TKJK, *The Prophet of Tabuse* (TKJK Headquarters, Tabuse, Yamaguchi Prefecture, 1954), from pp. 17–47.

4. Father J. Spae in *Missionary Bulletin,* July 1958, p. 440.
5. *Guidance to God's Kingdom, op. cit.,* p. 17.
6. *ibid.,* p. 6.
7. *ibid.,* p. 17.
8. *The Prophet of Tabuse, op. cit.,* p. 84.
9. *ibid.,* p. 121.
10. Spae, *op. cit.,* p. 444.
11. *Guidance to God's Kingdom, op. cit.,* pp. 4–5.
12. Both the Japanese and the English texts are given in *Guidance to God's Kingdom, op. cit.,* p. 12.
13. *The Prophet of Tabuse, op. cit.,* p. 67.
14. *ibid.,* p. 136.
15. *ibid.,* p. 79.
16. *Guidance to God's Kingdom, op. cit.,* p. 8.
17. *The Prophet of Tabuse, op. cit.,* pp. 129–130.
18. *Guidance to God's Kingdom, op. cit.,* p. 8.
19. The author would like to challenge the generally accepted conception that the burial system and the ancestor worship represent the greatest hindrance to the propagation of Christianity in Japan. This conception was relevant fifty years ago, but perhaps not now.
20. *The Prophet of Tabuse, op. cit.,* p. 123.
21. *ibid.,* p. 141.
22. *ibid.,* p. 143.
   (due to an editorial omission, there are no notes 23 and 24.)
25. *Guidance to God's Kingdom, op. cit.,* p. 10.
26. TKJK, *Tensei* (a monthly magazine issued by TKJK), February 1958, p. 15.
27. *The Prophet of Tabuse, op. cit.,* p. 157.
28. *ibid.,* p. 96.
29. *ibid.,* p. 153.
30. *Guidance to God's Kingdom, op. cit.,* p. 20.
31. *ibid.,* p. 3.
32. *Tensei, op. cit.,* May 1958, p. 12.
33. TKJK *Mioshie, The Divine Teaching* (TKJK Headquarters, Tabuse, Yamaguchi Prefecture, 1952), p. 14.
34. *The Prophet of Tabuse, op. cit.,* p. 105.
35. *ibid.,* p. 97.
36. *Mioshie-, op. cit.,* p. 28.
37. *ibid.,* p. 27.
38. *The Paradise of Tabuse, op. cit.,* opposite picture nr. 17.
39. *Guidance to God's Kingdom, op. cit.,* pp. 14–15.
40. *ibid.,* p. 41.
41. *Spae, op. cit.,* p. 443.
42. *Guidance to God's Kingdom, op. cit.,* p. 7.
43. *Guidance to God's Kingdom, op. cit.,* p. 8.
44. *ibid.,* p. 19.
45. *Mioshie-, op. cit.,* pp. 12–13.
46. *The Prophet of Tabuse, op. cit.,* p. 138.
47. *Guidance to God's Kingdom, op. cit.,* p. 6.
48. *ibid.,* p. 18.
49. *ibid.,* p. 18.
50. *The Prophet of Tabuse, op. cit.,* p. 46.
51. *ibid.,* p. 149.
52. *ibid.,* p. 128.
53. *ibid.,* p. 137.
54. *Mioshie-, op. cit.,* p. 28.
55. *The Prophet of Tabuse, op.*

cit., p. 91.

2. ITTOEN

1. Ittoen, *General Information about Ittoen* (Ittoen, Yamashina, Kyoto).
2. *Extract from Tenko Nishida's Kokoro no Kuzukago* "From a Wastepaper-Basket Mind") published in 1934.
3. *From What is Ittoen?,* published by Ittoen 1959, pp. 5–9.
4. One of Tenko-san's favorite poems, which he regards as a description of his own life.
5. Shu-ko-ge-man-gyo (Training-Empty-Flower-Thousand-Prac-tices) and Za-zui-getsu-do-jo (Sitting-Water-Moon-Training-Center)

3. VARIOUS OTHER NEW RELIGIONS

1. Chibusa Hiroike, *An Introduction to Moral Science* (Dotoku Kagaku Kenkyusho,-Kogane, Chiba Prefecture, 1942), p. 1.
2. The Sermon on the Mount plays a role and is included in the sacred writings of several new religions.
3. Hiroike, *op. cit.,* p. 150.
4. ibid., p. 3.

Bibliography

The following is only a short and incomplete bibliography. For a more comprehensive bibliography the reader is referred to Bibliography on the New Religions, *edited by Harry Thomsen, Christian Center for the Study of Japanese Religions, Kyoto, 1959.*

GENERAL BACKGROUND READING (ENGLISH):

Anesaki, Masaharu: *History of Japanese Religion,* Kegan, London, 1930.

————: *Nichiren, The Buddhist Prophet,* Oxford University Press, London, 1949.

Ariga, Tetsutaro: "The So-called 'Newly-arisen Sects' in Japan," *Occasional Bulletin,* Missionary Research Library, Vol. V, No. 4, New York, 1954.

Bouquet, A.C.: *The Christian Faith and non-Christian Religions,* Nisbet, London, 1958.

Bunce, William K., ed.: *Religions in Japan,* Tuttle, Tokyo, 1955.

Eliot, Sir Charles: *Japanese Buddhism,* Edward Arnold, London, 1935.

Hammer, Raymond: *Japan's Religious Ferment,* SCM Press, London, 1961.

Hiyane, Antei: "Non-Christian Religions in the Contemporary World-Japan," *Religion in Life,* Vol. XXV, No. 4, 1956.

Kishimoto, Hideo: *Japanese Religion in the Meiji Era,* Obunsha, Tokyo, 1956.

McFarland, Neill H.: "The New Religions of Japan," *Perkins School of Theology Journal,* Fall 1958.

Nielsen, Niels C.: "Japan's New Religions," *Christian Century,* October 9, 1957.

————: "Religion and Philosophy in Contemporary Japan," *The Rice Institute Pamphlet,* Vol. XLIII, No. 4, Houston, Texas, 1957.

Reischauer, August K.: *Studies in Japanese Buddhism,* Macmillan, New York, 1925.

Reischauer, Edwin D.: *Japan, Past and Present,* Knopf, New York, 1946.

Sansom, G.B.: *Japan, A Short Cultural History,* Cresset, London, 1931.

Schiffer, Wilhelm: "New Religions in Post-war Japan," *Monumenta Nipponica,* Vol. X, Nol, Tokyo, 1955.

————: "New Religions of Japan, "*Today's Japan,* No. 4, 1956.

Thomsen, Harry: "Japan's New Religions," *International Review of Missions*, July 1959.

Van Straelen, Henry: *Through Eastern Eyes*, Loveland, 1951.

Watanabe, Baiyu: "Modern Japanese Religions," *Monumenta Nipponica*, Vol. XIII, pp. 153–162, Tokyo, 1957.

GENERAL BACKGROUND READING (JAPANESE):

Inui, Takashi: *Kyoso—shomin no kamigami*, Aoki Shoten, Tokyo, 1956.

Niwa, Fumio: *Hebi to hato*, Asahi Shimbunsha, Tokyo, 1953.

Oguchi, Iichi: *Nihon shukyo no shakaiteki seikaku*, Tokyo Daigaku Shuppankai, Tokyo, 1953.

Takagi, Hiroo: *Shinko shukyo*, Million Books, Tokyo, 1958.

————: *Nippon no shinko shukyo*, Yuwanami Shinsho, Tokyo, 1959.

Takatomi, Takeshi and Nagata, Hiroshi: *Ikiru koto e no jonetsu*, Toto Shobo, Tokyo, 1956.

Takeda, Choshu and Takatori, Masao: *Nihonjin no shinko*, Sogensha, Tokyo, 1957.

Tosei Shuppansha: *Shinko shukyo to bukkyo* (second volume of *Gendai shicho to bukkyo*), Tokyo 1956.

————: *Shinko shukyo no kaibo*, Tokyo, 1954.

Watanabe, Baiyu: *Gendai nihon no shukyo*, Tosei Shuppansha, Tokyo, 1957.

BIBLIOGRAPHY ON THE VARIOUS NEW RELIGIONS

ANANAIKYO (ENGLISH):

Nakano Yonosuke: *A Guide to Ananaikyo*, Shimizu 1955.

————: *The Universe Viewed from the World of Spirit*, Shimizu, 1957.

DOTOKU KAGAKU (ENGLISH):

Hiroike, Chibusa: *An Introduction to Moral Science*, Kogane, 1942.

Spae, Jos. J.: "Dotoku Kagaku," *The Japan Missionary Bulletin*, December 1958.

ITTOEN (NON-JAPANESE):

Ittoen: *What is Ittoen?*, Ittoen, 1959.

Reichelt, Karl L.: "Hos Tenko Nishida", *Fromhetstyper og Helligdommer i Øst Asia*, Vol. II, pp. 85–94, Oslo, 1948.

Thomsen, Harry: "Ittoen, the Park of One Light," *Japanese Religions,* Vol. I, No. 3, Kyoto, 1959.

Zimmermann, Werner: *Licht im Osten,* Munich, 1954.

ITTOEN (JAPANESE):

Harakawa, Yoshio: *Ittoen no keizai o kataru,* Ittoen, 1958.

Nishida, Tenko: *Kokoro no kuzukago,* Ittoen, 1934.

————: *Zange no seikatsu,* Ittoen, 1936.

KONKOKYO (ENGLISH):

Fukuda, Yoshiaki: *Hand Book of the Konko Mission,* Konko Mission, San Francisco, n.d.

Nishimura, Shozen: Manual of Konkokyo Konko Hombu Kyocho, 1956.

Schneider, Delwin: "Konkokyo: A Religion of Meditation," *Contemporary Religions in Japan,* Vol. II, No. 1, Tokyo, 1961.

————: *Konkokyo,* International Institute for the Study of Religions, Tokyo, 1962.

Sato, Kazuo: *Konkokyo, A New Religion of Japan,* Konko Hombu Kyocho, 1958.

————: *Sacred Scriptures,* Konko Hombu Kyocho, 1933.

KONKOKYO (JAPANESE):

Konkokyo: *Konkokyo kyogi,* Konko Hombu Kyocho, 1954.

————: *Konkokyo kyoten,* Konko Hombu Kyocho, 1959.

Sato, Hirotoshi: *Konko Daijin,* Konko Hombu Kyocho, Vol. I 1953, Vol. II 1955.

KUROZUMIKYO (ENGLISH):

Hepner, Charles W.: *The Kurozumi Sect of Shinto,* Meiji Japan Society, Tokyo, 1935.

Kurozumikyo: *Kurozumikyo,* Omoto, Okayama, 1957.

Tanaka, Goro: *The Brief Outline of the Kurozumikyo, the Most Genuine Japanese Religious Faith,* Omoto, Okayama, 1956.

OMOTO (ENGLISH):

Omoto: *A Guide to God's Way,* Kameoka, 1958.

————: *Basic Teachings of Omoto,* Kameoka, 1955.

————: *Didactic Poems by Onisaburo Deguchi,* Kameoka, 1957.

————: *Memoirs by Onisaburo Deguchi,* Kameoka, 1957.

————: *Scripture of Omoto,* Kameoka, 1957.

OMOTO (JAPANESE):

Deguchi, Onisaburo: *Reikai monogatari,* 72 volumes, Kameoka.

PL KYODAN (ENGLISH):

PL Kyodan: *Essay on the Way of Life,* Tondabayashi, 1950.
————: *Guide to a Happy Life,* Tondabayashi, n.d.
————: *Perfect Liberty—how to Lead a Happy Life,* Tondabayashi, 1950.
————: *PL,* an illustrated pamphlet, Tondabayashi, 1958.
Spae, Jos. J.: "PL Kyodan," *The Japan Missionary Bulletin,* October 1958.
Tatsuki, Yuasa: "PL (Perfect Liberty)," *Contemporary Religions in Japan,* Vol. I, No. 3, Tokyo, 1960.

REIYUKAI (ENGLISH):

Kotani, Kimi: *A Guide to Reiyukai,* Tokyo, 1958.

RISSHO KOSEI KAI (ENGLISH):

Kamomiya, Jokai: "Rissho Kosei Kai," *Contemporary Religions in Japan,* Vol. II, No. 1, Tokyo, 1961.
Rissho Kosei Kai: *A Guide to Rissho Kosei Kai,* Tokyo, 1959.

RISSHO KOSEI KAI (JAPANESE):

Kamomiya, Jokai: *Bukkyo no honshitsu yori mita Kosei Kyogaku,* Tokyo, 1958.
————: *Kosei kyogaku,* Tokyo, 1959.
Niwano, Nikkyo: *Hokkekyo no atarashii kaishaku,* Tokyo, 1959.

SEICHO NO IE (ENGLISH):

Seicho no Ie: *Seicho no Ie,* a monthly magazine issued from 1953.
Taniguchi, Masaharu: *Divine Education and Spiritual Training of Mankind,* Tokyo, 1956.
————: *The Power of Faith,* Tokyo, 1935.

SEICHO NO IE (JAPANESE):

Taniguchi, Masaharu: *Iesu wa jujika ni kakarazu,* Tokyo, 1958.
————: *Seimei no jisso,* Tokyo 1937. One edition in 40 volumes, another in 20 volumes.
————: *Shin no chikara,* Tokyo, 1941.

SEKI KYUSEI KYO (ENGLISH):

Fujieda, Masakazu: "The Church of World Messianity," *Contemporary Religions in Japan*, Vol. 1, No. 4, Tokyo, 1960.
Sekai Kyusei Kyo: *The Glory*, and occasional newspaper in English issued from 1954.
————: *World Messianity and What It Means*, Atami, 1957.

SEKAI KYUSEI KYO (JAPANESE):

Okada, Mokichi: *Amerika o sukuu*, Atami, 1953.
————: *Kirisuto to Kannonkyo*, Atami 1949.
————: *Tengoku no fukuin*, Atami 1947.

SOKA GAKKAI (ENGLISH):

Brannen, Noah: "A Visit to Soka Gakkai Headquarters," *Contemporary Religions in Japan*, Vol. I, No. 1, Tokyo, 1960.
————: "A Visit to Taisekiji, "*Contemporary Religions in Japan*, Vol. II, No. 2, Tokyo, 1961.
Ikeda, Daisaku: *Soka Gakkai*, Seikyo Shimbunsha, Tokyo, 1961.
International Institute for the Study of Religions: "Soka Gakkai and the Nichiren Sho Sect," *Contemporary Religions in Japan*, Vol. I, No. 1, Tokyo, 1960.
Kobayashi, Sakae: "Soka Gakkai, a Strange Buddhist Sect," *Japan Christian Quarterly*, April 1958.
Kudo, Takuya: "The Faith of Soka Gakkai," *Contemporary Religions in Japan*, Vol. II, No. 2, Tokyo, 1961.
Makiguchi, Tsunesaburo: *The Theory of Value*, Soka Gakkai, Tokyo, 1953.
Murata, Kiyoaki: "Soka Gakkai, Communist Envy," *Japan Times*, June 25, 1959.
Soka Gakkai: *Doctrines of Nichiren Shoshu*, Tokyo, 1957.
Thomsen, Harry: "Ise or Daisekiji," *Japanese Religions*, Vol. I, No. 2, Kyoto 1959.

SOKA GAKKAI (JAPANESE):

Kohira, Yoshihei: *Shakufuku kyoten*, Tokyo, 1951.
Makiguchi, Tsunesaburo: *Kachiron*, Tokyo, 1953.
Saki, Akio and Oguchi, Iichi: *Soka Gakkai*, Aoki Shoten, Tokyo, 1957.
Toda, Josei: *Rissho ankoku ron*, Tokyo, 1952.

BIBLIOGRAPHY

Nakayama, Shozen: *The Missionary Spirit of the Foundress of Tenrikyo,* Tenri, 1958.
——: *On the Doctrine of Tenrikyo,* Tenri, 1957.
——: *On the Idea of God in the Tenrikyo Doctrine,* Tenri, 1954.
Tenrikyo: *Doctrine of Tenrikyo,* Tenri, 1958.
——: *History of Tenrikyo,* Tenri, 1954.
——: *Oyasato, Guide to Tenrikyo,* Tenri, 1958.
——: *Scriptures of Tenrikyo,* Tenri, 1952.
Ueda, Yoshinari: *The Outline of Tenrikyo Doctrine and Its History,* Tenri, 1955.
Van Straelen, Henry: *The Religion of Divine Wisdom,* Veritas Shoin, Kyoto, 1957.

TENRIKYO (JAPANESE):

Fukaya, Tadamasa: *Mikagura uta kogi,* Tenri, 1956.
——: *Tenrikyo nyumon,* Tenri, 1954.
Nakagawa, Kurakichi: *Choseki mikagura uta,* Tenri, 1949.
Nakayama, Keiichi: *Tenrikyo kyoten kowa,* Tenri, 1951.
Tenrikyo: *Mikagura uta,* Tenri, 1957.
——: *Ofudesaki,* Tenri, 1952.
——: *Tenrikyo gentenshu,* Tenri, 1952.
——: *Tenrikyo yoran,* Tenri, 1956.

TENSHO KOTAI JINGU KYO (ENGLISH):

Kitamura, Sayo: "The Dancing Religion," *Contemporary Religions in Japan,* Vol. II, No. 3, Tokyo, 1961.
May, Carlyle L.: "The Dancing Religion, a Japanese Messianic Sect," *South-western Journal of Anthropology,* Spring 1954.
Spae, Jos. J.: "Tensho Kotai Jingu Kyo," *The Japan Missionary Bulletin,* July 1958.
Tensho Kotai Jingu Kyo: *Guidance to God's Kingdom,* Tabuse, 1956.
——: *Mioshie, The Divine Teaching,* Tabuse, 1952.
——: *The Paradise of Tabuse,* Tabuse, 1953.
——: *The Prophet of Tabuse,* Tabuse, 1954.
Tokugawa, Musei: "Interview with Ogamisama," *Shukan Asahi,* March 11, 1956.

TENSHO KOTAI JINGU KYO (JAPANESE):

Tensho Kotai Jingu Kyo: *Mioshie,* Tabuse, 1947.
——: *Seisho,* Tabuse, 1951.
——: *Tensei,* a monthly magazine issued from January 1954.

Index